MY MOTHER'S DAUGHTER

Also by Tracy Clark-Flory

Want Me: A Sex Writer's Journey into the Heart of Desire

MY MOTHER'S DAUGHTER

FINDING MYSELF IN MY FAMILY'S FRACTURED PAST

TRACY CLARK-FLORY

GALLERY BOOKS
New York Amsterdam/Antwerp London Toronto
Sydney/Melbourne New Delhi

Gallery Books
An Imprint of Simon & Schuster, LLC
1230 Avenue of the Americas
New York, NY 10020

First Gallery Books hardcover edition May 2026

GALLERY BOOKS and colophon are registered trademarks of
Simon & Schuster, LLC

Interior design by William Ruoto

Manufactured in the United States of America

10 9 8 7 6 5 4 3 2 1

Library of Congress Control Number: 2025949514

ISBN 978-1-6680-8332-1
ISBN 978-1-6680-8334-5 (ebook)

For Mom and Kathy

CONTENTS

I am telling you your own past, I want to explain
it to you, I want to cure you of it . . .

—Violette Leduc, *La Bâtarde*

MY MOTHER'S DAUGHTER

PROLOGUE: SHAME

I'm standing in front of a red brick Victorian on the West Side of Chicago, thousands of miles away from my home in the Bay Area. The building's yellowing curtains are pulled tight, bare vines of ivy creep up the sides, and leaves blanket the walkway to the door—it has been unoccupied for quite some time. On one corner is a rounded tower with a pointed roof like a witch's hat. This place is brooding and ominous, like something out of a bad horror film. Looking up at a squat attic window, I half expect to glimpse a ghostlike blur of a girl—of my mom twenty years before she became my mom.

I imagine my grandfather's stylish white Chevy Malibu pulling up along this curb in 1965. I picture my teenage mom inside, wearing an A-line dress and a curled bob, pressing her face to the window, lightly fogging it with her breath. Her swollen belly was too big to be hidden by a girdle, which was why *she* had to be hidden away. Her eyes might have followed the same searching path that mine just did, up along the turret to that attic window. The first time I saw a photo of this building, I thought of Rapunzel locked in her tower.

When my mom was brought here, it was known as a "home

for unwed mothers," but let's call it what it was: an institution of shame. It was a place for bad girls—single women who had fallen off their pedestal. A place where they would be turned into future wives and mothers—*good girls*—but first they had to give away their babies. I am my mom's second child but the only one she raised.

She wasn't pregnant with me back then, but this building is part of my origin story. I understand that now. I spent so much of my life facing off with shame—as a young woman grasping for sexual empowerment, and as a journalist exploring taboo subcultures. I wanted to believe that I was free of that wagging finger, but I inherited my mom's shame, along with the world that shamed her.

And now my mom is gone.

Taking a step toward the home's wrought-iron front gate, I think of my mom taking these same steps decades earlier. Pulling off a glove, I wrap a bare hand around one of the gate's cold iron spikes, needing to make contact, wanting to feel its icy sting. This place is physical, touchable proof of the dividing line used to control women for thousands of years. *Good or bad, wife or whore, virgin or slut, mother or lover.*

And so I've come to stand at this gate—at shame's front door. I'm here for my mom, whom I still desperately miss. I'm here for the bad girls, for the women denied the pedestal and the women who fell off it, for the mothers who are also lovers, and for the parts of us that are punished and sent away. I'm here because, as much as this building feels stuck in time, its history is very much alive.

Almost a year ago, I started asking about what happened to my mom back in 1965, which led to questions about what happened to me—as her daughter, a woman in this world, a mother now myself, and a wife, too. After trying to run from the pain of my mom's past for most of my life, I suddenly rushed toward it, and there is only one reason. I found my mom's daughter, the baby she carried in her belly so long ago.

My sister.

1

DOWN THE HALL

I had never seen my sister before, but I recognized her.

It happened in the span of a single block. I had spent this Saturday morning with my husband, Christopher, and our four-year-old, Quinn, watching third-graders pop fly balls in a neighborhood park crisped by the California sun. Then Quinn announced that he wanted to learn to play baseball because he liked "the costumes," so we decided to grab a bat and ball from a big-box store.

Now, on the way home, I scrolled through emails on my phone as Christopher took our exit off the freeway, driving us past a taqueria, a massage parlor, and an autobody shop with one of those flailing inflatables. Working as a journalist for more than sixteen years, I developed a habit of compulsively checking my inbox, because I was often looking for a story.

Well, here was a story.

As Christopher came to a stop at a red light, a subject line caught my breath. "Your AncestryDNA results are in." A couple weeks earlier, I'd spit into a vial and dropped it in a mailbox, because I wanted to find my half sister. I had only learned about her when I was a teenager.

My mom got pregnant as an eighteen-year-old college student in the Midwest in the sixties. She was a white woman, and the father of her baby was a Black student from Nigeria, which added to the taboo of her out-of-wedlock pregnancy. Her father sent her away to a home for unwed mothers, where she finished her pregnancy, gave birth, and placed her baby girl for adoption.

After my mom shared these vague details with me—her white daughter—we barely spoke of it again. A friend called me "Twenty Questions Tracy" because I always seemed to have a follow-up, but I'd asked my mom hardly any questions about her past, and now it was too late. My mom had died from lung cancer almost nine years earlier.

I tapped the link for my DNA results as we turned off the busy thoroughfare and snaked up a hill to our home, just a ten-minute drive north from where I grew up in Berkeley, that famous bastion of liberal politics.

My first match was a woman named Katheryn. "Close family," it read. "27% shared DNA." Her profile picture revealed dramatically arching eyebrows, like mine, and high cheekbones that made me think of my maternal grandmother, Quen. I blinked and felt I was looking right at my mom.

It's her, I thought, gasping. *It's* her.

"*What*," said Christopher.

"I think I found my sister," I said in the disembodied voice of shock.

"Really?" Christopher asked.

"Really," I said.

Quinn let out an unsettled snore from the backseat, and I turned to look at him. He was slumped forward, chin to chest, worn out from our morning in the sun. He sat back up and nuzzled into the headrest of his car seat without opening his eyes. He looked just like my mom, even more so when he slept.

In the midst of my mom's terminal illness, I'd messaged a friend: "when my mom dies, i honestly don't know how i'm not going to kill myself." How shocking, then, to approach the decade anniversary of her death—to have lived so much without her, to be a mother myself, to have a four-year-old son with her face. When we looked at pictures of Quinn, Christopher often invoked my mom: "Deb Clark vibes," he said. The resemblance moved both ways: Once, I showed him a photo of my mom as a kid, and Christopher said matter-of-factly, "It's Quinn."

I turned back to my phone—to my sister, to *my mom*.

Katheryn's profile said that she was adopted and longed to connect with biological relatives for the first time, aside from her three sons. *Three sons. My mom's grandkids.* "It would be a gift, to be able to look into the face of another person, and see myself," Katheryn wrote. Family, she said, "is my world, and there is always room for more."

Christopher, who is white, parked on our street of single-family homes with distant views of San Francisco. From here, the glinting sprawl of the city was flanked by a bridge on either side, like a pair of arms reaching out to nearby Oakland and Sausalito.

Right under Katheryn's name was her location—Atlanta, Georgia—and a button reading "Message." I started typing with shaky thumbs. "I did this test purely because I was hoping to connect with you," I wrote. "I don't want to bombard you with information, but I believe that we are half sisters and I would be so happy to share more of what I know with you." I gave my phone number and email. "Please feel free to reach out to me," I wrote. Before I could overthink it, I hit send.

I realized I had been waiting for this moment most of my life—even before I knew that my sister existed.

....

I was seven years old and sitting with my parents at a Chinese restaurant a few blocks from our house in a quiet, hilly neighborhood in North Berkeley. Our waiter slid the check onto the table, past my soy-sauce-stained napkin, and my dad reached out to grab it. "E-T-P-T," I whispered, urgently. Those four letters didn't stand for anything. They made up the random code word that I used to signal to my dad that it was time for the game we played whenever we ate out, which was often. My dad let go of the check and smiled knowingly at my mom.

"Why don't you pay the bill and we'll head out to the car," he told her. The restaurant's door jingled as we opened it, and I could barely contain my laughter. "Tell her you *lost me*," I whispered. "Tell her you can't find me *anywhere*." I crouched down in the darkness of a nearby storefront. Just as my calves started to ache, the door jingled again.

"I lost her," my dad wailed. "Tracy, where are you? Where did you go?"

A squeal of excitement rose in my throat.

"You *lost* her?" my mom asked. "How could you *lose* her? Where is she? Where did she go? Where did my little bunny go?"

I leaped from the shadows with a "ta-da," and my mom doubled over in exaggerated relief. She wrapped her arms around me, and I sank into her as if she were a pile of fresh laundry—all warmth, softness, and floral scents. "There you are," she cooed, "my little bunny."

The Runaway Bunny was one of our favorite books to read together. In the story, a baby bunny threatens to run away from its mother and turn into various things to escape her—a bird, a cloud, a sailboat. "If you run away, I will run after you," says the mother bunny, who promises to shape-shift in turn. "For you are my little bunny." The mother bunny will not let go of her little bunny; nothing can keep her baby from her. Her mothering is a protective and irrepressible force. *I will run after you.*

Whenever my mom read those words, she would squeeze me a little tighter.

My mom held me tight, period. I was born premature with wet lungs and spindly legs that my mom worried she would break while changing my diaper. She breastfed me until she was raw, singularly determined to get me to a healthy weight. "You were pretty much laying on my chest for the first six months of your life," she would tell me later.

In my earliest memories, her arms seemed to never actually rest at her sides; they hovered ever so slightly, always at the ready. I can still hear her saying, "I just worry that . . ." The "that" could be me choking or falling down stairs or chipping a tooth. Any minor illness or injury of mine would have her consulting our household medical book, which was thicker than the Bible—a book my parents did not own—and filled with full-color photographs of weeping sores and rashes that looked like topographical maps. She tended to everything from my passing sadness to my shyness around other kids like wounds in need of dressing. "Oh honey, my *sweet* bunny," my mom would say, the entirety of her being poured into those words like a healing ointment.

It seemed my mom was always prepared for the worst thing that could happen; I had no idea that she had already lived it. When I was still in diapers, my paternal grandmother, Esther, who knew that my mom had placed a baby for adoption, pointedly told my dad of my mom's devotion: "She cares for Tracy as though she were two children." Esther didn't say this in front of me, because I didn't know yet about my sister, but I felt the doubled intensity of my mom's care all the same.

Sometimes it showed up as an absence. My dad took me to school on the first day of kindergarten while my mom commuted across the Bay Bridge to work at the graphic design company that she had cofounded. Much later, she would tell me what I already sensed: She was intentionally avoiding the anxiety of the goodbye, the moment of separation. The tightness of her grip could make it feel like there was no distance between us at all. That first big day of school, I was so nervous that I threw up on the steps to my classroom. Was it my nerves or my mom's nerves? Impossible to say.

My dad, on the other hand, was her opposite—a carefree, fun-loving Berkeley hippie who made a Peter Pan–like vow to never stop skateboarding, not even in old age. "I'll be skateboarding in my eighties," he liked to say. He had stories about naked hot-tubbing in the seventies and getting tear-gassed during the historic People's Park protests. The long hair of his youth was gone by the time I arrived, but it had been replaced with a bushy anti-establishment beard, which made him seem to me like even more of a cuddly teddy bear. On the weekends, the two of us would go adventuring at our neighborhood park, climbing through creeks and picking blackberries. I'd come home with wet shoes and purple fingertips.

My dad would place his skateboard at the top of the park's concrete hill and sit down on the black sandpaper board with me on his lap. He'd wrap me in a tight hug, lie back, and send us flying down the hill yelling, "Cowabunga!"

My mom stayed home, worrying about skinned knees and sprained ankles. Later in my life, she would tell me that her absence was strategic. "I didn't want you to absorb my anxiety," she explained. My mom, who got her master's degree in English literature with a thesis on the Romantic poets, liked to quote William Wordsworth: "Children come into the world 'trailing clouds of glory.'" Once, my mom told me with a reverent tilt of her head, "I just knew that you were *perfect* as you were and that it was my job to get out of your way." Here was the paradox of her mothering: holding me tightly and at a distance, trying to protect me from the world and from herself.

As a little kid, I just thought of my mom as a source of comfort and safety. She was the person who held wrung-out wet washcloths to my forehead during fevers and reminded me to tie my shoes before heading out the front door. Our love of *The Runaway Bunny* seemed a reflection of that care. Wherever I went, there she would be.

I didn't know that my mom had lost a child. I didn't understand that my favorite bedtime story could be seen as an allegory for her devotion to the child she kept. I didn't see the similar echoes in ETPT, this ritual of departure and return, but I *had* given our little restaurant game a name that seemed like an acronym, like it was waiting to be decoded.

Stories and games speak to us in funny ways—sometimes we feel the meaning more than we understand it. What I understood on some wordless level was that this dynamic of lost and found, attachment and separation, closeness and distance was an essential part of my relationship with my mom.

. . . .

Growing up, I often asked my parents for a sister. On one occasion, I begged. "Can you *please* get me a sister?" I said from the backseat of our car. I was eight years old, and we were driving down a tree-lined street dotted with elegant Craftsman houses and beat-up Volvos covered with liberal bumper stickers. "PEACE." "MAKE LOVE NOT WAR." "CLINTON GORE '92." My mom sat in front of me, and the setting sun made a halo of her curls.

"I want a sister," I said. "Why can't I have a sister?"

She was silent, frozen. My dad glanced over at her. I couldn't see her face, but I could see my dad's face seeing hers, and it told me everything I needed to know about what my question had done to her. "Honey, your mom got very sick when she was pregnant with you," he said. "We decided that it wasn't worth the risk to try again, and now it's a bit late for that."

I already knew this. My mom had been diagnosed with preeclampsia, a serious complication that can be life-threatening, and was put on bedrest for several weeks. Her blood pressure skyrocketed, and I was born premature. My dad watched her emergency cesarean, looking "white as a ghost," as my mom told the story. "You were so tiny, but long in all the ways," she said. "The first thing I exclaimed when I saw you was 'Look at those feet!' We joked that you would be a basketball player." My birth had almost killed her, but when she talked about it, she brimmed with a sense of wonder and comedy.

I understood why she wouldn't want to risk having another baby, but I felt my question had hit on something else that I wasn't supposed to know. I saw it in my dad's glance and my mom's icy quiet. I bet I'd seen it in my mom's face the very first time I asked for a sister—a twitch or a flicker of terror. It might have been why I kept asking. I'm not sure I longed for a sister so much as I longed for the whole truth.

Kids know so much without being told. When your mother carries a secret sadness, you become adept at reading between the lines. What is said creates the shape of what is not. I became an expert in glances and vocal tremors. I would study her eyes like the surface of the ocean, calculating the currents below. I learned the sounds of softening that secret sadness. The suctioned pop of the refrigerator door, the clink of a magnum bottle of cheap white wine, the tap of a glass placed on the kitchen counter, the glug of poured relief. The crinkle of a Ziploc bag full of weed, the click of a lighter behind a locked door, the sound of a tongue slightly loosened, of words subtly blunted.

I never thought, *My mom had a baby and gave her up for adoption.* But I did lie in bed at night imagining that I had a secret sister down the hall whom my parents were keeping from me. This idea made no sense—for one, there was no spare bedroom down the hall. There was only my dad's bedroom, where he often slept apart from my mom—a reflection of my parents' nontraditional belief in maintaining some separateness in their marriage. *What if it's really my sister's bedroom?* I thought. *But where is she during the day? Why don't I hear them putting her to bed? How does she eat dinner? When does she take baths?*

I would pull my floral comforter tight to my chin, eliminating the possibility of any rustling that might interfere with hearing my secret sister. I'd take a deep breath and puff out my cheeks. If I held my breath long enough, I figured, maybe I would be able to hear her. I would listen to the buzz of silence and think, *Was that her breathing?* One night it occurred to me that she might be holding her breath and listening for me. I coughed, theatrically, and waited in the silence.

By the time I hit middle school, my suspicions shifted. I went looking through the large wicker basket where my mom kept our family photos. Each set was tucked away in the worn paper envelope from the photo developer a few blocks from our house. "Presto Prints," it read in yellow lettering underneath a cartoon genie. I flipped through the envelopes, peeking in each, until I found the roll I wanted: my birth photos.

I was well aware of the scandals and dramas that defined the daytime talk shows that my mom watched after picking me up from school, and they seemed to offer a potential clue to my vague but insistent sense of a mystery at the center of my family. I asked myself a question. It materialized like a faint itch. *What if I was adopted?*

I was looking for proof that my mom was my mom, that I had come from her body. In the first image, a hospital gown was pushed off her shoulders to let me rest against her bare chest. I was a month early and weighed less than five pounds. Gazing down at me, her face swollen, she looked like she had just survived something—like she was *still* surviving something. *Would they have staged these?* I wondered. For all I knew, that was how adoption worked: The adoptive mother waited at the hospital for the handoff of the baby and then posed for photos.

Still, I couldn't explain my mom's hospital gown and bloated face. And I thought of the story my mom told about almost dying in childbirth. They might lie about an adoption to protect me, but I couldn't imagine them lying about a near-death experience. It was too elaborate. *I must be hers*, I thought, but I occasionally returned to those photos over the months, looking for clues.

When I was twelve, my mom's good friend Wini gave me a journal filled with writing prompts, including an "inner child" exercise with instructions to write a letter to one of your parents. I wrote:

Dear Mom,

Why did you have me? Was I a mistake? Do you really *love me? I can tell that dad loves me. I see it in his eyes. I don't see it in your eyes . . . I feel like your* [sic] *not my mom, that dad had me with another woman.*

The truth is that I was desperately wanted. My parents had already been married for seven years when my mom got pregnant with me at thirty-seven. Hers was what they called a "geriatric pregnancy." She had waited eighteen years before trying for a second baby—as many years as she had lived when she had her unplanned pregnancy. She had told me how she got some spotting early on with me, feared a miscarriage, and rushed to the hospital in tears, only to find that I was perfectly okay.

I often felt myself to be at the center of my mom's life. Still, it seemed that in some essential way she was not mine, not entirely.

I noticed how complex emotions sometimes took over her face when she looked at me, especially in my moments of joy. I might be tossing a Frisbee with my dad on our front lawn and notice a troubling micro-expression—the knitting together of her brows, conveying a certain ironic detachment, or a head-tilted half smile that said she was happy for me but not happy herself. In these moments, she seemed like an outside observer of something she had created—the architect of a home she had lovingly built but couldn't actually live inside.

There's a photo that my mom framed and put on our fireplace mantel in which I'm just over a year old and cuddling with my dad in bed one morning. My doughy body is comfortably splayed across his chest as if he's a pillow, and I'm smiling so big that my round cheeks look like they could burst. Over the years, my mom would reference that photo, which never left the mantel, talking about my look of ease and comfort. "I'm not always the cuddliest," my mom told me. "I'm just so glad that you have your dad to balance me out."

It was her favorite family photo, and she wasn't even in it. She often seemed just outside of the metaphorical frame, like she wasn't allowed to fully join us in these happy scenes.

....

When I was sixteen years old, I sat in the passenger seat of my mom's car outside of our neighborhood drugstore with two prescriptions in my lap. The paper bags and their stapled-on sheets of instructions crinkled emphatically as I clicked my seat belt. The label on one bag read: "Accutane." My dermatologist had prescribed it to treat the pimples that had dotted my face since junior high. It was a last-resort kind of drug, one that required you to pledge not to get pregnant because of the risk of severe birth defects.

In the other bag was a pack of birth control pills. I had not yet had sex, but I had every intention of doing it soon. It was unthinkable to ask my parents to let me go on birth control for that express purpose, but acne had provided a convenient alibi: I could tell them that my dermatologist was making me do it.

As I sat there with my crinkling prescriptions, my mom erupted. "Are you having *sex*?" she shouted. The word "sex" came out in a squeal, like a car coming to a screeching halt. Her voice was filled with anger, accusation, and, most of all, terror.

I had never seen her like this. When my mom was upset, she fell silent—there was no explosion, just an internal collapse. If she was really annoyed with me, she might say, "Watch it, kid," or she would simply deploy my middle name—her mother's first name—as a warning. "*Tracy Quen*," she'd say, all italics, and I'd understand the meaning perfectly well. In the car that afternoon, there was no warning, just a sudden screaming question about whether I was having sex. My mom had seen past my alibi after all.

"No," I yelled. "The doctor said I *had* to go on birth control. I told you."

I noted the sheen of sweat at her temples, the flush in her cheeks, and how her curls seemed to frizz out, as if electrified by emotions. Ours had been what you would call a sex-positive household. I don't remember any single "sex talk" so much as my parents taking every opportunity to underscore that sex was a good, healthy, and loving act. My mom had even referred to it as "the glue of marriage," to which I'd said, "*Ew*." Now, suddenly, the topic of sex had sent her into a panic.

A few weeks later, my mom and I sat down at the kitchen table at right angles to each other. "I have something I need to tell you," she said. "It's serious."

The moment slowed and expanded. My mom folded her hands tightly on the table, pressing her fingertips into her skin. I heard a finch chirping in the olive tree outside, a delivery truck rumbling down the street, the subtle tick of the antique grandfather clock on the wall. I rubbed my thumb across the rough wood grain of our kitchen table and felt my toes against the cold tile floor. I sank into the before of whatever was coming next.

"When I was eighteen—" she started, all the color draining from her face. "I had sex and I got pregnant."

The room tilted.

"I had the baby, a girl, and I gave her up for adoption," she continued.

I heard my heartbeat in my ears, and my vision jumped in sync with it. My mom said the phrases "I wasn't able," "what was best for her," a "better life." Her voice was distant, like it was coming from across the house even as she sat right next to me.

I thought I might throw up, which seemed like a potential exit from this unbearable moment, as if I could purge myself from it. My whole life I'd been living with a shadow, gazing into its mysterious darkness, trying to make out certain subtle contours, and now here I was, spun around by the shoulders and pointed at exactly what had cast it.

Beyond my own experience of shock, I could see my mom's face saying, *Please don't destroy me please don't reject me please don't hate me please don't punish me.* It said: *I hurt enough already.* I would not destroy or reject or hate or punish. I was taken over by this new sensation of falling, as if a trapdoor had opened underneath me. I was falling away from the conversation but also away from the world my mom had built for me. *Only child. Family of three.* Now there was a fourth.

Of course, my sister had been in the room with us all along.

"My father sent me away to a home for unwed mothers," she continued. "It was like a camp for pregnant girls." I pictured a home just like ours, only filled with bunk beds and sleeping bags. I flashed to my own memory of sleepaway camp in the woods, writing a letter home and messily scrawling "Dear Mom." She had never been just mine.

Then my mom told me that my sister was Black. "Her father was Nigerian, which made the pregnancy even more taboo," she said. "We met at college. He was captain of the soccer team."

I don't remember feeling surprised that my sister was Black. My parents and I were white, and we lived in an overwhelmingly white neighborhood, but I did have Black relatives. My closest family members—my cousins Ari and Conroe Jr. on my dad's side—are mixed. Their dad, my uncle Conroe, is Black and married my aunt Sue in 1968, the year after the Supreme Court struck down laws banning interracial marriage in *Loving v. Virginia*.

Not that I thought about that—or much of anything—in the moment. I was too preoccupied with the sensation of falling. I heard my mom say that she had listed herself and our home phone number on an adoption registry, and something about adoptions being "closed" back then. Babies were placed for adoption without any identifying information about their birth mothers, who were left without any identifying information about their babies' adoptive parents.

"In case she ever wanted to find me, I wanted to make myself available," she said. "Someone might call the house looking for me, and I don't want you to be surprised."

As I nodded in slow motion, my mom scrunched up her eyes. She might have decided in that moment to hold off on the full story. Only later did I learn that her grief over the adoption had landed her in a mental institution—for weeks or months, she couldn't remember. "The loony bin," she would wryly call it. My mom didn't just lose her baby; she lost her grasp on reality, too.

"Do you have any questions for me?" she asked gently.

"Do you . . . wonder about her?" I asked.

"*I think about her every day of my life*," she said in a gush of a whisper that sounded like air being let out of a tire.

I had the sensation of my body breaking off into atomized little pieces and floating off on a breeze like dandelion seeds. All this time, my mom had harbored this other aching love.

"Could you try to find her?" I asked.

"Some people hire private investigators, but I don't want to interrupt her life," she said firmly. "It could be very painful for her.

She might have struggled quite a bit. I would understand completely if she never wanted to hear from me. I don't think that it's my right to barge into her life. It is *not my right.* But I would love to be fully available to her if she ever wanted."

We sat there in silence for a moment before my mom spoke again. "Any other questions, honey?" she asked. I was filled with them. *Why couldn't you keep her, how could you leave her, could you have left me, where is she now?* But I told my mom I didn't have any. I went up to my bedroom, closed the door, and lay down in my bed. I was still. I gripped the comforter. I held my breath. I listened for my secret sister down the hall.

Then I sighed out the air and breathed in the truth of my sister who wasn't secret anymore.

2

THE CALL

A couple hours after messaging Katheryn on Ancestry, I was sitting in our breakfast nook with Quinn, watching him press red Play-Doh into a mold to make a miniature hot dog. Christopher was in the next room folding laundry on the dining table, creating a cityscape of clothing piles. All I could think about was my sister. *My sister.* The phrase kept knocking around my brain like a pinball setting off bells that reverberated throughout my entire body.

I decided to stalk her on the internet. I pulled out my phone and did a quick search, which turned up Katheryn's Instagram feed. I found snapshots of homemade food alongside a series of selfies with playful filters—a flower crown, cat whiskers, a shining disco ball. In one image, she looked radiant and glamorous in a bold pink lip. The caption announced, "Single, not sorry." I smiled.

I kept scrolling and learned that Katheryn was into skin care—she sold organic oils, sprays, masks, and scrubs. Under an image of river rocks stacked in a tower on her windowsill, she wrote a one-word caption: "Balance." I thought of my mom, who had hung an illustration of a tightrope walker by our front door. "Life is all about balance," she had said.

I noted Katheryn's love of nature and the hashtags on one of her photos of a backyard sunset: "#blessed" and "#livingmybestlife." You couldn't trust the accuracy of a person's hashtagged existence on social media, but it seemed possible that my sister was indeed living her best life.

My phone buzzed. The selfies disappeared, and an unknown number showed up on the screen. Underneath the number it read, "Atlanta, Georgia."

My sister had never called my childhood home. After my mom died, my dad disconnected their landline. When he told me, my first thought was of my sister. *She can't find us now.* Eventually, I'd considered a DNA test but resisted—I didn't trust a billion-dollar corporation with my genetic material. But a few weeks earlier, a friend had told me about the family secret she uncovered with a DNA test. "Screw it," I'd said, ordering a test right away. "They can *have* my DNA."

And now my own phone was ringing. As a kid, I'd listened for my sister on so many nights while holding my breath. Here she finally was, a trilling ringtone, a series of digits on my lock screen.

I stood up and answered the phone. A warm and confident voice was on the line, thanking me for reaching out. I listened from somewhere outside of my body as my sister—*my sister*—explained that she'd taken her DNA test a year ago but hadn't gotten many matches. I breezed past Christopher, still standing over the laundry piles, and gestured wildly for him to keep an eye on Quinn.

"The only reason I did it was to find you," I said, breathless. I was running up the stairs two at a time, needing to find quiet for this most important phone call of my life. I hadn't known what I would say to my sister, what words I could possibly use to explain the 27 percent match of our DNA. I'd thought only of finding her.

I stepped into the guest room and walked to the window, which overlooked a roaring freeway, the flat expanse of neighboring Richmond, and a Chevron refinery with earth-toned oil tanks and spewing smokestacks. To the left I could see a stretch of sparkling blue bay and the improbable elegance of the Golden Gate Bridge. To the right was Mount Tamalpais, which cut sharply into the sky, higher than any surrounding mountains. I often stood here for important conversations; it grounded me to look at the water and the rolling hills, these constant backdrops of my life in the Bay Area—more constant than even my mom.

"So, what can you tell me?" she asked.

"Well, my mom, Deborah Clark, got pregnant when she was eighteen years old," I said into the phone, my voice quaking. "She placed her baby for adoption. I believe that baby was you."

I realized there was something else that had to be said, and quickly, before she had the chance to hope. "She died," I added softly. "Several years ago." This was the time distortion of grief; it had been nearly a decade.

"I'm sorry to hear that," Katheryn said. "I apologize for asking this, but how did my mother die?" Those two words shocked and thrilled me: "my mother." She didn't refer to our mom as her "biological mother" or "birth mom." There was no qualification or caveat, it was simply and matter-of-factly: *my mother.*

"Lung cancer," I said.

I had revealed and destroyed our mom in the space of a few seconds.

We went on to cover the basics of our lives. I was thirty-eight, lived in the Bay Area with my husband and four-year-old. I'd worked as a journalist for more than sixteen years, writing about—dot-dot-dot. "Women's issues," I told her. This was the euphemism

I sometimes defaulted to when I was worried about being judged or misunderstood. It was true that I had written about gender and pop culture, topics often dismissively filed under "women's issues." I'd started my career as a feminist blogger and until recently had worked as a feature writer at a feminist website. According to the internet, though, I was a "sex writer."

I had built my career writing about sex from every angle and in every format—advice, cultural commentary, personal essays, and investigative reporting. Just a year earlier, I had published a memoir about my own sexual coming of age. Reviewers called my book "intimate," "provocative," and "bold." I was none of those things in this moment with my sister. I deployed the women's issues euphemism and, before she could ask any questions, mentioned my latest gig, which was easier to talk about. A few months earlier, I'd taken a job at a tech start-up, writing for a women's health app.

My sister was fifty-six and managed a call center. She had grown up in Chicago and moved to Atlanta as an adult. She had three sons, seven grandkids, and three adoptive siblings, including a sister. Usually, she went by Kathy. Both of her adoptive parents had passed away, but she had been raised by "an incredible woman," in her own words.

My mom, keeper of the big book of maladies, had worried about her daughter, but her worst fears hadn't come to be. "I've lived a blessed life," Kathy said with a richness in her voice that made what she was saying feel patently true. "I've lived a very blessed life." She didn't qualify or caveat this, either. "I really, truly believe that God's got my back," Kathy added.

I had figured that I would be welcoming my sister into *my* family, but here I was with one kid, no grandkids, and no siblings aside from her. My mom's side of the family had largely passed away.

Meanwhile, Kathy had a whole world of immediate family. I had assumed that her DNA search would have come from a lifelong existential ache, but it turned out she had ordered an Ancestry test because her adoptive siblings had talked her into doing it with them. She had never even looked into adoption registries, because she hadn't grown up with a feeling of loss. Kathy already had a mother.

Insecurities started to whisper at the periphery of my mind. *She doesn't need another sister. You've spent your life longing for her, and all this time she had no idea that you even existed. Why should you even matter to her? She's so well adjusted. Grateful and grounded and confident. Not neurotic, like you.*

Kathy cut through the whispers with a question. "Do you know who my father is?" she asked. I had only vague details. "He was the captain of the Indiana University soccer team," I said. "He was African. Nigerian. Maybe an exchange student?" I offered to reach out to one of my mom's college friends—maybe she would know something. "I would love that, if it's not too much trouble," she said.

Kathy had been on her way out the door for dinner when she got my message, and she needed to go. "Obviously, we'll talk again," she said. "There are a lot of questions swirling in my head." I could imagine. Suddenly, I had my own. Some of them were about the circumstances of the pregnancy. Most of them were about the parts of the story that Kathy didn't yet know: the home for unwed mothers and the mental institution.

For most of my life, I had been interested in questions about my sister. *Who is she? What happened to her? Where is she? Is she okay?* Now this other question came into view. *What happened to my mom? What happened to* our *mom?*

....

As soon as I got off the phone with Kathy, I emailed Sharon, my mom's best friend from college, hoping that she would have some details about my sister's dad. Two days later, I was working on my laptop in our sunny breakfast nook when Sharon's response landed in my inbox. It turned out I had my facts wrong. "I was under the impression that Deb met him elsewhere—at Purdue? I think that's where she was before I met her," Sharon wrote.

Kathy's father was Nigerian and captain of the soccer team, but not at Indiana University. "She didn't come to IU until after the whole saga had been finished," Sharon explained. *The whole saga.* I texted my dad right away.

"Did Mom go to Purdue before IU?" I asked.

"Not sure," he wrote back.

How was it possible that the people closest to my mom were unsure of the most basic details of this life-changing event? Her husband of thirty-five years, her daughter, and her best friend from college were all grasping for vague recollections and details never shared. "I know very little about it all . . . she thought I'd be 'too shocked' to hear the full story," Sharon wrote.

It was hard to picture Sharon being shocked by a teenage pregnancy. After college, she and my mom ended up in the Bay Area, and Sharon eventually became a fixture of my childhood and part of the circle of friends whom my mom called "the Berkeley family." I knew Sharon as a dope-smoking, wisecracking character, not a pearl-clutching prude. Sharon, who was white, was also a lesbian, and I imagined that she had endured the homophobia of the Midwest in that era.

In any case, shocked or not, Sharon knew just enough to make a difference. All I needed was a yearbook.

My reporter brain had already moved several steps down the path, anticipating the need to call the university library, but it was much easier than that. I popped some leftovers in the microwave for lunch and stood at the kitchen counter doing an internet search. It was a matter of seconds before I found a virtual collection of Purdue yearbooks. I clicked on the year in question: 1965. I navigated to the athletics section, then to the soccer team. I ran my finger along the text on my screen, scanning the list of names, looking for that word: "captain." He stood in the back of the team photo, squinting in the bright sun of the soccer field.

His name was Babajide.

I clicked over to Babajide's senior portrait. He was captured in black and white as a twentysomething young man wearing a suit and tie. He had an inviting face and a genuine smile. I felt his charisma right through my computer screen. He looked ready with a joke. Not a goofy, adolescent one—something incisive and revealing. His face was heart-shaped, and the tops of his ears stuck out just a little. Babajide was the only Black man on the page. The yearbook was a sea of white faces.

"I think I found my sister's father," I texted my dad, ignoring the beeping of my lunch in the microwave.

The day before, my dad had come over to pick up Quinn for "Grandpa time," as he did every Sunday morning. We had sat down over coffee to talk about the big news of my sister but kept finding ourselves at a loss for words. "Deb's other daughter," he had said, his voice catching like water in an eddy before rushing onward. "Her first."

Now I had some basic details to hash out with him via text—like whether my mom had told Babajide about the pregnancy and adoption. "Definitely not," my dad texted back. "Not sure her parents even knew who the father was."

I took a deep breath, flattened my palms against the cool tile counter, and slowly breathed out. My mom had never told this young man in the suit and tie about the pregnancy. Babajide must be around eighty years old now. If he was still alive, this news could rip his world apart. I found myself interrogating my mom in my mind. *Why would you? How could you?* And then—I don't know how to explain this—I realized that I'd known this all along. I remembered that she had *told me his name.*

I flashed to a memory of me and my mom in the living room of my childhood home. I was in my twenties, having driven across the bridge from my apartment in San Francisco to visit my parents. My mom was sitting in a blue armchair with white stuffing spilling out where our cat had scratched a hole in the upholstery. I was perched in front of her on a wicker ottoman. I could hear myself saying, "What was his name?" and her giving his first name, followed by his nickname: Jide. "I looked him up online once," she said. "He works in the oil industry in Nigeria."

I had pushed this memory into the attic of my mind, but now the conversation with my dad had pulled it tumbling down.

"Why didn't you tell him?" I had asked my mom.

"I didn't want to bother him," she had said. "I didn't want to burden him."

She had never told Babajide—not even in the decades that followed, after finding him online. *Why didn't it eat away at her?* I wondered. Then the shadow of another thought moved over me: *It did.*

....

In Kathy's junior-year high school portrait, she wore a pink satin headband with a small bow on top and a matching T-shirt with pink stripes. Here was the girl my mom had thought about every single day of her life. I remembered a concept from the philosopher Alan Watts, whose work I had recently started reading during what I sometimes joked was a spiritual crisis. He suggested that the universe was looking at itself through our eyes—in other words, we humans were *of* the universe and gave it consciousness. *Through my eyes, my mom is looking at her daughter*, I thought.

I had emailed Kathy several family photos, including a sampling of images of my mom ranging from her twenties into her sixties. I'd also thrown in a recent photo of Quinn, with his apple cheeks and messy mop of hair, which we were still cutting ourselves at home. He was her *nephew;* she was his *aunt*. These words, their webs of meaning, took my breath away. I hadn't just found my sister—I was mentally redrawing my family tree.

Kathy had responded to my email with a handful of her own pictures, including this school photo. The next image in Kathy's email, a selfie, showed her as she was now. She had a glint in her eye and a vibrant smile. She wore a tiny dot of a nose ring and a choker-style necklace with a silver pendant etched with the image of a tree. Her closely cropped hair was bleached blond. She exuded an improbable mix of hipness and elegance.

My sister is cool, I thought, grinning.

I scrolled down to a photo of my mom's three grandkids, my nephews. It looked like it was taken at a family dinner at a restaurant. Two of Kathy's sons, Sean and Justin, were seated, and the youngest, Devin, stood crouched between them with his arms slung across their backs, looking thrilled to be with his brothers. Sean and Justin had something of my mom's eyes. Her ineffable essence. I marveled at the familiarity of Devin's smile. His teeth and cheeks. The shape of his chin.

Sean was just a couple years younger than I was, and Justin a couple years younger than he was, and it struck me that my sister and mother had raised children around the same time. I imagined the way my mom would have regarded her biological grandkids. Face tilted, loving smile, total delight. That was the way she looked at my group of high school and college friends. Many of them were guy friends I'd made through my boyfriend Snow, a charismatic transplant from New York who dabbled in "extreme" Rollerblading.

Toward the end of high school, Snow moved into our house, as his mom struggled with alcoholism, and he ended up staying for several years, long after we broke up and I went off to college. He came to think of my mom as his "other mom," which sometimes made me feel jealous, but it also fueled my sense of the radical possibilities of love and care freed from the constraints of the traditional nuclear family.

Our friends would often hang at the house on the weekends and might pop into the kitchen to grab a soda but end up chatting with my mom for half an hour—because she was inquisitive and funny and listened like no one else. There could be something holy in her attention, a rare and undiluted presence. "Your mom is the best therapist I know," my mom's friend Margie, an actual therapist, once joked to me.

Staring at the photo of Kathy's sons, I thought of how a white neighbor had taken notice of our friend group back then. Snow was Irish and Japanese, and our friends were Asian, Black, Latinx, and white. Our neighbor was a white Berkeley liberal and a professor who wined and dined academics; she knocked on our door once to ask after the cars parked on our street and the people who came out of them. She acted as though she was concerned about street parking—there was plenty of it—but it seemed she was trying to sort out who some of these boys were and what they were up to. My mom would say her name, Betty, the way people would say Karen now. "*Betty* wants to know why there's a car parked in front of her house."

I remembered how my mom told me that, as a teenager, she went head-to-head with her father, arguing for the importance of the civil rights movement; she cherished James Baldwin's blistering critiques of racism, classism, and the church. Even her post-college move to the Bay Area was a privileged attempt at finding a like-minded community. A quintessential image for me as a teenager was my mom watching Fox News and shouting in outrage at the TV screen. "I do it just to get my blood pressure up," she would say with a smile.

I realized that this reverie was unconsciously casting my mom as "cool for a white person," a better-than-Betty white person. I was reviewing my mom's credentials for loving and relating to her Black grandchildren, gathering hard evidence for what I felt to be true: that her love for her grandkids would have both transcended race and emphasized it. She understood that claims toward "colorblindness" were an insult that ignored the impacts of systemic racism. My mom would have tried—sincerely and imperfectly—to thoughtfully hold her daughter's and grandsons' Blackness as central to their experience in the world.

I was doing the same for myself, reviewing my own credentials for loving and relating to my Black relatives, casting myself as a better-than-Betty white person. I'd been thinking, too, about the Black family members I'd grown up with, which suddenly felt like a preemptive version of the "but I have Black friends" defense. In this idiotic credentialing, there was a straining toward colorblindness, a wish for race to not matter.

Scrolling back through the photos in Kathy's email, I glimpsed the fear behind my wish. I was terrified that race was actually an essential part of my family's story.

....

I was sandwiched between Margie and Wini, two of my mom's longtime best friends. They were white women in their seventies and eighties, respectively, and each had a shock of soft silver curls. Of all my mom's friends, I had stayed closest with them. Margie wore a purple corduroy jacket that had belonged to my mom. On her dining room table were a handful of plastic takeout containers with steam escaping from the seams—but before we ate, they wanted to know everything.

Ever since my mom died, the three of us had been meeting up regularly. They were both members of the Berkeley family, and I had recently taken to calling them my "slothy aunties." It was an inside joke: One year they had missed my birthday by a few days and given me a card with a cartoon sloth on the front and a message apologizing for being slow. They had signed it, "Love, Your Slothy Aunties."

Slothy or not, they had been there for the big events in my life that my mom had missed: a wedding, a miscarriage, a pregnancy, a layoff, a birth, a baby. We would often go out to restaurants and have hours-long conversations; we would leave only as waiters started sweeping the floors and stacking chairs. This time we were doing takeout at Margie's house, and the major life event was finding my mom's daughter.

"She hardly talked about the adoption," Wini said. "But it was always there."

"I can't believe you found her, TQ," Margie said.

"And the fact that I had *just* enough information to find her dad, too," I said.

"It's almost like your mom was leaving you breadcrumbs," Margie said. "Like she knew you'd need them one day."

"Can you even imagine her being able to see—" I started before my voice cracked.

I felt their heads land on my shoulders, their arms squeeze across my back. This moment of bodily closeness brought me back to one of my earliest memories: placing my ear to Margie's pregnant belly and trying to listen for the baby inside.

Margie was Sharon's ex. They had gotten pregnant in the nineties in the midst of what some fearmongering articles would call a lesbian "baby boom," and their son, Ben, would come to feel like a cousin to me. I knew nothing of those articles at the time; it was clear to me that Margie and Sharon were a family, we were all a family, and there were a million different ways of being a family.

Now I think how lucky I was to have my first close encounter with pregnancy happen in this queer context. It was a positive example of family existing outside of straight married life, and that was true even after Margie and Sharon broke up. We all kept getting together for the usual "Berkeley family" holidays and parties hosted by my mom. She had made sure of it.

Wini and Margie pulled back and looked at me.

"It's a lot," I said. "I'm still processing."

I made a point of avoiding eye contact with Margie, because I knew I would lose it. She was a longtime therapist with probing eyes and a great hug; Margie used terms like "transference" and "cognitive dissonance" in casual conversation. Wini wasn't a therapist, but she was quick with the kind of earthy, knowing, affirmative "mmm" that sometimes made her seem like one.

"You know, I went to a home, too," Wini said.

"What, really?" I asked.

I already knew that Wini had gotten pregnant as a teenager in California, but I didn't know this part of her story. "I signed the adoption papers and everything," she explained. Then Wini said in a voice that bordered on a roar, "I went and got my baby back." Her baby's father hadn't signed the adoption papers yet, and with the help of an attorney, she successfully reclaimed her own motherhood. By the time I was born, Wini's son was all grown up, and she became a grandmother not too long after.

"I remember your mother saying, 'I wish I could have done what you did,'" Wini said. "Something like 'I wish I could have been strong like you.'"

....

It had been only a week since I'd connected with Kathy, but a handful of books about adoption and homes for unwed mothers had already piled up on my desk. Obsessive research came naturally to me as a journalist. I often carried stacks of books around the house with me—from my office to the living room to the kitchen table to my bedside. Christopher called my book stacks my "teddy bear" and my "security blanket" because of how I clung to them. His metaphor felt especially appropriate now. It was like I was carrying a part of my mom around the house with me.

Except there was nothing reassuring about this security blanket; reading these books felt like watching a horror film starring my teenage mom.

In just a couple days of reading, I learned that my mom had been one of an estimated three million girls and women, most of them unwed, who surrendered their babies between 1950 and 1975 in the United States. In the pre-*Roe* era, thousands of parents sent their young pregnant daughters away each year to the maternity homes that had sprouted up across the country in response to the "problem" of premarital sex and pregnancy. The visual proof of their taboo sexuality was hidden behind the walls of these homes. No one would know—not their neighbors, not their friends, not even their extended family. Lies were told about staying with an aunt in California or going off to boarding school. Even the fathers of so-called illegitimate babies were kept in the dark.

The idea was that these girls and their families would be spared the community judgments and social repercussions of unwed pregnancy. Never mind the judgments and repercussions that had already arrived: The workers in these homes could be rigid, strict, and punishing, sometimes even acting as though they were going to burn "witches at the stake," as one doctor put it at the time. It's an apt historical comparison: During the witch hunts, the accused were often single mothers and "promiscuous" women. As the feminist scholar Silvia Federici puts it, "Once exorcised, denied its subversive potential through the witch hunt, female sexuality could be recuperated in a matrimonial context and for procreative ends."

Many of these homes for unwed mothers had started as actual family homes. They were often Victorian mansions that had housed a family before being used as a tool of *the* family. These places sometimes made a terrifying first impression, as the historian Rickie Solinger explains in *Wake Up Little Susie*. In recalling their stays, women compared the homes to prisons, asylums, and leper colonies. They were controlled by house rules, like having their mail screened by staff members or going on supervised neighborhood walks while wearing fake wedding bands to disguise themselves as respectable married mothers-to-be.

Inside these homes, they were schooled in "appropriate" womanhood with lectures on makeup, cooking, and social etiquette. Days were filled with domestic chores and ladylike recreational activities, like sewing and knitting. An out-of-wedlock pregnancy was seen as a failure of femininity, which was why many homes immersed these women in wifely activities. They prepared them for another shot at becoming a proper woman, wife, and mother.

Most of these women were white, and maternity homes typically had a "white only" policy. After World War II, divergent cultural mandates for Black and white unwed mothers emerged and were gradually institutionalized. Single Black women were expected to raise their own children, in part because of racist stereotypes about Black women's hypersexuality, which ruled out the possibility of "redemption." When Black unwed mothers *tried* to place their babies for adoption, they were sometimes threatened with charges of child abandonment.

White women, who were assumed to be inherently pure and innocent, were expected to vanish into these "systems of redemption." Through a combination of social norms and public policies, the threat of unwed white women's "sexual power" was turned into "pathetic powerlessness," explains Solinger. Single women who had sex and got pregnant outside of marriage were shuttled into institutions that worked to control and contain them.

This was part of a broader attempt to reinforce marriage and the white middle-class nuclear-family norm. Black women were seen as "socially unproductive breeders," Solinger writes, while white unwed mothers were seen as "socially productive breeders," because their babies could be adopted by white married couples who struggled with infertility. This period came to be known as the Baby Scoop Era—adoption agencies were just *scooping up babies.*

In these homes, adoption was not just overwhelmingly common; it was commanded, coerced, and sometimes even forced. These women were expected to give away their babies to white married couples and pretend that the pregnancy had never happened. My sister was mixed, though, and placed with a Black family, in part due to the prejudice of white adoptive families.

As I crashed through my stack of books with a pen in hand, my understanding of my mom's teenage pregnancy started to shift. I'd seen her as a victim of a bad predicament: My mom had gotten pregnant as a teenager in the Midwest in the sixties—when contraception was taboo for single women and abortion was illegal—and she'd made the difficult choice of adoption. I'd thought of the home for unwed mothers as a result of that personal decision.

Now I saw that she had been pulled into a system designed to both oppress her as a woman and maintain her white privilege by punishing her sexual rebellion and pushing her toward marriage.

That system contained white women's sexuality and reproductive capacities within the patriarchal household. It aligned them with—and helped to maintain—white men's power. *That* was the context of her choice.

I questioned whether it could be called a choice at all.

3

SCARLET LETTER

I folded open a notebook and double-clicked a mechanical pencil. It was the same brand of pencil my mom always used to write grocery lists and sketch landscaping designs for her garden. There she was, in my mind's eye, sitting in our light-strewn kitchen, brushing away eraser bits with the back of her hand before drawing the cloudlike outline of a shrub on graph paper. Some days my mom could feel so lost to me—a sun-bleached photograph slowly fading to white—but then something as simple as the click of a pencil could bring her back in a vivid flash.

I found myself scrawling a list:

whore
loose
slut
ruined
bad girl
promiscuous

It was a word cloud of my reading over the last several days, a litany of the judgments that white unwed mothers faced in my mom's era. These labels weren't stuck in the past. We were just over a year past the end of Donald Trump's first presidency, which had brought the relentless slut-shaming of Stormy Daniels, the porn performer at the center of his hush-money scandal. Those words were alive in our culture and politics—and in my body, too.

Each word felt like a match lit against my skin. It was the fire of shame but also the hot flame of self-recognition, like having my name called unexpectedly in class.

....

My first viral personal essay was titled "In Defense of Casual Sex."

It was 2008. I was twenty-four, living in San Francisco, and working at the online magazine *Salon*, where I wrote for our feminist blog. My editor asked whether I wanted to respond to a series of books about hookup culture, including one warning young women that they were ruining themselves for love and marriage by sleeping around. I had slept around and I didn't feel ruined, and I wrote as much in my essay. I argued that young women were "putting feminist ideals of equality into sex by refusing shame and claiming the traditionally male side of the stud/slut double standard."

Trolls filled the comments sections and my inbox with words like "tramp" and "cum dumpster." I printed out the cruelest remarks and taped them on my fridge: Every morning, as I opened the door for milk or eggs, I smirked at these names men had called me. At the time, I told friends that it felt like inspiration—a reminder of exactly what I was fighting as a feminist. Later, I saw that I was also trying to inure myself to the insults.

This was five years before my mom died, before we even knew

she would get sick, and my parents often came into the city on Sundays to take me out to brunch. When my mom saw my hate-filled fridge collage, she was not amused. "Honey, they're so angry," she told me. "These men are *not* laughing. They don't think it's funny at all. They worry me." I sighed in response. "Oh, Mom, don't worry," I told her. "They're just idiots on the internet."

My hookup essay landed in a sex-writing anthology, which led to a reading in Berkeley at Good Vibrations, a famous sex-positive adult toy store, just a few minutes away from my parents' house. "What a hoot," my mom said when I told her. "How *fun*. Am I allowed to invite friends?" Her enthusiastic support was not new; I had been writing about sex ever since joining my college newspaper, and occasionally, I asked my mom to edit my pieces. She took a red pen to a printout of my story about the outrage at my all-women's college after Larry Flynt's *Hustler* magazine published a homophobic and objectifying exposé of our on-campus sex-positive, queer-led dance party.

"Nail those doofuses," she said, handing me her notes.

The night of the Good Vibrations event, my parents drove me to the reading, the three of us laughing about our wholesome family outing to a local sex shop. My dad parked in front of the store, and I read my essay out loud for practice. "I think you should slow down," my mom said. "Let your words sink in." I read the essay again. "Good, *great*," she said. "That line about withholding sex not being women's 'sole superpower'? It's the setup for a funny moment. Try pausing a beat before saying 'coitus isn't women's kryptonite.' "

I had to go into the store ahead of time to chat with the event organizers, so my parents went to the bar next door. By the time they showed up in the audience, my mom was flushed pink from a couple of margaritas. She gave me a strained *You can do it* smile from the audience. I watched her riffle through her purse, shift in her seat, cross and uncross her legs. Her enthusiasm from the car had been replaced with anxiety.

My own feeling of nerves—about reading about my sex life for a couple dozen strangers—was amplified by my mom's unease. I stood in front of a wall of vibrators and started to read from the book, which trembled in my hands. Glancing up, I saw my dad and several members of the Berkeley family smiling at me, but my mom couldn't meet my eyes. Midway through the essay, she fell into a coughing fit.

My eyes focused on the words on the page, but in my periphery, I saw my mom with a fist to her mouth, her face turning red as she tried to hold in her cough, her body trembling from the effort. She would have coughing fits sometimes—in a couple years she would be diagnosed with emphysema—but the timing of this one felt meaningful. In retrospect, it seems a physical manifestation of anxiety, a paroxysm of panic.

After the reading, Margie came up and gave me a hug. "She did so great, didn't she?" she said. My mom took a deep breath. Her voice was ragged when she spoke. "Yes, she survived," she said with a weak, wobbling smile.

At dinner with my parents afterward, I confronted my mom with a wavering voice. Did she think I did a bad job? "No, honey, you were great," she told me. "I was expressing my own relief, my own nervousness. I worry for you sometimes." A pause. "You're so much braver than I was," she added. My mom didn't mention her teenage pregnancy or being sent away, but I felt the implication. Her first pregnancy was often inferred when she spoke about her past: "You're so much more together than I was at your age," she had told me when I'd finished college. "It took me six years to graduate." She hadn't explained *why* it took six years, because I already knew: She had been sent away and then locked away.

In this post-reading moment, I realized that my mom, who had been punished for her sexuality, had a daughter who was writing about her sexuality for hundreds of thousands of people to read on the internet. I had gone viral defending casual premarital sex, the very act that had brought her world crashing down around her. *My poor mom,* I thought. *She worries too much. Things are different now.* I *am different.*

....

"Now companies are sending me sex toys at the office," I told my mom one afternoon, a few years after my Good Vibrations reading.

I was visiting home from my apartment across the bay, and she was sitting in her usual spot at the kitchen table, right next to a stack of magazines. I'd been featured in an article about the next generation of feminist activists for a publication geared toward older women, and she kept half a dozen copies on hand. Inside the magazine, several of us twentysomethings were captured in a two-page photo spread. They had styled us in soft makeup and prim dresses, but the cover line screamed, "FEMINISTS IN FISHNETS?" The magazine couldn't seem to decide whether it wanted to portray us as respectable daughters or matricidal Electras.

In my case, at least, the fishnets bit was starting to feel accurate. After several years as a feminist blogger, I had been officially reassigned to cover the sex beat, because it was the topic I was always finding excuses to write about anyway.

"I don't even write about sex toys," I continued to my mom.

"What a riot," she said.

"I don't want to just be some Carrie Bradshaw," I said.

"You're not."

"I want to write about sex with the same seriousness that's applied to any other aspect of our culture."

"Totally," she said. "Sex is one of the most vital parts of our world."

"I want to challenge all the shame and taboo."

"I think that's wonderful, hon."

In the years that followed, I took a special interest in reporting on taboo subcultures. I hiked into the Santa Cruz Mountains with men dressed as leather horses and latex hounds to report on a kinky "fox hunt." I sat in the office of a New Age sexual healer, where I scribbled in my notebook and a woman squirted onto my foot as she orgasmed; I delighted in this off-color detail, never failing to note in my retellings that the experience left a weathered patina on my shoe. It's like I was flirting with the idea of being permanently marked by my subject matter; I already knew that the Google search results attached to my one-of-a-kind hyphenated byline were a certain kind of forever.

The first porn shoot I ever reported on was for the BDSM-themed series *Public Disgrace*. I watched as a bound woman named Rylie was paraded around a San Francisco bar so the beer-swilling men in attendance could spit on her bare flesh. It was a staged fantasy of disgrace: The film's director had briefed the men on what they could and could not do to Rylie, who was into "rough sex" and had a safe word in case she felt uncomfortable. After that shoot, I curled up in my bed in the fetal position; the disgrace felt all too real to me.

"You don't seem like a sex writer," strangers told me more than once. I'd long cloaked myself in the signatures of good-girl respectability: girl-next-door loafers and turtlenecks. Years later, one of my editors would observe that I came to work in this era dressed in "cardigans buttoned all the way to the top," looking like I had something in me "fighting to get out."

Publicly, I pushed for acceptance around risqué topics; privately, I struggled with my own sense of embarrassment. I launched a sex advice column in *Salon* titled "Am I Normal?" after noticing that most people's sex questions boiled down to a fear—born of the taboo around talking about sex—that their bodies and desires made them a little freak unlike everyone else. People wrote in to ask about sexist fantasies, infidelity, painful sex, and armpit fetishes. My answer to the column's titular question almost always boiled down to: yes. "You're normal, I'm normal, we're all normal," I seemed to say.

At one point, I starred in a documentary web series called *The Sex Confessional*. We wheeled a custom-built mobile confessional booth with ornate wood trim and red velvet curtains all over San Francisco—a bowling alley, a record shop, a hill with a view of boxy pastel houses. I would listen through the wooden grate to people's stories about having a blood-sucking fetish or trying to keep the spark alive in a monogamous marriage. The tongue-in-cheek idea was that folks were confessing their "sins" to me and our cameras, but there was no penance in this confessional. I was just there to listen, validate, and empathize.

I unburdened myself of my own "sins," too, writing candid personal essays about my sex life—not just on the internet but in glossy women's magazines. When it was just me and my laptop screen, I could ignore the potential for embarrassment, but when my work came up at family gatherings or with new acquaintances, I rushed to change the topic. Around this time, my college alumnae magazine interviewed me about my career, and I said, "My aim is to be shameless." Those words ended up as a pull quote in the magazine—big block letters right next to my smiling headshot, a photo of me wearing a high-necked shirt with a demure Peter Pan collar.

It's true that something in me was "fighting to get out," but I was also fighting to get rid of something.

• • • • • • • • • • • • • •

I met Christopher in my early days at *Salon*, where he worked as a designer and occasionally illustrated my stories. He played in a local indie rock band and had the mussed hair to match, along with a pair of tattooed swallows peeking out from his shirt above either collarbone. In a critical sorting error, I concluded that he was adorable but not my type. Then, after we'd been friends for seven years, I looked at him one day and went, "*Oh.*"

Here was a tender, thoughtful, handsome, intelligent, and hilarious man whom I'd often called "the best." In college, he had taken women's studies courses, hung out with radical queer activists, and gotten his sex education not from mainstream internet porn but rather *The Whole Lesbian Sex Book*. Within six months of our first date, we mutually proposed, swapping rings on a cliffside overlooking the spray and swells of the Pacific Ocean.

When I published a personal essay for *Salon* about getting married, a misogynistic blogger announced that I had "won the mating game." Linking to several of my pieces from over the years, he suggested that I'd cheated the system by embracing "absolute sluttery" before settling down. He seemed to marvel at my maneuvering, as though I had outwitted the dividing line of the wife/whore dichotomy. I was unsettled by his hateful attention, but I also felt a tiny surge of pride at his incredulousness over my "win."

In a sense, Christopher and I *were* trying to get away with something. We walked down the aisle to the *Mission: Impossible* theme song in a nod toward the sexist and moralizing pressures placed on traditional marriage—from domestic inequality to lifelong monogamy. *Impossible* pressures. During a wedding speech, a relative referred to Christopher as a "brave man" for marrying me. I was not only a woman with a past but a woman who had *written about* her past.

Several years later, I started working on my memoir, *Want Me*. By then my mom was gone. I had also just become a mom myself—a motherless mom. I wrote my book during maternity leave, hammering away on my keyboard during Quinn's naps, often with him sleeping on me as I contorted myself into a series of impressively unergonomic positions. Sometimes I worked in the dark, save for the glow of my laptop screen. Nothing except his cries could stop me from writing not even, in one instance, noticing some of his poop on my pants leg.

In my cocoon of darkness, this moment of maternal transformation, I felt that I was writing for my life. Motherhood—as gendered idea and institution—arrived with its set of normative demands, including that I cease to exist as a sexual being. My coming-of-age memoir—so rooted in what sex had taught me about myself—felt like a form of resistance.

I wrote about growing up in the nineties, wedged between shouts of "girl power" and the breast-flashing of late-night *Girls Gone Wild* infomercials. I was trying to tell a generational story about navigating the competing pressures of commercialized feminism and sexualized pop culture. I showed how plumbing the depths of our sexual culture as a journalist helped me to confront those competing pressures—not to mention the tyranny of the "male gaze" and the unfinished work of the sexual revolution. The book jacket eventually read: "With a vague aim toward sexual empowerment, she set out to become what men wanted—or, at least, understand it."

I put words to paper about those parts of myself that were supposed to not exist now that I was a wife and a mother; those parts that were never really supposed to exist in the first place. I wrote about masturbating to porn and faking countless orgasms and experimenting with "rough sex." I unflinchingly detailed my fantasies and pornographic tastes in the interest of feminist cultural analysis; I quoted Jacques Lacan and Judith Butler alongside discussions of tube sites and sex dolls. I wanted to capture the difficulty of finding yourself as a young woman in our partially changed world.

I talked about my mom's teenage pregnancy, too, but only in passing. After being sent away, my mom felt "marked with a scarlet letter for the rest of her life," I wrote. I ended up "making the scarlet letter into my career." I saw this as an ironic juxtaposition, a poetic coincidence. For some brief context, I'd skimmed the ebook preview of a history of homes for unwed mothers, but I hadn't read the whole thing. It felt tangential to my own narrative—a footnote, an aside. It was my mom's story, not mine.

After my book was published, people called me "brave" a lot. I didn't feel brave. In fact, when they said this, I heard, "You should be afraid." I heard, "Aren't you ashamed?" Intellectually and politically, I was not ashamed. I was proud of my work and believed in the importance of writing about sex with seriousness and honesty, especially as a woman. I knew what it meant to say the unsayable; I got regular emails and DMs from young women telling me that my book had changed their lives. They said it made them feel less alone. It helped bring them greater pleasure, understanding, and self-acceptance.

That had been my wildest hope for the book. I had distilled my own decades of searching and grasping into a couple hundred pages of text with the belief that it might help other young women on their way. "If I never accomplish anything else in my life, I have this," I told Christopher when I showed him one of those reader messages. "This should be more than enough." He nodded emphatically. I often felt that Christopher believed in the value of my work more than anyone, sometimes even me.

When it was just me and my laptop screen, I could hold on to that sense of purpose. I could tap into that confidence when I played the part of a sex writer giving a podcast interview or stepping on a stage for a reading. The moment I tried to incorporate this identity into my "real life," I disassembled; all the parts didn't fit. At a holiday gathering with Christopher's family on the East Coast, one of his cousins asked me the title of my book as a Christmas song jingled in the background. What a simple, easy, friendly question, but it felt impossible to answer. I mentally zoomed out and saw myself standing in the midst of twinkly lights and pine garlands, festive ties and knit tights, as kids raced around the house in slippery socks. I took a deep breath. "*Want Me*?" I said, wrinkling up my face.

Sometimes I wondered what it would mean for my child to grow up with a mother like me—a mother with a bookshelf full of titles like *Hard Core*, *The Erotic Mind*, *Girls & Sex*, *Powers of Desire*, and *I Love Dick*. A mother who had written a memoir with a cover featuring an illustration of a naked woman. Never mind all the revealing details he might one day find inside that book, including a passage about discovering a new sense of eroticism during my pregnancy.

I felt especially indecent introducing my work into our suburban parental existence, even though said parenthood was brought into existence most often *by sex*. Such are the paradoxical demands of maternal virtue. "A mother is a woman whose sexual being must be invisible," writes the author Jacqueline Rose in the essay collection *Mothers*. "She must save the world from her desire—thereby allowing the world to conceal the unmanageable nature of all human sexuality, and its own voraciousness, from itself (as if sexuality never exists outside the bounds of married life)." In my day-to-day life as a mom, I made my sexual life as invisible as I could, which was easy enough until the topic of my work came up.

At a *Paw Patrol*–themed birthday party, a fellow mom asked what I wrote about. "Um, I, well—" I said, nervously scanning the surrounding landscape of popped balloons, half-eaten pizza slices, and piñata detritus. "*Sex*." During a playdate in our backyard, another mom asked what my book was about. I lost all access to words and looked to Christopher pleadingly in the hope that he would answer for me.

Later, I told my therapist, "I was so incapable of forming a coherent sentence about what my book was about. I was fluttering and flailing. I felt adolescent, childish—like this pathetic, embarrassing little girl." My therapist's response was quick and precise: "It sounds like you're describing shame." It was as if she had turned on a light in a room that I hadn't even realized was dark.

A few months after my book's publication, I met Margie for dinner. So many years ago, she had beamed with pride at my

Good Vibrations reading as my mom fell into a panicked coughing attack. Now she had become one of the stand-in mother figures whom I turned to after my mom's death. I told her about my little-girl shame opposite all these declarations of bravery. She smiled. "Bravery doesn't mean that you don't feel afraid," she said. "It means that you do it anyway."

I thought about it for a second and told her, "It doesn't feel like I have a choice. It feels more essential than that—like breathing."

. . . .

Sitting with the list of slurs that set my skin on fire, surrounded by my stacks of history books, I thought back to my earlier understanding: *My mom was marked by the scarlet letter, and I turned the scarlet letter into my career.* I kept repeating it to myself like a koan. It didn't seem like poetic irony anymore. It felt like more than a coincidence. I tried replacing the "and" with "so." *My mom was marked by the scarlet letter, so I turned the scarlet letter into my career.* I knew that my mom had been stuck in her experience of shame. What if I was, too?

The question seemed obvious and rhetorical as soon as it formed in my head. I'd designed a career that demanded a constant face-off with shame. I wrote things that got me called "cum dumpster" on the internet and left me red-faced and sputtering at family gatherings. I reported on taboo subcultures that required me to confront my own judgments, embarrassment, and discomfort. Many of those subcultures explicitly eroticized shame—like the BDSM-themed porn shoot that had left me curled up in the fetal position.

Of course, I tried to "challenge all the shame," as I'd told my mom: writing an advice column to tell people that they were normal and sitting in a damn confessional absolving people of their sins. But my own fundamental sense of normal and absolution was another story. I was a sex writer who went to forbidden places while maintaining a safe turtlenecked, note-taking distance. I had written a "brave" coming-of-age memoir that had helped other young women feel less alone, but I could barely talk about it in my "real life." Shamelessness was my aim, but it was not my result. My career was like exposure therapy that didn't take.

It seemed uncanny, and maybe a little far-fetched, that this mysterious event from my mom's past had so dramatically shaped my own life. But I couldn't deny the familiar heat of those words: "whore," "loose," "slut," "ruined," "bad girl," "promiscuous."

This was not just my mom's story, I realized. It was mine, too.

4

FEELINGS WHEEL

"Hey, kid," Sharon said, answering the phone like an old-timey film star.

I had emailed with more questions about my mom, but addressing them all over email was too much typing for her. "Arthritic fingeeees," Sharon wrote. So we scheduled a call instead. It had been a few years since we had seen each other in person, having drifted apart in the wake of my mom's death, but the familiarity of her voice, which alternated between a low conspiratorial hum and a sharp laugh, made it feel like no time had passed. Together, we started piecing together a rough timeline of events: In the fall of 1966, nearly a year after my sister was born, my mom transferred from Purdue to Indiana University, where she met Sharon in the dorms.

"I'd just come out, and my girlfriend was living on the same floor as me. We had a tight-knit crew in the dorms, a *gang of gals*," she said with a smile in her voice. "They protected us from the powers that be. Your mom was part of that."

After being sent away in shame, my mom had fallen in with women who either lived on the sexual margins or wanted to protect those who did. This made perfect sense, seeing as both lesbians and unwed mothers were demonized as sexually deviant. The same was true of any woman who fell outside the white, marital, heterosexual, and procreative norm.

"What was she like back then?" I asked.

I scrawled down fragments of Sharon's response in my notebook as if she were an interview subject: "really not happy, really quiet, elusive. enigma. never spoke. rarely shared her opinion." My mom would intently listen to the chatter of the "gang of gals" while silently smoking a cigarette, Sharon said. Sometimes she would smirk or laugh, but she didn't join in—except this one time when Sharon dared to joke about Bob Dylan's "funny-sounding" voice. "He's a *poet*," my mom spit back. Other than defending her favorite musician, my mom was "basically a mute," Sharon explained.

I had recently found some photos from this period at my dad's house. They showed scenes of intimacy and silliness: young women fully clothed and giggling in an empty bathtub, getting ready with face masks and shower caps, and lounging in nightgowns with cigarettes perched between fingertips. My mom was in the background of only a couple shots: smoking, laughing, and listening, just like Sharon said.

One day in the spring semester, she vanished from the dorms.

"Very few people knew why she left," Sharon said. "Much later, she told me that she stopped showering and that kind of thing. I don't know if she was hearing voices or what. She had a schizophrenic break, was my understanding."

I knew that schizophrenia could run in families, and it struck me as odd that I didn't know the exact nature of my mom's institutionalization or the diagnosis that had gotten her there. I remembered learning about schizophrenia in a college Psych 101 class and noting with alarm that it often showed up in your twenties. *What if I'm on the verge of a schizophrenic break?* I had thought, staring at my textbook. *What if* worrying *that I have schizophrenia is a sign of schizophrenia?* I'd recognized the unreasonableness of this fear, which only made me more fearful. *See, maybe I* am *out of touch with reality.*

"Schizophrenic." All these years later, the word still made my hair stand on end.

The next day, I called Margie for a reality check while walking barefoot in our backyard. I recapped my call with Sharon as I paced in front of a mound of bright green aeoniums. They had been propagated from my mom's garden—once a lush, magical oasis exploding with color and texture. The quintessential image of my mom was her in a fleece L.L.Bean vest, listening to talk radio through earbuds while holding a garden hose, the arcing spray of water reflecting a shimmery rainbow.

After her death, it was the succulents that best survived without her regular care. Christopher and I had rescued armfuls of cuttings, which now blanketed our yard and deck. "Plants have wheels," my mom liked to say, because she was always moving them around her garden in search of the most harmonious composition.

I stopped to gently rub a waxy leaf between my fingers. "Do you think my mom had a schizophrenic break when she was locked up?" I asked.

"No, I think it's more likely she had a trauma-induced psychosis, given the circumstances and everything we know about the rest of her life," she said.

"Okay," I breathed. "Got it."

"Your mother was *traumatized*—by being sent away and by the adoption," she said. "There was no trauma-informed care back then, you know. You can only imagine the care that she got or didn't get in the wake of her trauma, and then she was only further traumatized by being locked up in a mental institution."

Traumatized. I was looking at a part of our garden path where the gravel had worn away to reveal a torn piece of black woven weed barrier—like a fissure, an exposed seam, a rip in the fabric of reality.

I had never considered that my mom had been traumatized, but it fit with what I'd learned in my reading. Adoptions in that era left many women stricken with grief and suffering from mental health issues, ranging from anxiety to addiction to post-traumatic stress disorder. Many suffered for the rest of their lives. I'd always seen her as tough: She had *been through some shit.* Now I saw how thoroughly she had been stuck in it.

"That trauma was never healed," Margie said. "It's very common to sort of clamp down around the trauma, contain it inside of a box, and never again let it out, because it would feel like it threatened to completely overpower you. So, knowing your mom, I think that's what she did. She clamped down, she didn't talk about it, and she numbed it. I think we can see that in your mother's relationship to substances as well."

My stomach somersaulted. "Mm-hmm," I said, as though I was not at all surprised. It was the first time anyone had ever mentioned her smoking and drinking to me. I'd thought I was the only one who had noticed.

As I kid, I watched my mom disappear into her room multiple times a day, only to emerge with heavy-lidded eyes and smelling slightly of skunk. She drank out of small red plastic cups that made it hard to tell what was inside, but I watched the refrigerator door enough to know that it was often white wine. Even into my twenties, my stomach knotted whenever I detected a remoteness in her eyes or a slight warble in her voice. She could be so powerfully *there*, more present than anyone I'd ever known, and then vaguely absent, like part of her had been secreted away.

"Your mom was so deeply empathetic, emotionally insightful, and connected to other people," Margie said. "But she wasn't connected to herself or her own emotions."

"Yep," I agreed.

"Your mom had trouble with her own feelings," she said.

The two of us sighed in unison.

"She tamped them down, boxed them up, like she did with her trauma," Margie said. "That was part of her survival strategy."

....

In my first days at work after finding Kathy, I couldn't box up my own emotions—I got sideswiped by them. I wasn't just working at a "women's health app," as I'd described it to my sister. The company had launched a virtual platform for pregnancy and postpartum education before broadening into sexual and reproductive health. The start-up's founder, Erica, a Black woman with an intersectional feminist ethos, was a former doula known for writing a holistic book on pregnancy, birth, and motherhood. Often I found myself writing copy about exactly those topics for the company's website, newsletter, and Instagram account.

This job was my first foray outside of journalism—a decision I made as things got rocky at *Jezebel*, the feminist publication where I'd worked for years. Accepting a job at a start-up had felt like leaping to a life raft—or, really, a venture-backed yacht filled with celebrity investors. Since finding Kathy, my choice had started to seem weirdly prophetic, given how the job overlapped with my new interest in my mom's teenage pregnancy, but my work was also leaving me in tears.

I cried while researching the benefits of trauma-informed care for pregnancy and childbirth, as I thought of Margie saying, "There was no trauma-informed care back then." I cried while reading about forced sterilization, a horrific practice with a long history in the United States, including among women of color, poor people, unmarried mothers, and "promiscuous" women. I cried while watching an educational video featuring Erica flexing a replica of a pelvis and holding up models of a cervix in different stages of dilation.

I was immersed in the physical facts of pregnancy and the politics of it, too. I had recently written some copy for the company's Instagram account about reproductive justice, a feminist framework arguing for "the human right to maintain personal bodily autonomy, have children, not have children, and parent the children we have in safe and sustainable communities," as the activist organization SisterSong puts it. This is an intersectional approach led by Black women that emphasizes not only the right to *not* have kids, but also the right to *have and raise* kids, and in adequate environments. It crucially pushes beyond the issue of individual "choice" and calls for a collective movement concerned with all forms of oppression that impact people's reproductive lives, from inadequate wages to police brutality to inaccessible prenatal care.

I had also started exploring concepts that were brand-new to me, like "matrescence," the complex transition into motherhood, which comes with all sorts of changes to your body, hormones, emotions, and identity. Then there were fascinating phenomena like "microchimerism," where cells pass between a fetus and a pregnant person, and even between a fetus and a subsequent sibling. These hitchhiking cells could migrate throughout the body, showing up everywhere from cardiac tissue to the brain, and they could persist years after pregnancy. In the days after my DNA match with Kathy, I thought of microchimerism and lost my breath picturing her cells in my heart and head, glinting like flecks of gold.

My throat closed and tears poured.

Luckily, I worked from home. The start-up was remote-friendly but based in Los Angeles with an earnest, feelings-forward company culture—a shock to my system after spending so many years immersed in the cynical and irreverent world of New York media. At the start of every virtual all-hands meeting, we took turns sharing how we were doing with the help of a "feelings wheel," which functioned like a color wheel, only it depicted the full spectrum of human emotion with labels like "triumphant," "enraged," "warm-hearted," and "dismayed." Given the feelings wheel and our focus on pregnancy, I'd thought nothing of mentioning in a small staff Zoom meeting several weeks earlier that I had taken a DNA test in the hope of finding my sister.

"So, my mom got pregnant at the age of eighteen," I had told the *Brady Bunch*–like boxes of friendly faces on my laptop screen. "She was sent away to a home for unwed mothers to protect the family from sh—"

I hadn't seen it coming, but as I started to say "shame," my throat seized. I choked out the rest of the story while waving my hand in front of my face.

"Sorry," I said as the faces on my laptop smiled sympathetically. "I didn't think I would cry. *Jesus.*"

I had always been able to talk about my mom's teenage

pregnancy in a contained and matter-of-fact way, but just the act of dropping that vial of DNA into the mailbox had loosened something in me—and now it seemed a dam had broken.

I had experience with returning to work after life-changing news. After my mom's terminal diagnosis, I had gone back to my job as a twentysomething sex writer. I was changed, dizzied, and sleepwalking, but I went through the motions of the "before," feeling like a pod person, a human body invaded by an alien life-form. This time I felt more like an alien invaded by a human body. It seemed clear which one was calling the shots. Ever since finding my sister, I'd felt like someone had taken my rib cage and gone *crr-aack*—just splayed it open like butterfly wings. I felt the sensation of my beating heart without armor—*but also without a cage?* New York–media me cringed at this thought, even caveated as it was with an inflection of irony. *Too many feelings wheels.*

• • • • • • • • • • • • • •

I waited several days to email Kathy about finding her dad. I was worried about coming on too strong. I had already emailed after our exchange of family photos, but I hadn't heard back. My internal monologue reminded me of my dating experiences: *Do I sound desperate? Was it weird when I said that one thing? Am I more invested in this than she is?* But bigger than my worry of coming on too strong was my worry about having this life-changing information in my sole possession. Every minute of her not knowing felt like holding on to a winning lottery ticket that might also be nuclear codes.

That simple Google search, the all-too-easy yearbook discovery, had unleashed marvelous and terrifying possibilities. It could change Babajide's life. It could change Kathy's life, too. Just *how* remained unknown.

"I wanted to let you know that I got much better information about your birth father after talking with Deb's good college friend," I wrote. Kathy had called her "my mom" during our phone call, but it felt presumptuous to refer to her as "our mom," like the "our" would be assuming a sense of closeness as biological sisters that she might not want. It seemed too distant to call her "your mom" and too cold to use "birth mom," so I'd landed on using her first name, a decision I ceaselessly interrogated as soon as I hit send. "I think I've likely found his name, too," I continued. "I want to make sure I'm not overwhelming you with information, though. I'd imagine this is a lot to take in. If you're interested, I'd be happy to share my notes."

She wrote back in less than twenty minutes and told me that she'd been thinking of me all week. "You don't have to worry about overwhelming me," she wrote. "I want to know EVERYTHING!! I am so happy to hear from you and that we connected, and to find out I have a little sister." She added a blushing smiley face. "I will be the first to admit that I wish I was better at this stage," she wrote. "I worry about just picking up the phone and calling you. I feel like I am not sure if I know what to say and I don't want to be awkward. I tell myself that I am probably overthinking it." *Wow*, I thought, *we* are *related*. "I want to really get to know you better, if that is something you are interested in," she added.

"Hah, welcome to the club—I've been doing a lot of overthinking myself," I wrote back. "I'd love nothing more than to chat more and really get to know each other." I shared my notes about her dad. I linked to his yearbook photo. I explained that he was never told about her. Twenty-four hours later, she wrote: "I absolutely think this is my father." A distant cousin with the same last name had shown up on her Ancestry results. Kathy said she was looking forward to talking again and asked for a good time to chat, so I gave her a bunch of different windows.

Then I checked my inbox for days with no response. *Did her dad not knowing change things? Was my response too cold? Did I not express enough enthusiasm? Did I fuck it all up? Should I push harder? Let her come to me? Is she just chiller about this whole thing? On a different timeline? Am I being desperate?* My mind churned with worry and longing. I relayed all of this to my therapist in a phone call. It was our second weekly session since I'd found Kathy. The first one had been devoted to my basic telling of facts: the DNA test, our Ancestry messages, the back-and-forth of the first phone call. Now we were really getting into it.

My therapist brought up the concept of object permanence, which babies develop in their first year of life. They begin to realize that an object continues to exist even when it can't be seen. When a parent leaves the room, the baby might start to have separation anxiety because now they understand that the parent continues to exist—and when will they come back? I was confused: This sounded like the kind of attachment issue that an *adoptee* might struggle with.

"It seems like your sister is very warm and loving," she said. "Like she's incredibly open and genuinely wants to get to know you. So, we might wonder what happens for you in the silence. We might ask, 'Why can't I hold on to the security of my connection to her?' "

This wasn't a problem for me just with my sister. I saw rejections where there were none. In conversations with friends, coworkers, and even family members, the subtlest look or intonation could bring about a landslide of self. *They don't like me. They hate me. I am bad.* The ground would fall out from under me. My conversations with my therapist often circled around my attempts at parsing these minor interactions.

"I feel like there's this . . . *toxic sludge* in my body," I had recently told Christopher, motioning with my hands as if trying to expel it. I imagined thick gray muck squished between muscle and bone, filling every internal gap with the sodden weight of worry and fear. I'd lived with those emotions as a backdrop for a long time. Since I was a teenager, I had mockingly referred to myself as a worst-case scenarioist. I tried to anticipate all the bad things that could happen—from conflict with friends to romantic snubs to professional rejection to the innumerable ways that one could be dreadfully injured or straight-up die, interpersonal rejections being right up there with existential threats.

Why can't I hold on to the security of my connection to her? I asked myself. My brain was a jumble of connections: *Because my mom gave my sister away as a baby and longed for her ever after? Because I never felt secure in my attachment to my mom because she was always yearning for her other daughter? Because I wasn't enough to fix her sadness, so I believe there must be something wrong with me?* It struck me: I'd titled my memoir *Want Me* in reference to the way I'd channeled my own desires into being desired by men, but now it sounded like the bare, pleading wish behind my questions in that long-ago journal exercise: "Why did you have me? Was I a mistake? Do you *really* love me?"

. . . .

I was sitting with three women friends around the firepit in my backyard. We had met years earlier while pregnant and taking a childbirth class, where we watched our instructor squeeze a baby doll through a model of a pelvis and took turns holding ice in our palms to simulate the pain of childbirth, an exercise that we all laughed at darkly after we'd experienced the real thing.

I had just shared the news about my sister, and Stacy was pulling objects out of her woven purse: a pillar candle, tins of loose incense, a matchbook, and a deck of tarot cards wrapped in a silk scarf. She placed each on a black wrought-iron table that had belonged to my mom. Next to it, the flame of the firepit licked the cold night air. Stacy had a taste for "woo-woo" stuff, as she put it, and she happened to be a therapist. I was *swimming* in therapists.

"I brought a few things," she said. "In case we wanted to get witchy tonight."

"*Yes*, witchy moms' night," I said, feeling instantly embarrassed by my enthusiasm.

The four of us had been knotted together by our experiences of pregnancy, labor, and the postpartum period—in part by talking about the disillusionments of motherhood. Just the first of those disillusionments: We had all taken our childbirth class with the hope of having a vaginal birth, armed with stats about the overabundance of cesareans and a vaguely feminist cynicism toward the medical establishment—and yet all but one of us had been pushed toward a surgical birth.

And we were the lucky ones. We had access to a progressive $375 childbirth class taught by a lactation consultant who offered free breast-and-chest-feeding advice postpartum. We all paid for doulas, who are known to reduce the cesarean rate. We all were white: Black babies are more likely to be born through cesareans, which carry greater risks of complications, and Black women are three times more likely to die from a pregnancy-related cause than white women, for reasons ranging from chronic stress to medical racism.

Despite these privileges, we walked away from childbirth with a sense of having been tricked and cheated. This sense didn't end with childbirth—it showed up at every stage of motherhood. We felt it in the impossible expectations placed on moms, the lack of paid parental leave, the challenge of feeling heard in postpartum doctors' appointments, the cost and unavailability of childcare, the unpaid labor of parenting, the household inequities in heterosexual relationships, and on and on. Similarly, Amanda Montei writes in her memoir, *Touched Out*, that her experience of motherhood "felt forced, compulsory, staged." She had wanted to become a mother, but her experience "was immediately tainted by what I hadn't known before consenting," she explains, connecting this dynamic to the many coercions and violations of rape culture.

There is so much that becomes known only by stepping into motherhood—and that's no accident. Motherhood is romanticized as the ultimate fulfillment of a woman's life, but as Montei argues, it's an institution that has been designed—in America especially—to exploit women's "bodies and psyches, to put them to work for free and call it love, then to gaslight them into thinking they have done something wrong that led them there."

I found that talking with other moms was an antidote to that self-blame. My "mom friend" gatherings made me think of feminist consciousness-raising circles during the sixties and seventies, when women got together to talk about the issues in their lives as a means of awakening to their shared oppression. The incense and tarot cards weren't a typical feature of our get-togethers, but there was something inherently witchy and transgressive about women comparing notes, especially when it came to the business of reproduction.

In fact, I'd learned in my recent research that many of the women targeted by the early modern witch hunts worked as midwives. They used herbs for contraception, abortion, and pain reduction during childbirth—a direct challenge to beliefs around women's punishment for Eve's original sin. The persecution of witches served to invalidate lower-class women healers, replacing them with bourgeois male physicians, destroying "a vast body of knowledge that women had transmitted from mother to daughter over the generations," writes Silvia Federici in *Witches, Witch-hunting, and Women.*

This history wasn't the reason for my enthusiasm over the possibility of a witchy moms' night, though. Officially, I liked the idea of tarot cards as an inkblot test: Maybe a random assortment of archetypal cards, viewed through the lens of a pressing personal question, could tap into some deep inner wisdom—the thing you knew without knowing. Unofficially, I wanted to talk to my mom. I never would have said this out loud—it seemed foolish and superstitious and intellectually indefensible. Then again, maybe I had inherited the centuries-old shame of women being burned at the stake for daring to imagine a world beyond patriarchal reason and control.

Stacy had me light some incense as an offering for our ancestors. Then I cut the deck of cards while asking out loud, "What does the universe want me to know about my sister, my mom, and me?" Stacy started flipping over cards in a row—left to right, then up to down—forming a Celtic cross. She leaned back and surveyed the table, nodding.

"I see a story of love, one that moves backwards and forwards in time," she said.

Her hand hovered over another card in the spread.

"I see conflict or tension or difficulty of some sort," she said.

I winced. I didn't want conflict or tension or difficulty of *any* sort with my sister.

"It could just be the conflict of the pain that is resurfaced in returning to your mom's past," Stacy said. "I also see that finding your sister is part of your spiritual path. You are healing your mother's trauma."

I wondered how much of this was in the cards and how much of this came from what Stacy already knew of my life. Six months before finding my sister, I had started meditating and reading deeply about spirituality: Buddhism, Zen, Taoism. I'd chalked it up to a desperate search for stability amid career uncertainty, but the timing felt weirdly poetic, not unlike the fact of working alongside a former doula while revisiting my mom's teenage pregnancy. Just in time for meeting my sister, who told me that she had been blessed, I had transformed from an arrogant atheist into someone actively exploring my sense of connection to something bigger than myself.

"The big story, the real story I see, is one of love," Stacy said, passing her palm over the full spread. "It's all over these cards: love, love, love."

She tapped the air with each repetition of "love." The bangles around her wrist clinked like a bell. My backyard had been swallowed by darkness, leaving just the four of us lit by the glowing fire. We could have been anywhere and in any time, save for the familiar whoosh of cars on the freeway in the distance.

"It's like, 'Okay, universe, I get it.'" She laughed. "*Love.*"

"Okay." I nodded. "Love is good. I like love."

5

GOOD AND BAD

My hotel room in Los Angeles had chipped concrete walls that turned out to be wallpaper made from photographs of the building's *actual* concrete walls. That morning I'd flown in for a long, lingering business lunch with my boss at an exclusive club in West Hollywood, where they made me put a sticker over my phone camera lens because they didn't want civilians taking photos of celebrities, and where the actor Jon Hamm sat down right next to me.

I had been so starstruck that it wasn't until now, back at my hotel room and settling in for my one-night stay, that I realized: This was the same man who played Don Draper on *Mad Men*, a show that dramatized the gendered tumult of the sixties, the very period that had recently overtaken my brain. On the show, Draper's secretary, Peggy, gets pregnant out of wedlock, places her baby for adoption, and is hospitalized with a "psychoneurotic disorder." Draper urges Peggy to move on and forget her baby, delivering this preposterously false line: "This never happened. It will shock you how much it never happened."

Days before this trip, I had underlined a sentence fragment in Ann Fessler's *The Girls Who Went Away*, a book about this era of maternity homes and adoption: "they discovered that moving on and forgetting was impossible." As I dug my pen across the page, it occurred to me that rooting around in my mom's past was not only about understanding her, and myself, but also a way to insist: *This happened.*

Now the world outside my floor-to-ceiling hotel window had fallen dark. The apartment building across the way was a disorganized checkerboard of windows—pitch black, bare and bright, covered and glowing. I pressed a button to automatically lower a sheer privacy screen, cracked a can of sparkling wine from the minibar, and opened my laptop, feeling pulled to search my inbox for my mom's name.

I sometimes returned to my mom's emails around Mother's Day, her birthday, or the anniversary of her death. I could lose hours—an entire day, even—clicking through these messages, alternating between tossing my head back with laughter and blowing my nose into a wad of tissues. These emails from my mom spanned the eight years between my college graduation ("I hope you know how very proud of you we are") and the months before she died ("For me, nothing is harder than knowing what I will miss of your life").

They showed everything in between, too: my mom marking my birthday ("You have been an absolute treasure"), asking random questions ("Do you like oatmeal cookies?"), and coaching me through breakups. "The loneliness, I think, can be endured when you have a vague 'faith' in the idea that things will get better," she wrote after an especially bad breakup. "I know that is hopelessly corny and meaningless, but also true. Ick!!!" She ended that email by telling me about a pair of shoes she had gotten me as a present before jokingly warning, "Do not go out and tell your friends that your mom is so dense she thinks new shoes will fix your pain."

I loved how these messages seemed to press play on a long-lost tape of her voice, which I missed so very much. But what I was specifically interested in was an exchange I remembered in which I'd asked about her sexual coming of age—and there it was, a message that was starting to hold so much more meaning.

I had emailed her explaining that I was writing a blog post about "the current generation and how the aesthetics of porn are influencing teen sex." It was 2009 and I was in my mid-twenties, working as a feminist blogger. I'd asked what kind of "cultural ephemera" had defined her teenage understanding of sex. "Sex was something boys were expected to want and actively seek and girls were to be the gatekeepers, a job made easier by an attitude that females just want to cuddle and do not have a sex drive," she wrote back. "At least, good girls didn't have a sex drive." She added: "No one was kidding."

At her high school in suburban Indiana, there had been a fad of wearing a circle pin, "a round, unbroken symbol of one's virginity." Mothers, she explained, often "seemed to present [sex] as a bleak obligation," a "duty in marriage." Her older brother kept *Playboys* in his room. "Our family was really rather prudish so I think it's amazing that it was totally accepted," she wrote. When she was alone in the house, she sometimes checked out the *Playboys*: "I'm sure my parents would have been horrified if they had known."

I thought of her father, John, a classic fifties patriarch who drank too much and "ruled like a tyrant," as my mom had put it. He married her mother, Quen, right out of high school. Quen was good at playing the part expected of a housewife as John brought home the bacon. He was a Midwestern farm boy without a college education who helped build a big-time plumbing and heating company, eventually amassing wealth. "Your grandfather is rich," my mom told me when I was little, and I pictured Scrooge McDuck diving into piles of gold coins. John liked to dress Quen in furs and fine jewelry to show off his success. She had a life of financial comfort but also silent misery. My mom always called it a "deal with the devil."

It was only as Quen was on her deathbed in her sixties that she broke her silence. She called the whole family into her room, including my mom, who held me, then a six-month-old baby, in her arms. I was flushed and fat-cheeked opposite Quen, whose face was gray and sunken from the ravages of ovarian cancer. "You were the love of my life," Quen said, looking at her husband of over four decades, "and I should have left you the day I married you."

She had tried to leave once. In high school, my mom came home one day to find her mom packing her bags, but my grandfather got Quen to stay by telling her that he would die first and then she would be free.

As everyone looked on, Quen continued: "You promised me a second chance. You promised me a better life, a happy life." I was far too little to remember "the speech," as my mom called it, but I grew up hearing about it. Every time my mom told the story, I knew that she was handing me operating instructions for this life of mine. She was warning me about how a woman could find herself imprisoned in sex and marriage. The lesson I took was that I could escape imprisonment through the right series of choices. *No deals with the devil.*

Taking a long, slow sip of my minibar wine, I realized that Quen had looked back on her lifelong marriage with regret, while my mom had grieved her first child "every day," as she had told me.

The parallels between their stories were suddenly obvious: In one of the books stacked on my desk back at home, the pre-*Roe* practice of placing unwed mothers' babies for adoption was compared to a Faustian bargain in which something of spiritual importance is traded for superficial benefits. Women could relinquish their children in exchange for a return to normal life, and they were often tricked, manipulated, or coerced into accepting this deal with the devil.

I thought of my grandmother packing her bags in a frenzy in the sixties, long before Indiana legalized no-fault divorce, which allowed people to end marriages without having to prove "wrongdoing." I imagined my grandfather begging her to stay and promising that she would be rid of him soon enough. I wondered if he also reminded her of the harsh realities that she would have faced as a single mother—and if those were the same arguments that he made a few years later, when my mom found herself single and pregnant.

In both their cases, the "devil" was the nuclear-family ideal—as constructed by white middle-class patriarchal values. Here were two generations of women strong-armed by feminine expectation. My grandmother played by the rules and was punished for it; my mom broke the rules and was punished for it. The real lesson in these maternal parables: There is no way to win in a system rigged for oppression, only different ways to lose.

Turning back to my mom's email, I could see how her eventual sexual rebellion might have emerged from her understanding of her mom's deal with the devil and the "cultural ephemera" of her time. She recalled "endless 'sex' comedies," including those with Rock Hudson "chasing an outraged Doris Day." It had seemed to her that "the 'game' between men and women was very high-stakes—for the woman." There was also the hit 1960 film *Where the Boys Are,* about spring break in Florida, "where the 'bad' girl who has sex tries to kill herself," she remembered. The cultural "emphasis on hostilities between the sexes" made her feel "like we were destined to be enemies on a very fundamental, survival level," she said.

My mom ended her email with: "I don't know if this is worth anything to you, but I hope so." *More than you ever could have known*, I thought. Before I had any conscious thought to do it, I hit the reply button and watched an empty window pop open. "To: Deb Clark," the address field read. I gasped and clicked it closed, as though I'd opened a portal that was supposed to stay shut.

....

I decided to do some reading about *Where the Boys Are.* "The film mainly focuses on the 'coming of age' of four girl students at a midwestern university during spring vacation," Wikipedia told me. One of the girls, Melanie, "loses her virginity on her first date." When the first guy abandons her, she moves on to Guy No. 2, whom she sleeps with, too. Then, Wikipedia explained, Melanie goes to meet Guy No. 2 in a motel room, but Guy No. 1 shows up instead. And here was a major detail that my mom had omitted: He rapes her. It's not just "sex" that drives her to a suicide attempt. "Melanie, her dress torn, walks into traffic," explained the dispassionate summary. "Just as her friends arrive, she is sideswiped by a car and is rushed to the hospital." And then I read this line: "Ultimately, the girls resolve to act more maturely and responsibly."

"More *maturely* and *responsibly*?" I screeched at my laptop. "She was *raped.*"

I looked behind me at the door to my hotel room, remembering myself as a woman traveling alone. I clicked out of Wikipedia and started googling again. I learned that this morality tale about premarital sex had been adapted from a novel of the same name written by Glendon Swarthout, a college professor who had overheard some students talking about spring break. He'd asked to follow them on their vacation to Fort Lauderdale and then channeled his judgments of youth culture into this book-turned-film, which stoked fears about young women's sexual behavior.

Those fears were only further stoked by the film's cultural impact. Despite its cautionary tale, *Where the Boys Are* popularized the fantasy of a collegiate beachside bacchanal. After its release, the number of spring breakers in Florida more than doubled. Fast-forward to the mid-eighties, and there were not just twenty thousand but *hundreds of thousands* of spring-break revelers in Florida. In 1986, two years after I was born, MTV started broadcasting from spring break in Florida. Soon spring break became a defining symbol of youthful sexuality and rebellion.

This pop-cultural moment from my mom's coming of age had helped build the notion of spring break, a staple of my own coming of age. As a teenager in the nineties, I spent hours, days, *whole weeks* lying on the living room couch in a spring-break stupor, watching MTV's wall-to-wall coverage of misbehaving coeds. There were beachside dance parties, where barely clothed college students ground against each other to the pop songs of the moment, but also reality-TV series, including one that promised an "undercover" look at spring break.

The resulting images were burned into my retinas: a tequila shot slurped out of a pierced belly button; two girls and one guy kissing one another at the same time in a move they dubbed "the triple kiss"; a wet white T-shirt suctioned to a young woman's breasts as she bounced around onstage in front of hundreds of screaming men.

Spring break had inspired that other pop-cultural staple of my adolescence: *Girls Gone Wild.* The infamous VHS video series started in 1997 with footage of mostly white college-age women flashing their breasts during spring break in Fort Lauderdale. The series was the creation of Joe Francis, a man who would eventually be accused of a great many things, including coercing and tricking women into performing in these films. As a teenager, I sometimes stayed up late to catch *Girls Gone Wild*'s infomercials, which featured censored previews of women flashing their breasts—for beads, a free T-shirt, or just the attention of TV cameras.

Spring break seemed to grant permission to let go of any inhibitions. The usual rules did not apply. The girl next door could let loose, under the influence of peer pressure, alcohol, or free swag. Spring break was a temporary, sanctioned state of debauchery, one where girls were not just allowed but encouraged to be a little bit bad.

Spring break. Bad girls. Wild girls. I felt myself hurtling back through time. Suddenly, I was a sixteen-year-old high school sophomore on a beach in Hawaii. *Was it spring break?* Oh god, it *was* spring break. I'd been invited to a party on the beach, where I met a boy who seemed older than the sixteen he claimed. He stole some rum for us from a convenience store and rubbed my back as I threw up from too many swigs. My clearest memory from the night: He laughed when a local girl drunkenly stumbled, and he called her "Trashy Ashley." Then he kissed me before leading me to a poolside cabana and pulling the curtains closed. This boy guided me through a series of firsts—everything but losing my virginity—while my peripheral vision started to blur.

Just a few minutes before curfew, I ran through the dark back to the condo my parents had rented down the beach, my feet slipping inside Steve Madden platform sandals, my bladder straining against tight denim cutoffs, the edge of my T-shirt crusted with ejaculate. I was moving forward through space, but it felt more like falling—skin tingling, stomach lodged in my chest. That cabana was like doing a cannonball into adult life. Alongside the thrill was the threat of consequences. Not only was I young, drunk, and alone at night, but I had also just done the kind of thing that got a girl nicknamed Trashy Ashley. My eyes darted left and right, my head wheeled around, searching for danger in the shadows of tropical plants and beach chairs.

It was another year before I lost my virginity to my boyfriend Snow. My mom quickly got over her initial panic at the thought of me having sex: Snow and I came up with the idea of a romantic getaway in nearby Santa Cruz, but we were too young to rent a hotel room on our own, so my mom booked it for us. I didn't tell her that the whole point of the trip was to lose my virginity, but she probably had her suspicions. She was making space for me to come into my sexuality—safely and without having to hide.

My mom must have thought of her own experience losing her virginity, which I asked her about once in my twenties. It happened at a high school party with a boy from her class. "I wanted to just get it over with," she said. "Virginity felt like a burden." Her attitude sounded jaded, but her view of sex was not. It never made sense to her that sex was something women simply refused or endured. She had a sex drive; she wanted to do more than cuddle.

All the influences of her childhood had suggested that men and women were, in her words, "destined to be enemies," but my mom still believed that sex could be an experience of "friendship and beauty." She reached for its potential.

"Sex," she told me once, "can be a mutual gift."

....

My West Coast women's college was the antithesis of the *Girls Gone Wild* infomercials and MTV spring-break specials. There were no flashed breasts or belligerent frat boys in my turn-of-the-century dorm. Any "girl-on-girl" make-outs happened behind closed doors, without any boys to see, which felt to me like the philosophical conundrum of a tree falling in the woods with no one to hear. Did *anything* exist without a man there to see it? I took women's studies classes where I read about phallocentrism, the male gaze, and the feminist porn wars of my mom's generation.

Sometimes I climbed into my dorm room's twin bed and watched porn on my laptop, always with my headphones in so the neighbors couldn't hear the moaning women on my computer screen. I had started watching porn as a teenager because it seemed like a guidebook to sexiness, a way to get "good" at sex. Then I discovered its capacity for giving *me* pleasure, the kind that came from images of women with insatiable appetites—for men, sex, ecstasy, adventure.

My own desire had long felt outsize and in excess. In middle school, my friends had passing celebrity crushes, while I ran a daily Leonardo DiCaprio newsletter that led me to spend hours every afternoon writing in the style of a barely suppressed squeal. In high school, while other girls passed notes in class, my best friend, Meredith, and I drew elaborate manga-style cartoons about imaginary adventures with real-life crushes. Back then my mom called me "boy crazy" with a knowing and appreciative smile. I never lost that sense of being crazy for boys, and then for men.

The moaning women on my computer screen felt like an affirmation of that craziness. Granted, they were performing a straight male fantasy about women's desire, but it was the best endorsement that I had found. For a long time, shame and taboo looked to me like freedom—take the classic pornographic tropes of the cock-hungry housewife and the busty librarian. Women exploded out of their prim and proper roles, losing all feminine respectability. They were undone by the largeness of their desire—or their bosom, which threatened to pop the buttons on their ladylike cardigan. Of course, the fantasy was rarely about a woman recognizing the full complexity of herself outside of restrictive feminine roles.

This was not so far from the collegiate bacchanal that I'd grown up on: going "wild" was a slide between extreme states. Good to bad, tame to wild, innocent to sinful. The naughty librarian finally let her hair down, but eventually, she slid back; the hair returned to the bun. The point *was* the contradiction, the momentary lapse. The cultural ideal wasn't unrestrained sexual liberty but rather walking a thin line. To quote Ludacris from a popular song at the time: "We want a lady in the street but a freak in the bed." I loved that part; I mouthed the words every time.

After college, I moved to San Francisco and got my job as a feminist blogger. At the end of each workday, I would return to my tiny studio apartment and glance up at the built-in bookshelf by the front door that I'd ornamented with signifiers of my twenty-something self. On that bookshelf, I had a figurine of Angelina Jolie as the video game heroine Lara Croft. She stood in a silver skintight bodysuit with an empty black holster around one thigh. I had placed the miniature toy gun in her hand and positioned her arm at a right angle to her body. Any man I brought home was greeted by this sex symbol pointing a gun at him. She was all lips, boobs, and combat boots.

There were loads of books, too—mostly on sex and feminism. Some had titles like *Whores and Other Feminists* and *Jane Sexes It Up*, a third-wave sex-positive feminist anthology featuring a cover image of a topless woman with Bettie Page–style hair. The book's title covered the space between her legs like a "censored" bar, but you could tell: She was wielding a strap-on.

Another pointed gun, I guess.

There was a collection of DVDs of *Sex and the City*, a series that featured women dating around, having sex, and buying pink vibrators shaped like bunny rabbits. "The only place you can control a man is in bed," Samantha said in one episode. "If we perpetually gave men blow jobs, we could run the world." Against those DVDs, I had propped a small-scale print of the poster for the 1958 campy sci-fi film *Attack of the 50 Foot Woman*. In it, a woman in a miniskirt and bikini top towered over a freeway with a car in one hand. A group of men fled at her feet, one considering a deadly leap from an overpass just to escape her. She reached toward the rodent-size men with sharp red fingernails like bloodied claws.

The claws. The blow jobs. The pointed gun. The *boobs*. I saw women's bodies and sexuality as a weapon. You could say I saw women's bodies and sexuality as heterosexual men often have—a threat to patriarchal power—only, I idolized women's bodies and sexuality as power *within* patriarchy.

Taking men home, casually and without any commitments, was empowering, or so I thought. This was what modern women could do, right? Have sex like a man—freely and unabashedly. But I did not have sex like a man, at least not according to the masculine stereotype of sexual selfishness. I walked my partners past the sex symbol with the firearm before promptly dispensing of the metaphorical gun. We fell into bed, and I lost touch with any sense of what I wanted beyond being wanted. I catered to my partner's every erotic whim and faked all my orgasms, instead taking pleasure in giving pleasure.

I insisted on my right to have sex, but I had sex that was indelibly shaped by the world in which I lived.

....

Sitting in my Los Angeles hotel room, still hunched over the glow of my laptop, I saw a theme in my mom's emails, in Quen's story, and in my own: women attempting to escape their mothers' fate. My mom rebelled against her mom's unhappy existence—not only Quen's deal with the devil but also the idea of sex as a "bleak obligation" and a marital "duty." She reached toward the potential of sex as a source of "friendship and beauty," "a mutual gift," something she made clear that she had actually found with my dad.

I rebelled against what I perceived to be my mom's unhappy existence. Sex may have been something she wanted to rescue for herself, but first it had been her downfall; it had gotten her punished in ways that were every bit as enduring as her own mom's Faustian bargain. So I approached sex as battle, grasping for power and control. I'd grown up with stories about Quen's deathbed speech. I saw that there were dangers in marriage, too: It could steal your future and identity, causing you lifelong pain.

I also saw an interwoven cultural story. Contemporary feminist research suggests that the virgin-slut dichotomy has morphed over the decades into a confusing and contradictory continuum. The traditional sexual double standard holds that women's sexuality is passive—being desired—and men's sexuality is active—doing the desiring—while dividing women into "good" and "bad" categories, depending on how they meet those gendered expectations. White, heterosexual, middle-class women—whose race, sexual orientation, and class protect them from being automatically seen as bad—can claim good-girl status by abstaining from sex until marriage or at least a committed relationship with a man. But the traditional sexual double standard was complicated in the nineties and 2000s by pressures to be sexy as well.

Girls and women are supposed to perform desire and pleasure—to seem really into sex with men while not being *too* into sex with men. If you're too into it, you suffer the consequences of shame, humiliation, and a bad reputation. If you're not into it enough, you're a prude. No one knows what "too much" or "too little" means because the definitions are subjective and ever shifting, so we're never really safe. As the feminist scholars Deborah Tolman and Jennifer Chmielewski point out, this mandate serves the same function as the traditional sexual double standard: the control of women's desire and sexuality.

With my generation, there also came new demands toward sexual empowerment—or what the researcher Rosalind Gill calls "compulsory (sexual) agency." You should be sexy *and* empowered, the world seemed to say. The scholar Laina Bay-Cheng highlights how emerging neoliberal feminist ideologies started to place an emphasis on individual choice and striving, as opposed to the feminist imperatives of social justice and collective action, which require cooperatively challenging oppressive systems instead of just finding ways to personally excel within them. Now women are judged based on "the degree of control" they appear to have over their sexual behavior.

These judgments are dependent on race and class. "Some girls are bolstered or shielded by race and class privilege," says Bay-Cheng, while others have to "ceaselessly work against racist and classist stereotypes of hypersexuality and irresponsibility." As the academic Patricia Hill Collins puts it, "Whether a woman is an actual virgin or not is of lesser concern than whether she can socially construct herself as a 'good' girl." Privileged white women are given more leeway to experiment sexually—and even play with being bad, as I did—in part because they are allowed the assumption of goodness in the first place.

Navigating social and cultural pressures around sex used to mean walking a tightrope—my mom had fallen off that tightrope, landing in an institution designed to get her back on it. These days it was more like women had to contort themselves through a field of lasers.

The intended destination of the traditional sexual double standard remained: The sexual influences of my youth had included not only raunchy TV spectacles but also reactive cultural commentary about settling down. Women's desire was portrayed as a danger to marriage: We were told that casual sex could damage our ability to love. We were told to go ahead and marry "Mr. Good Enough" instead of searching for "Mr. Right." Otherwise, some argued, we would end up sad, lonely, childless, and filled with regret.

This commentary was often defended as well meaning and pragmatic—feminist, even. Now it felt so clearly reminiscent of old warnings about the danger of becoming the slut or the whore. *Sex can ruin you. Marriage is safety.*

....

Back when I asked my mom about the cultural ephemera of her youth, I had been expecting a narrative of generational change. In a sense, I'd gotten it: her sneaking glimpses of *Playboy* and watching a morality tale about a girl who has sex on spring break, opposite my unfettered access to internet porn and misbehaving coeds on MTV. By now, though, I understood that the rules for being sexual as a woman in the world had changed over the decades but, in some insidiously sneaky ways, had also stayed the same. You could point to endless markers of real political change—and just as many cultural phantoms that only looked like progress.

I was a product of the political and cultural realities of my time, as well as the pain of my mother's life that I had so desperately wanted to escape. The same was true of my mom—and, almost certainly, the mothers who came before her. The belief that I could dodge my mom's fate had helped to obscure the ways I was mired in the same essential muck. I had "forgotten" details about my mom's past only for them to resurface all these years later. I wondered if I had blocked out parts of my mom's story simply because it was too painful and too relatable, too revealing of the constraints I faced in my own life.

I closed my laptop and glanced at the glowing bedside clock. It was after midnight, a bedtime that was usually unfathomable to me as a parent, but Quinn would not be running in to jump on the bed at seven a.m. Earlier in the night, Christopher had sent me a video of Quinn in his gray-and-white-striped pajamas, cuddled up in the same cushy glider where I'd breastfed him in the first year of his life. In just a few months, he would be turning five and heading off to kindergarten. "Mommy, I love you," Quinn had said in his sweet, breathy baby voice before leaning in to kiss the camera as though it were my cheek. Then he said his usual: "Good night, sweet dreams, I love you," delivered so fast that it sounded like "Gonighsweedrluhyou."

I sent back a video for Quinn to watch when he woke up in the morning, complete with my own kiss of the camera. Then I slipped between the crisp hotel sheets, turned on my bedside light, and opened a book: another history of homes for unwed mothers in the pre-*Roe* period. I had no idea that we were a few weeks from returning to that era.

6

OUR MOM

I emailed the registrar's office at Purdue, explaining matter-of-factly that my mother was dead and, for reasons undisclosed, I wanted her transcript. I didn't mention that my mom had dropped out after getting pregnant as a freshman in the sixties. I omitted the part about how finding my long-lost sister had sparked all these pressing questions, some of which the transcript could help answer. All I explained was that my mom was dead and I wanted that transcript.

I got an email back: "So sorry for your loss." I smiled, feeling touched by this expression of sympathy. Then I kept reading: "Please provide the obituary." They were requesting proof of my loss. "Will do, thank you!" I wrote back with false cheer. Anything to get that piece of paper.

Soon they told me the transcript was in the mail—a post-marked piece of her. It felt like I was waiting on a letter from my mom, like I'd tapped into a dimension where she existed and could write letters and yet somehow still relied on the United States Postal Service. What a treat to receive a new piece of my mom almost a decade after her death. A paper version of her. One that had existed in a rusted file cabinet in the back of an administrative building for more than half a century. What other documents could I request? What other records could I amass?

An envelope arrived, stamped with the university logo, and I tore into it with my thumb, as she must have torn into her acceptance letter. There was a photocopy of a typewritten transcript with blunt letters that gradually lost their inky boldness as the text continued down the page. She had spent her first semester with unprecedented freedom, living in the dorms an hour away from her home in northern Indiana. This brought a series of underwhelming letters: C, D, B, D, C, C. One of the worst grades was in Personal Hygiene. The best was in Physical Education.

I laughed, thinking of all the times my subpar high school grades, including repeated failures in algebra, had led to grave family meetings. She never mentioned her own college record or that she had *nearly failed Personal Hygiene.*

These were the grades that she took home with her for Christmas break, once again under her father's roof and rules. When I was a kid, we had flown across the country several times to visit Grandpa John, who seemed harmless enough in his old age, but I also noted that my mom refused to ever leave me alone with him. *Those grades*, I imagined him saying to her. *Is that what I'm paying all this money for?* How this would have riled my mother, her intellect being her ticket to freedom.

It wasn't just that her smarts had gotten her into a good school and away from suburban Indiana, where she had been expected to go to church every Sunday dressed in her most demure and ladylike clothes. Her smarts, paired with her toughness, had allowed my mom to hold her own against her dad. He never hit her; he favored emotional violence. When I was a kid, she told me if he was in a mood and she looked at him the wrong way, he would eviscerate her with words. I remember having to ask her what "eviscerate" meant. "He would make you feel less than human," she clarified.

My mom called him a "bulldog," and yet she could debate him and win. Her dad was smart, but she was smarter. "If only you had been a son," he told her. She had relayed this detail to me more than once, and I heard the pride in her voice every time. It was a conditional and caveated pride. Her father had approved of her intelligence, he had seen it and understood it, but he had also discounted its worth because she was a woman. He thought there was something "perverted" about a woman who was strong and smart like that, my mom had told me.

I imagined my mom returning to school after winter break, relieved to be free of her father's roof and rules. Counting back from my sister's birthday, I guessed that my mom got pregnant in those early days of the new year. She might have come back to a snow-covered campus, the steps to every building walled by shoveled white. The timing adds a certain romance: Crackling fires. Banging radiators. Coats and gloves and hats. All the layers that had to be taken off. The cold of one's skin. The shock and delight of meeting another body and creating new warmth.

Maybe she met Babajide at a back-to-school party after a few drinks sipped out of a flask with gloved hands. I could picture her crossing the threshold of some bedroom. Finally, again, a taste of freedom.

I doubted that she used any form of contraception. The birth control pill, especially, was often hard to get for young single women. Later that year, 1965, the Supreme Court ruled in *Griswold v. Connecticut* that married couples had a right to contraceptives—but big hurdles persisted for unmarried women, and some state bans continued for single people. The Pill was portrayed as a promoter of "promiscuity," including on college campuses. Some college health officers tried to dissuade unmarried women from going on the Pill, and controversies broke out over doctors who did prescribe it to single students. It wasn't until 1972, the year before *Roe,* that the court extended the constitutional right to contraceptives to unmarried people. At that time, most young and sexually active single women reported rarely or never using contraception.

After that night with Babajide, there must have been a missed period. This was well before at-home pregnancy tests hit the market in the United States in 1977, ten years—*a whole decade*—after they were thought up by the product designer Margaret Crane. When Crane first pitched her idea at the pharmaceutical company where she worked, a manager told her, "What if a senator's daughter, unmarried, found she was pregnant and jumped off a bridge?"—the concern being that the pharmaceutical company would be blamed for the girl's suicide. The subtext is that an unwed pregnancy led to such shame that it could drive a girl to end her own life. Pharmaceutical companies wanted no part of that shame, didn't want to be tainted by it, and "were afraid of . . . aligning themselves with the 'fast women' who desired a fast test," explains the journalist Pagan Kennedy.

My mom—one of those fast women, those girls so hopeless they might jump off a bridge—could have confirmed her pregnancy only through a test at a doctor's office. The results would have told her what she already knew: Her life was about to change forever.

"Abortions were illegal, but I knew girls who had gotten them," my mom had told me when I was in high school. "I believe in the right to choose, but it wasn't the right choice for me." Now I wondered about the tricky nature of the word "choice." An illegal abortion would have carried risks, which fundamentally changes the decision. I knew the risks were much greater for women of color: In the sixties in New York City, abortion accounted for one in two childbirth-related deaths among nonwhite and Puerto Rican women; it was one in four for white women. The illegality of abortion made the procedure dangerous—for reasons ranging from untrained practitioners to a lack of sterilized equipment to the difficulty of getting antibiotics.

The first outcome of my mom's decision to continue her pregnancy was that she would leave school. At the time, most colleges expelled girls for getting pregnant; it would be another ten years before they had any federal protections against this kind of discrimination.

Indeed, the transcript's story ends there. She enrolled in a handful of classes with titles like Social Problems and Elementary Psychology, but in the second semester she didn't get any grades at all. The transcript reads: W, W, W, W, W. It makes me think of the five W's of journalism, which apply to so much of my search around my mom's past. I would find myself turning to them over and over, from every angle: who, what, when, where, why? An answer to a few of those W's: On February 10, 1965, she withdrew from all her classes.

I could only guess at what happened next: She returned to her father's roof and rules. I could feel her dad's whiskey-fueled rage in my rib cage, how he would have made the walls of the house shake upon finding out that his daughter had gotten pregnant. Even as an adult, my mom was afraid of him. Once when I was a kid, she went to visit him after he fell onto his shot glass and broke a rib. Alone in the house with her elderly father, she called my own dad in a panic. "She didn't feel safe," my dad told me much later. "And I couldn't really understand it—he was this frail old man. You could have tipped him over with your pinky finger, but she was scared of him." I can only image her fear at eighteen, single and unexpectedly pregnant.

Did she tell her dad that her baby's father was Black? I had a vague memory from our first conversation about the adoption. "It would've enraged him," my mom said. Or was it simply "It enraged him"? That one word made all the difference. Whatever it was she said in that moment, I'd flashed to imagining my grandfather's face overtaken by a scream—the scream from an iconic civil rights era photo that I'd recently seen in my high school history class. In that image, a young white woman yelled at a young Black woman—Elizabeth Eckford, one of the Little Rock Nine—as she walked to high school during desegregation.

I wondered, too, what part Quen might have played in those early conversations. White women are subjugated by patriarchy, but they often work to uphold it to protect their own relative privilege via proximity to white men's power—including by voting for politicians who are intent on curtailing women's freedom but gesture toward defending the privilege of the white men with whom they share a bed, a mortgage, and the binding legal agreement of marriage.

My dad was pretty sure that my mom's parents never found out that the father of her baby was Black, but I couldn't be certain. No matter what my grandparents knew, the truth is that race was key to my mom being sent away, because it was at the heart of the very notion of the fallen woman and the protective institution of homes for unwed mothers.

. . . .

There was a shift in the nineteenth century in the United States when white women were "no longer portrayed as sexual temptresses," writes the feminist scholar bell hooks. Growing economic prosperity among white Americans led to a movement away from fundamentalist Christianity. Instead of being portrayed as "sinners," white women were desexed and cast as pure, innocent, and virtuous. Meanwhile, Black women were seen as the stereotype of "female evil and sexual lust." The hypersexualized jezebel stereotype was used to justify the rampant sexual abuse of enslaved Black women. "As American white men idealized white womanhood, they sexually assaulted and brutalized black women," writes hooks.

The image of the jezebel made "pure White womanhood possible," argues Patricia Hill Collins. Similarly, the myth of the Black male rapist was used to try to legitimize untold injustices against Black men, including lynchings.

The counterpoint to the jezebel was the stereotype of the loving, passive, and maternal mammy, which was used first to "justify the economic exploitation of house slaves" and then adopted to "explain Black women's long-standing restriction to domestic service," writes Collins; the mammy was depicted as "caring for her White children and 'family' better than her own." Crucially, the mammy image did not romanticize the notion of Black women as actual mothers. "American culture reveres no Black madonna," writes the sociologist Dorothy Roberts in *Killing the Black Body*. "It upholds no popular image of a Black mother tenderly nurturing her child."

A set of idealized feminine values known as the "cult of true womanhood" emphasized the importance of piety, purity, submissiveness, and domesticity, but it was implicitly designed for white women only. "The conception of motherhood confined to the home and opposed to wage labor never applied to Black women," writes Roberts. "While Victorian roles required white women to be nurturing mothers, dutiful housekeepers, and gentle companions to their husbands, slave women's role required backbreaking work in the fields." After emancipation, many Black mothers were forced by economic and cultural circumstances to work outside the home, she explains, including as "domestic servants in white people's homes."

True womanhood—*good* womanhood—was built on ideas of "bad" Black women. It was reserved for white women, provisionally. There were strict terms and conditions. In the Victorian era, right alongside these racially constructed ideals, a white woman "lost the privilege of whiteness" when she got pregnant outside of marriage, as the academic Elaine Tyler May puts it. She became a "fallen woman."

To fall, you must first be positioned at some height. Reigning cultural values placed white women on a pedestal of virtue. They were imbued with goodness—a goodness that could be lost. Black women were cast as "bad girls" from the start. There was little distance to fall. There was no redemption. No repair. No reform.

There would have been no homes for unwed mothers without white femininity, white culture, and white respectability, as they all intersected with the middle class. All these things are built on the existence of a Black "other." In many ways, the race-based approach to unwed motherhood in the post–World War II era worked to maintain that otherness.

White unmarried mothers were redirected toward marriage and the middle-class nuclear family. Meanwhile, in raising their children, Black unwed mothers faced a host of associated costs—from lost education to lifelong poverty. Racist laws and policies also directly targeted Black unwed mothers with surveillance, harassment, and welfare restrictions, as well as imprisonment and sterilization. The visibility of Black single mothers was used to support campaigns for everything from school segregation to restrictive public housing policies, and all against the backdrop of a growing civil rights movement.

The racially divided approach to unwed motherhood was designed to prevent individual women's further sexual misbehavior, but it also worked against shared rebellion. Black and white women's reproductive fates were determined along diverging paths, obscuring their shared interests in reproductive justice. As Collins argues, the control of both white and Black women's sexuality and reproduction is "essential in reproducing racialized notions of American womanhood."

Maternity homes were part of a broader racist effort at the time, but they were also part of a centuries-old history of using women's bodies for white supremacist aims in the United States, starting in the earliest colonial days. White settlers saw population growth among Europeans and enslaved Africans—and the genocide of Indigenous people—as key to their claims to land, wealth, and political power. They developed laws, policies, and a culture to support those ends, as explained by Solinger and Loretta J. Ross in the book *Reproductive Justice.*

Take, for example, the 1662 law that defined the status of a child as either enslaved or free based on the status of the mother. This turned "the fertility of the enslaved woman into the essential, exploitable, colonial resource," as her pregnancies enriched "the holdings of her owner," write Ross and Solinger. Enslaved women couldn't claim the "right to choose their sexual partners, the right to enter into a legal marriage, the right to mother and protect their own children, or even the right to *know* their own children," who were often sold to new enslavers.

These early population-control strategies were "fundamental to racializing the colonies and then the nation, establishing (and fortifying) the primacy of whites," explain Ross and Solinger. White women—seen as both chaste and fertile—were cast as "the fundamental creative symbol of the white nation," and a "precious resource." The nineteenth century saw the rise of laws criminalizing contraception and abortion—the primary aim being "to make sure that white women brought their pregnancies to term and so gave birth to all the white children necessary for populating the white nation," write Ross and Solinger.

By the end of the century, all states had banned abortion.

This pattern continued into the early twentieth century. Eugenicists set on "racial betterment" conspired with politicians to criminalize interracial sex and target certain people with sterilization—including, notably, women of color. Immigration laws served to defend the "white identity" of the country, and public health officials promoted contraceptives in poor Black communities with the aim of curtailing Black fertility. Federal aid for poor mothers further underscored racial divisions by excluding the "children of 'immoral' unmarried mothers and most women of color."

All these laws used "reproduction to regulate who could live in the United States, who could become a citizen, who could live where, who could be 'white,' who could love and have sex with whom, who could marry, who could be born," write Ross and Solinger.

The postwar approach to unwed pregnancy was a continuation of this disturbing legacy. It was part of an attempt to "make sure that the *right* white women were having as many white babies as possible and that these children were being raised in the *right* white families," write Ross and Solinger. After *Roe*, the maternity homes were shuttered—but the history of using women's sexuality and reproduction for white supremacist aims in the United States did not end.

It still has not ended.

....

Two months after our DNA match, my sister and I got on the phone again. Over the last weeks, I'd made a few attempts at setting up a time to talk, but no plans had materialized. A couple times Kathy had gone silent for long stretches while I told myself stories that made me feel like I was lost in the wilderness: *She doesn't need a sister. She already has one. I'm no one to her. She didn't even know that I existed.* Each time she reemerged with a loving, emoji-filled email, and I clung to those messages, reading them again and again, like an incantation that could help me believe in the strength of our connection.

The reality was that Kathy had been working sixteen-hour days, managing the launch of a brand-new call center for a housing lender. "That's why I have been MIA lately. But I literally think about you every day," she wrote in an email that made my body turn to warm mush. Meanwhile, I had been working a job with flexible hours and "unlimited" vacation, which allowed me to freely fall into obsessive research about our mom.

Now on the phone, as with her emails, Kathy was showing me that she was excited to build a relationship as sisters beyond the fact of our DNA. "I'm so excited to have a little sister," she told me. I was sitting at the window in our guest room, once again looking out at the fixed landmark of Mount Tam across the bay. I watched as a slow-motion wave of airy fog poured over the mountain's sides, filling the sloping forest below. "I get to be a big sister," Kathy continued. "I was always the baby of my family."

I wanted to know absolutely everything about her life, so we started at the beginning. She told me that her adoptive parents, Marguerite and Willie, were Black and had raised four adopted children, all of whom were mixed and had white mothers, just like my sister. Kathy's adoptive mom had been born in 1918 in Mississippi. "I'm pretty sure she was born on a plantation, but she tried to keep that from us," Kathy said. "I think she was ashamed. She was a very proud woman." Marguerite had been approaching fifty years old when she adopted Kathy.

Although Kathy didn't have her own original birth certificate, she knew that she had been born in Chicago. Their family lived on the South Side in a neighborhood Kathy described as predominantly Black and lower-middle class. In addition to caring for her four adopted kids, Kathy's mom regularly fostered children throughout her life. "She took in babies during the crack epidemic," Kathy said. "They cried a lot and no one wanted them, but my mother could handle it." Marguerite had wanted to become a mother but had not been able to have biological children for reasons that were not entirely clear to Kathy.

Her mom stayed at home with the kids while Willie worked full-time on the Ford assembly line and took security gigs on the weekend. Kathy described Marguerite as ingenious and penny-pinching, a woman who would sell homemade popsicles to neighborhood kids during the summer and sock away the money to buy better opportunities for her children. With savings and the help of a scholarship, they sent Kathy to a predominantly white private Lutheran school. "My mom wanted me to experience different cultures," she said. "She wanted me to be able to talk to anyone. She was determined to expose me to all sorts of different things."

My white mother's child had been adopted by a Black woman who had been born on a plantation; a Black woman who had raised three other white women's biological children. Kathy's Black adoptive mother had sold popsicles to give her better opportunities in life while her white biological mother had pursued an education and a career. Another resounding, bell-clanging thought: My mom and sister had been sent away by my grandfather, whose wealth had defined not just my mom's opportunities in life but mine as well.

My grandfather had started my college fund, which allowed me to graduate without any student debt. The money my mom inherited after his death was part of why my parents were able to support me during an unpaid college internship, which turned into my first journalism job right after graduation. It was essentially my grandfather's money that was passed along to my dad after my mom's death that was part of what allowed him to help me and Christopher with the down payment on our house. Plenty of white adoptees in that era were cut off from the wealth of their biological families, but my family's fracture spoke to the inheritance gap between white and Black Americans, which was caused by a long history of injustice—from slavery to land theft to redlining—that contributes to the broader racial wealth gap.

I glanced out the window and saw that the wave of fog had transformed into a solid wall that was advancing across the bay.

"I didn't even know I was adopted for the first decade or so of my life," Kathy continued.

"Wow," I said. "How did you find out?"

"The kids in the neighborhood would call me 'Oreo cookie,'"

Kathy said. "I was like, 'What? I'm not white.' So one day when I was thirteen, I went home and said to my mom, 'Why are they calling me that?' "

That was when her mom told her. The news was a shock but not destabilizing. Her mother was her "world," as she put it, and the fact of the adoption didn't change that. "I was raised as a Black woman," she said. "I feel like a Black woman. I am definitely *seen* as a Black woman. And my mom really taught me to love myself. She gave me confidence in who I was. Some of my siblings struggled with finding out they were adopted, but I didn't. It just seemed obvious to me: It was 1965 in Illinois. My father was Black. My mother was white. I figured somebody forced my mother to give me away."

It wasn't until Marguerite died of breast cancer, when Kathy was thirty-five years old, that she felt like her world crumbled around her. "It was the first time I really felt anxious in my whole life," she said. "Just not having my mother around."

Kathy wanted to know the backstory of her adoption, but I found myself tripping over the language. "I'm sorry," I said. "I don't know how to refer to her—is it 'our mom'? Your 'biological mom'? I've been calling her by her first name in my emails because I don't want to say the wrong thing, but that feels weird. What's most comfortable for you?"

" 'Our mom' is great," she said, and my cheeks flushed from the rush of it.

The fog had reached my backyard, but now it felt like a hazy cocoon. I told Kathy how our mom had been sent away to a home for unwed mothers to protect the family from the shame of her pregnancy. For the first time, I shared some of what I was learning about the history of these homes—their sexist and racist aims, and how adoptions were often coerced. Then I got to the part I most wanted her to know, the piece that felt like a tragic testament to our mother's love for her. "After the adoption . . . our mom had a mental breakdown," I said. "She was swallowed by her grief. She was committed to a mental institution."

"Wow," she said. "Wow."

"Yeah. She got out and returned to school, all of that," I said. "She moved to California and built a life for herself here. But it never left her. She was very clear that she thought about you every single day of her life. *Every single day.*"

Kathy took a wavering breath. "I'm so sorry to hear that our mom suffered," she said. "As a mother, I can only imagine her pain. I can only imagine what that does to you to have your baby taken away." She paused. "It makes me so sad for her."

I folded over my lap with my head in one hand and the phone cupped to my ear. I was so sad for our mom, too.

"What else can you tell me about our mom?" Kathy asked. "What was she like? What was she into?" All Kathy had to go on were the photos I'd sent. I realized that I was our mother's emissary: If my sister was to have any relationship with her, I would have to facilitate it. I felt I was being called upon to write my mom's cover letter—her LinkedIn profile—on a cosmic level.

I picked some key bullet points: Our mom majored in art history and got her master's in English literature. She fled the conservatism of the Midwest as soon as she could, heading straight for the liberal Bay Area. She was artsy and intellectual, working at an art gallery in San Francisco, selling stained glass at craft fairs, and eventually starting her own graphic design business. Nature was her church and she had a spiritual connection to her garden, which she tended every day, and which landed her a spread in

Better Homes & Gardens. She was emotionally wise and had an almost telepathic level of empathy. "Also," I said, "our mom could be fierce, biting, and tough—and she would not take shit from any man."

"I think my two moms would have really gotten along," Kathy said.

I glanced at the time on my phone and realized we had been talking for over four hours. I'd been drinking water the whole time. Now my bladder was so full I'd already unbuttoned the top of my pants. I considered the possibility of muting my phone long enough to go to the bathroom undetected by my sister but decided against it. I crossed and uncrossed my legs. I unzipped my pants. I tried pacing the hallway outside the bathroom. I could have easily asked to call her back in a minute, but I didn't want to interrupt things. I felt we could talk all day long. I didn't want to risk ending it. Peeing myself actually seemed preferable. Then my sister said that she had to go. "We'll talk again soon," she said.

Tomorrow would not be soon enough, I thought.

7

RAPUNZEL

Florence Crittenton is the kind of name you never forget.

Back when I first heard it, Florence made me picture a severe Victorian matron with a stiff black dress and cinched white apron. Crittenton made me think in quick succession of "critters" and then those bug-eyed, havoc-causing monsters from the eighties horror film *Gremlins*. Maybe it wasn't that the name was inherently memorable but that it was forever etched in my mind when my mom told me as a teenager, "We weren't given pain medication. It was punishment for our sins. I remember the other girls' screams."

She had seen smears of blood on the floor, too.

I figured she was talking about the hospital where she gave birth, but for me, those details were forever tied to Florence Crittenton, one of the major organizations that ran homes for unwed mothers in that era. There was so much she didn't talk about, but this she wanted to convey: pain, screams, and blood—the horror of it all. I knew that some women emerged from maternity homes feeling like they had been given mercy, a great kindness, and even lifesaving care. For many others, like my mom, it was more like hell.

After learning that my sister had been born in Chicago—nearly an hour away from my mom's childhood homes in Indiana—I knew where to look. Some light sleuthing brought me to the address of the former Florence Crittenton Anchorage on Chicago's West Side. This place was my best guess as to where my mom had been sent. When I plugged the address into Google Street View, my stomach dropped at the sight of it on my laptop screen: a red brick Victorian building with snaking ivy, boarded-up windows, and one rounded corner that rose towerlike into its own pointed roof. *Like a witch's hat*, I thought. The building made me think of rumbling storm clouds and clapping thunder—a cheap Hollywood rendering of a haunted house.

I clicked back and forth on this virtual street, trying to see the building from different angles, somehow feeling like it might be revealed to be a false front on a soundstage. Instead, noticing a small attic window on the rounded corner, I tumbled right into a fairy tale: I pictured Rapunzel up there, letting loose her waterfall of golden hair.

At the thought, I opened another tab to remind myself of her story and gaped at the resonances.

A woman craves rapunzel, a salad green that grows in a witch's garden. The woman's husband steals some for her, but her desire is irrepressible, so he steals some more, only to be caught by the witch, who promises the wife as much rapunzel as she wants, so long as they surrender their firstborn baby. Out of fear, the man agrees. The witch names the baby Rapunzel, after the mother's damning desire (for stolen lettuce greens, an echo of Eve's apple), and locks the child up in a tower. Years later, Rapunzel lets down her long locks for a wandering prince, who in some versions impregnates her out of wedlock. She is sent away into the woods to give birth and "suffer[s] greatly."

I started copying fragments of text from the fairy tale and pasting them into my Notes app. I ended up with an accidental poem:

> she longed for some
> It was her greatest desire
> This desire increased with every day
> she devoured eagerly
> It tasted so very good to her
> her desire for more had grown
> such a longing came over her

Here was an ode to a woman's desire, minus the original language around reckoning and suffering. *How can we rewrite what is written for us?* I thought, staring at that attic window and feeling pulled back in time. *What can we edit out of the stories we're given?* I was starting to see that this was exactly what I'd spent so much of my life trying to do. Ever since that day at the kitchen table when my mom's secret was finally revealed, I'd wanted to believe that I could erase the punishing language from her cautionary tale and claim only the good parts for myself. In my twenties, I had tried to prove that longing and devouring and eagerness could be mine. That I could unleash my desire without being locked away in a tower.

Now, in my thirties, I had landed in exactly the place intended by these homes: marriage and motherhood. Monogamy. You could say that my *desire* had been locked up in a tower of sorts: an institution designed to control women's sexuality. And yet it was also true that my desire had found a fuller expression inside of my marriage. With Christopher, things were intimate, hot, vulnerable, and playful. There were no more faked orgasms. I joked that we needed more words for sex, because this act that we shared felt definitionally unlike what I had been doing before. These days the dilemma of my desire was the context in which I felt safe enough to authentically explore it.

....

The Florence Crittenton Mission opened in 1883 in New York City's red-light district, just a few doors down from a notorious brothel. It was founded by the wealthy white businessman Charles Crittenton, whose daughter Florence had died of scarlet fever at a young age. He was a man driven by "a supreme pity for the fallen woman and a burning desire to lead her to a Christian salvation," wrote Otto Wilson in a 1933 book on the history of these homes.

A leather-bound reprint of this old five-hundred-page doorstopper had recently shown up at my house, and I'd drawn exclamation points in the margins when I realized that many of these "fallen women" were not unwed mothers but rather sex workers. Crittenton's evangelical "rescue bands" would invade "concert halls, saloons, and disorderly houses," bringing back "many a street walker," as Wilson put it.

Soon the Salvation Army started opening similar homes in the United States after "rescuing" sex workers in England. Crittenton, nicknamed "the brother of girls," traveled across the country, spreading the word of his mission and funding additional homes, which were run by evangelical women. It was in these early years that the Chicago Anchorage opened in a "dark, dingy, forbidding" apartment—long before being upgraded to a Victorian mansion.

It was staffed with a matron and a missionary, and a "pure white lily" was placed in the window "where the draperies parted in the center," wrote Wilson. "For years this beautiful emblem of purity was kept in the window of the 'Anchorage' as an invitation to girls to come in and lead a better life."

As these homes sprouted up across the country, they ran into a problem: Sex workers didn't want to be saved. "Rescuers" could sometimes successfully recruit sex workers during nightly walking tours of red-light districts, but these women wouldn't stick around for long, as the historian Regina G. Kunzel explains in *Fallen Women, Problem Girls*, a book about the earliest history of homes for unwed mothers. Turns out, "women do not voluntarily restrict their own liberty unless forced to do so by illegitimate pregnancy," as the superintendent of a Crittenton home put it in 1926.

So, in the first two decades of the twentieth century, these homes narrowed their attention to a more captive audience: unwed mothers. White ones, specifically. Some homes accepted Black women, but in restricted numbers.

The white girls and women in these homes were cast as passive victims to "rogues, scoundrels, and unscrupulous cads" who had seduced and abandoned them. As a result, these "fallen women" were seen as deserving of sisterly sympathy. They were led through daily prayers and religious services, and schooled in the womanly arts, taking classes in everything from cooking to ironing. Back then the aim was always to keep mothers and babies together; in fact, Crittenton and Salvation Army homes required residents to agree to keep their babies.

If these mothers couldn't get married, to the father of their baby or otherwise, they could get placed as a married couple's domestic servant. Either way, redemption was found in a patriarchal household.

The twenties marked the beginning of a shift of power away from the evangelical matrons who built these homes. Social workers started claiming expertise around "illegitimacy" and unwed mothers, introducing a language not of sisterly sympathy but rather "science" and "treatment." Through the social-work lens, unwed mothers were transformed from passive victims into a threat to the American nuclear family. Unwed motherhood was blamed on "feeblemindedness," an ambiguous and unscientific term that tied notions of women's promiscuity to low intelligence, and which was used by a growing eugenics campaign to justify involuntary sterilization.

As an explanation for unwed motherhood, feeblemindedness presented a problem: How could you explain unwed mothers who were smart? There came another diagnosis: "sex delinquent."

These women were seen as aggressively and dangerously sexual, and a symptom of a larger "girl problem" in the culture. Single, urban working-class women were challenging middle-class values of chastity and testing the bounds of sexual respectability, explains Kunzel. These young women were free to take their pioneering sexual attitudes to dance halls and movie theaters, places of darkness and close bodies. "Social workers called on 'sex delinquency' to explain a female sexual agency that was visible, even flaunted in these new venues," writes Kunzel. Maternity-home case records started reflecting if an unwed mother liked going to the movies or amusement parks—they might even label her a "dance case."

As with feeblemindedness, though, this diagnosis presented a problem: How could you explain unwed mothers who weren't working class? This was especially problematic in the forties, with growing interest in maternity homes from white middle-class unwed women. These women of relative status weren't sex delinquents.

No, no, no. A new diagnosis was born: These girls were neurotic, repressed, and psychologically unwell. Unwed pregnancy was seen as the act of a conflicted psyche, as though these women had subconsciously willed their pregnancies into existence. It was explained by masochism, Oedipal issues, rape fantasies, paternal attachment, overbearing moms—you name it. Theory after theory piled out of the clown car of psychoanalysis.

Now, against the backdrop of the "postwar white family imperative," the unwed mother wasn't seen as morally weak but rather mentally ill. Her illness was seen as the "psychological inability to form a sanctioned relationship to a man," as Solinger explains. This "illness" could be treated through marriage or, at least, "preparing herself for a marriageable future," which was where the homes came in. Proper womanhood was achieved through a man—and so was motherhood. As a result of this shift, the unwed mother, deemed unfit for motherhood, was actively pushed toward adoption.

As ever, this approach to white unwed motherhood was plainly racist. Black unwed mothers were not seen as mentally ill; they were seen as having "the absence of psyche," explains Solinger. They were thought to be "naturally" promiscuous and maternal, assumptions that arose directly from the stereotypes of the sexed-up jezebel and caretaking mammy. In 1965, the influential report *The Negro Family: The Case for National Action* introduced a new stereotype: the Black matriarch. Black single mothers were blamed for a range of social problems, including poverty. "The matriarch represented a failed mammy, a negative stigma to be applied to African-American women who dared reject the image of the submissive, hard-working servant," writes Patricia Hill Collins.

Around the same time, following the approval of the Pill in 1960, Black women were aggressively targeted with birth control campaigns centered not on the value of reproductive rights but on population control. The Pill was presented as Black women's "public health duty." When it came to white women, however, the Pill was cast as an enabler of promiscuity and an agent of dangerous social change. A 1968 *Reader's Digest* article warned, "Everyone knows what The Pill is. It is a small object—yet its potential effect upon our society may be even more devastating than the nuclear bomb."

Alongside the growing countercultural movement of the sixties, the white unwed mother was recast from "a species of mental patient" to "a sexual revolutionary," writes Solinger. Her pregnancy was blamed on a breakdown of social values—it was the "neuroses of the era," not the neurosis of the white unwed mother herself. But that isn't to say that the earlier stigmas disappeared. The primary narrative had shifted, but the entire cast of negative stereotypes remained.

In 1965, my mom and her fellow residents at the home probably got hit with it all: fallen woman, problem girl, mental patient, and dangerous rebel.

. . . .

It all started with sex workers.

I felt like a match had been lit against my skin again, just like when I'd written that list of words in my notebook a couple months earlier. *Whore, loose, slut, ruined, bad girl, promiscuous.* As a teenager, I had idolized sex workers, taking mental notes as I watched the porn star on my computer turn the blow job into an art form. In my twenties, I had sometimes visited strip clubs on drunken nights out with friends, sitting at the tip rail and gazing up at the dancers, whom I saw as aspirational models of desirability. *I mean, look at them. Just* look *at them.*

I felt myself to be pretty straight, but my jaw dropped at the sensual beauty of their performances. The flipped hair, the swinging hips, the clicked Lucite heels—like Dorothy, only they were transporting the audience wherever we wanted to go. Often I'd felt that they were transporting me into a world of forbidden womanhood.

Of course, my mom had her own connection to forbidden womanhood. Once, in my twenties, I sat with her at the kitchen table—the same table where she had delivered the news about my sister. We were talking about my sex life, without actually talking about my sex life.

I told her about a straight woman friend who had said something about penises being gross, a necessary evil of sorts, and another straight woman friend who had never watched porn and wanted to know: *Did they actually have sex in those films?* In sharing my surprise at what my friends had said, I was also saying something about my own relationship to sex.

For me, it was fun, exciting, and intriguing, as an activity and a topic. "It's the most interesting thing in the world," I had breathlessly told a recent partner, but only after having enough drinks that I was compelled to say what I really felt. I couldn't fathom having never watched a single porn clip.

"It makes me feel like an alien species," I told my mom.

She slapped the table in recognition. "I know exactly what you mean. When I was younger, I felt . . . *unusual* for a woman," she said. "Men seemed to think I was, too, because I enjoyed sex. I didn't see it as a burden. I think it scared them a bit."

Ah, I thought, *that's where I get it from.*

She went on to explain that men were also put off by her intellect and independence. "I really thought I would end up having affairs for the rest of my life, just being a mistress," she said. "I really did not see myself being a wife. I couldn't imagine settling down with someone who didn't see me as an equal human being, and I also couldn't see myself living like a nun."

Until she met my dad, it seemed to my mom that marriage required a compromise that she wasn't willing to make, but she wasn't willing to give up on sleeping with men, either. My mom wanted sex *and* freedom. So she resigned herself to the idea that she would play the role of the other woman, the wife's foil and antagonist.

It was more than an idea: A few years after being sent away, she started an affair with a married man, whom she would take a train to meet in clandestine locations. She became the kind of woman who not only had sex outside of marriage but also directly threatened the institution.

I ended up spending a good chunk of my journalism career writing about forbidden womanhood, which is to say: sex work. After years broadly covering the sex beat, I narrowed my focus in my late twenties to writing about the porn industry. I covered policies and practices that impacted sex workers, like health regulators' attempts at mandating condoms in adult films despite performer protest. I reported on laws that purported to fight "sex trafficking" while really just putting sex workers' lives in danger.

I was passionate about sex workers' rights—more so than any other feminist cause. My father-in-law once asked me why. He was visiting us from Boston, and I was on my way out the door to cover a local rally for International Whores' Day, a global celebration of sex workers' rights. I stumbled through my response, partly because of the awkwardness of talking about sex and politics with my father-in-law, but also because so much of my "why" felt beyond words.

"I guess I can't stand the hypocrisy of our sexual culture," I told him. "The way that, say, pornography is a wildly popular and ubiquitous form of entertainment, but then sex workers are punished with shame and stigma—not to mention legislative assaults that are ostensibly meant to 'protect' them but that actually make their work less safe."

I paused to think, my face burning hot.

"I feel like sex workers are often the canaries in the coal mine, you know?" I continued. "Especially around technology and censorship and free speech—but also cultural attempts at controlling women's sexuality more broadly."

At the time, I was only beginning to be able to articulate that last point, thanks to the words of various sex-worker activists in the books lining my shelves. As the legendary Margo St. James once explained, the concept of "whores" is used to "keep all women in line" and "the punishment of the prostitute is the example set by the system." That "punishment" isn't just the criminalization of prostitution but also the stigmatization of sex workers.

All women live with perpetual pressure to prove ourselves as "virgins" or "wives." Jill Nagle calls this "compulsory virtue," a play on Adrienne Rich's concept of "compulsory heterosexuality." When a woman fails at "compulsory virtue," she faces "whore stigma," a "social and legal branding of women who are suspected of being or acting like prostitutes," writes the sex-worker activist Gail Pheterson.

The punishment of sex workers was essential to getting women to accept unpaid work within the nuclear-family home—again, it was the example set by the system. In the late nineteenth century, women were pushed out of paid factory work, the "family wage" was introduced, and the ideal of the breadwinning husband took off, as Silvia Federici explains. The housewife was an invention of capitalism designed to service "the male worker physically, emotionally and sexually," and without being paid a wage. The housewife's compensation for her unpaid labor was *respectability.* She was paid in approval and esteem, relative to the shame directed at sex workers.

Federici also specifically notes that "the destiny of the unwed mother . . . has been a constant warning to women that anything was preferable to 'losing one's honor' and being considered a 'slut.' " Of course, whore stigma arrived long before the housewife. "Like the profession of prostitution, the division of women into wives and whores is as old as (patriarchal) history," writes Nickie Roberts in *Whores in History.*

The feminist historian Gerda Lerner places the earliest rumblings of patriarchy five thousand years ago, in 3100 BCE. This social system—the same one now irreverently referenced by countless "Fuck the Patriarchy" coffee mugs—developed over the course of thousands of years. In her book *The Creation of Patriarchy*, Lerner argues that it emerged from a complex host of factors—from the tribal trade of women for marriage, which she says paved the way for the very notion of private property and social class, to the emergence of monotheistic beliefs linking women's non-procreative sexuality to sin and evil.

Lerner also notes that Middle Assyrian law severely punished "harlots" for veiling in public, an act reserved for only "respectable" women. It codified the notion of "good" and "bad" women. Ever since, writes Lerner, "the sexual control of women has been an essential feature of patriarchal power."

Then as now, whore stigma targets sex workers, but it "implicitly controls *all* women," creating a cultural sense of "illegitimate or illicit femaleness," Pheterson explains. It applies to any woman who challenges expectations around heteronormative marriage and motherhood, too—from a divorcée to a woman who speaks out against domestic violence. It's the fundamental underpinning of the more popularly recognized phenomenon of slut-shaming—which has its own storied history, from Eve on down.

In the years after that awkward conversation with my father-in-law, I came to better understand my interest in sex work through this lens of sexual control, but I hadn't seen the link to my mom, which now felt like another puzzle piece dropped into place. Absent whore stigma, these homes—these "systems of redemption"—would have had no reason to exist.

Without even realizing it, I had been writing against what had been done to my mom.

. . . .

Despite how much the histories of homes for unwed mothers told me, I still longed to peer inside this particular home. Then I found a way in. One afternoon at home on my lunch break, I was scrolling through a Facebook group for birth mothers and adoptees with ties to Florence Crittenton. I noticed a comment from someone named Toni, a woman in her seventies who had stayed at the Anchorage in 1968, three years after my mom gave birth. Toni had been nineteen years old at the time. I clicked through to her profile and found a photo of her grinning next to a young woman around my age whom I imagined to be her daughter—the child she'd had so many years after being sent away.

Right away, I messaged Toni to ask if I could interview her to learn more about the particulars of my mom's experience. She was happy to talk, as long as we did it through email. "That gives me as much time as I need to try to remember," she wrote. "It was over 50 years ago, and not really something I worked to remember all these years."

Toni described the home as a beautiful old mansion with "lots of dark wood trim, huge rooms, nice, ample furnishings." Her roommate cried so much that Toni had to change rooms to escape the torment. "She was in a lot of emotional pain—we all were, but some of us, like me, were able to stuff it down in a gigantic effort of denial," she said. This helped Toni in the short term; in the long run, it left her with PTSD. She recalled one young woman who was in such denial that she refused to believe she was even pregnant.

The "inmates," as Toni called them, cleaned the house and took turns helping in the kitchen. In their free time, they could dance to music on the record player or take art classes; she remembered there being a kiln for ceramics. Her descriptions were sparse, but the home and the young women were coming to life, as though she had unpaused a movie midscene. Music crackled over the record player, hips swayed, and arms flowed. These women's pregnancies had been hidden away—from the world and even themselves—but in this imagined transcendent moment, their bodies moved freely. Meanwhile, the kiln hummed and glowed, baking the clay vessels inside.

I thought of these girls as vessels. I thought of how clay has to harden to break. Quinn had recently made an unbaked clay bowl for me. After leaving it to dry for half a day, he tried to smooth out its rough texture and broke it in two. The metaphor was right there: These women were seen as damaged, a problem to fix, but the purported solution was so often what made them fall to pieces. My mom wasn't broken by sex or pregnancy. She was shattered by a shaming institutional response that required her to abandon essential parts of herself, including her baby.

I read on through Toni's email, and the movie in my head resumed again. She described a maintenance man who was a "lech," as she put it. "He made us think he needed to show us something in the basement, where he would try to kiss us on the lips." I saw him in the dim light of the basement, clad in dirty coveralls, lunging toward the opportunity of a woman already debased in the eyes of society. "I guess I wasn't the only one who got kissed—I got up those stairs really fast for being nine months pregnant," wrote Toni.

I imagined the tops of thighs hitting round underbelly as girl after girl ran up those stairs—month after month, year after year, because they were all too embarrassed to tell, because they told themselves they deserved it, because who would believe them, anyway?

There was also a "haughty and judgmental" nurse—Toni thought her last name might have been Smith. She was "not one to 'cozy up to,'" she wrote. While having them line up for their prenatal exams, Toni said this nurse barked at the girls, "For god's sake, clean the toilet tissue off your pubic hair." My stomach knotted at the familiar vulnerability of a paper gown, spread legs, and gloved hands. It knotted more at the thought of being shamed as unclean by the person wielding those gloved hands. And yet more at the thought of those gloved hands belonging to an employee of an institution created by shame. An institution that had in its earliest days displayed a "white lily in bloom" as an inspiring symbol of purity.

A few weeks after I found Toni, an email landed in my inbox that brought Mrs. Smith to life, and in her very own words. I'd reached out to the library at the University of Illinois Chicago, which houses the records from the Anchorage, including nineteen different boxes of printed materials ranging from board meeting minutes to financial records. There were also copies of the resident-run newspaper, including from the year my mom was there. A librarian sent me a digitized copy of the issue published on October 7, 1965, just four days after Kathy was born.

On the second page: a note from none other than Mrs. Smith, who had just returned from vacation. "Now, don't forget how keen my hearing is, particularly after 10 PM, lights out, then I hear everything," she wrote. She continued with what felt to me like gallows humor, "Remember my bit of advice: to report all warning signals so we can go to the hospital in style, not a mad rush like women going to a bargain sale." It was the residents' gallows humor that made me burst out laughing. A "Who's Who" column posed cheeky riddles:

> Who is most likely to sleep through her own labor?
> Who is most apt to miss her urine specimen bottle?
> Who didn't know they had a mole on her belly button until it turned inside out?
> Who has the sexiest nightgowns in town?

There was also a gossip column that reported humorous scoops from each dormitory-style room:

Room 1. It seems this room has an awfully hard time convincing its roommates that they're in labor.
Room 2. We would like to pay our respects to our two deceased friends, Mr. and Mrs. FLY. They had an unfortunate encounter with a book on communism.
Room 3. It seems Room 3 is a haven for unwed mother mice and other friendly rodents that happen to be passing by.
Room 4. Some goofball in this room can't tell the difference between hard boiled eggs and raw eggs; especially when they are for her roommate.

I loved these women and their ability to joke about urine specimen bottles and "unwed mother mice." I wanted to hang out with them. *Can we be friends?* I thought. Their sense of humor—irreverent, slant, and just the right amount of silly—reminded me of my mom. *Maybe she got it from this place. Maybe that kind of sensibility emerges from trauma. Maybe my mom passed it down to me.*

Room 12 brought it back to Mrs. Smith, suggesting that "there should be a spare carton of 'medicated' cigarettes on hand" for her. I read this and thought, *Hi, Mom.* I could just imagine her quipping that Mrs. Smith needed to smoke a joint, already.

What if it *was* my mom? Of course, I didn't know that my mom was in room 12—I hadn't even been able to confirm that she had been at this home. Even still, the thought thrilled me, but it felt dangerous, too—as if, with each additional piece of information uncovered, I was gradually casting a spell whose aim and outcome I didn't quite understand. The digital yearbook, the home address, and these library archives hadn't just unlocked information about the past—they had the power to change the future, too.

It absurdly called to mind *Back to the Future,* which I'd watched so many times as a kid, fascinated, above all, by the existential threat of time travel. You might undo your own existence. Here I was, visiting wrongs from the past: my mom being sent away and my sister being given away. These wrongs were not just essential to who I had become; they were essential to my having become at all. If my mom had not been sent away, if my grandfather had agreed to help support her as a single teenage mother, he never would have become my grandfather.

In the realm of philosophy and physics, there is something called the grandfather paradox: What happens if you travel back in time and kill your own grandfather before he has kids? My paradox was this: traveling back in time and mourning the events that had made my own life possible.

8

SORRY ABOUT HER

I was hit with a sudden memory of Christmastime when I was around eighteen. My mom and I were walking out of a drugstore near our house. A man was standing out front wearing a Santa hat and a red apron. He rang his bell and said, "Merry Christmas, ma'am! Would you care to donate to the Salvation Army?"

I smiled as young women are taught to smile at anyone and everyone who demands something of their time. My mom did not smile. Instead, she vigorously shook her head. "No," she told him firmly. "*No.*" Then she turned to me and said loudly enough for him to hear, "Those people will *never* get my money."

I was embarrassed, and not just because I was a teenager with a parent who was threatening to make a scene. I was specifically embarrassed as a teenage girl whose mother was stepping outside the bounds of feminine appropriateness. I glanced apologetically at the bell ringer as if to say, *Sorry about her.* As we made our way to the car, my mom explained—something about the Salvation Army and her teenage pregnancy.

Looking back, I felt this made no sense. I was sure that she had told me she'd gone to a Florence Crittenton home. *What did the Salvation Army have to do with her being sent away?* I figured that maybe she had stayed at a Florence Crittenton home and merely despised the Salvation Army for running similar homes, but then I asked my dad. "She always mentioned them together when she talked about being sent away," he said.

I decided to go digging through old belongings at my dad's house. I didn't know what I was looking for—I just felt pulled to search through my things. I stepped into my childhood closet and pulled out a big cardboard box into which my dad had tossed a bunch of old papers and belongings. On the top was a binder full of breathless notes written in multicolored gel pens with my best friend, Meredith, about our various high school crushes. At some point, I had tucked the notes into plastic binder sleeves as important artifacts of teenage longing.

Underneath this binder of desire was a piece of paper I had never seen. It was a copy of my mom's application for an adoption registry. This was the registry she had told me about when I first learned about my sister. Birth parents submitted information, like the when and where of the birth, so they could be found in a database if their biological children ever came looking. My mom's handwriting was just as I had remembered it—blunt, rounded, and precise—except for her answer to the field "HOSPITAL (Birth Place)." She wrote: "Florence Critednon." It looked like the *d* was written on top of an *n*, as if she had messed up in the flow of writing and tried to correct herself.

Still, it was a misspelling of Crittenton.

This was bizarre for my mom, who had prided herself on accuracy in writing. At her graphic design company, she had copyedited all their print materials, catching misspelling and grammatical errors as well as errant commas and spaces. This misspelling reminded me of a kid trying to spell words they hadn't seen and had only ever heard people pronounce.

After "Florence Critednon," she wrote a slash and then: "Salvation Army." Here on paper, I had proof of my dad's memory of her mentioning these organizations in the same breath. I found that the Salvation Army's Booth Memorial Hospital was not too far from the Anchorage. It had housed unwed women in dormitory-style rooms, as a 1967 newspaper article reported, "through their pregnancy and delivery, until the day they leave—usually without their baby." At that time, only 11 percent of women at the hospital kept their babies. As at the Anchorage, they spent their days doing "handicraft activities," visiting an on-site beauty parlor, and meeting with social workers who helped them "plan for the future."

Over the last weeks, I had tried and failed to locate the Anchorage's records, but an archivist at the Salvation Army walked me through the process of accessing their files. We talked on the phone, human to human, lamenting "how things worked back then." These days, she explained, they tried to help families who came looking for information about decades-old adoptions—but first there were a few legal requirements. As requested, my dad sent along notarized proof that he had power of attorney, a photo of my mom's death certificate, and a check for twenty dollars.

Then we got a letter back. "Our attorney reviewed your application and found that the Power of Attorney does not appeal [*sic*] to be sufficient to warrant the release of confidential records." *What the fuck.* I reached out to the nice archivist again. Had the grounds for accessing records changed overnight? "I am sorry, I would recommend you contact an attorney for guidance," she wrote.

At her email, I stood up so forcefully that my computer chair rolled across the room. The human-to-human connection was gone. Lawyers were involved, and now only lawyers could be involved. "How could she, how *dare* she," I said, pointing a finger at my laptop. Then I started shouting: "She made us jump through all these hoops—a twenty-dollar check, a death certificate, a notarized copy of power of attorney. Only to lawyer up? Fuck them. *Fuck* those people!"

I thought of my mom shaking her head at that Salvation Army bell ringer and the way she spit, "Those people will *never* get my money." I was a million miles away from that teenage feeling of being embarrassed of my mom.

This bureaucratic roadblock felt like a decades-on reenactment of my mom being silenced around her pregnancy and the adoption. I drafted and deleted responses to the archivist's email, talking to myself and typing so hard the keys stuck. This wasn't insurmountable—I could try calling a lawyer friend. Maybe down the line Kathy would request her original birth certificate from the state of Illinois, which would reveal exactly where she was born. In the meantime, I emailed Ann Fessler, who wrote *The Girls Who Went Away*, to see if she could crack this riddle.

It was one she had never come across, despite interviewing over a hundred women for her book, but she took a stab in the dark, revealing something that had never occurred to me: My mom might have gone to one home for a while and then switched.

Maybe she was that unhappy.

9

UTERINE SCREAM

I woke up to a news alert on my phone.

The headline used the word "overturns." With my mind still blurred by sleep, this sounded mild and temporal, like what you did with a playing card in a game of Uno. *To turn over.* Well, turn it *back* over. Draw another card, for god's sake. My mental haze burned off as soon as I tapped through to the story. "Supreme Court Overturns *Roe v. Wade.*"

In theory, I'd known it was coming. Several weeks earlier, just in time for Mother's Day, a draft of the majority decision had been leaked from *Dobbs v. Jackson Women's Health Organization*, which explicitly unraveled the constitutional right to abortion. Still, I had hoped for some unforeseen loophole, an eleventh-hour pardon.

"Fuck," I said to Christopher, rolling over in bed. "*Roe v. Wade—*"

Quinn came into the room in a thumping sprint, leaping onto the bed superhero-style. He crawled under the covers between us, our scruffy dog, Hank, splayed out on a pillow above his head. Christopher placed his hand on my shoulder.

"It happened?" he asked.

"It happened."

. . . .

A few hours later, I was driving down the coast for a solo vacation that I'd planned months earlier. Christopher and I did these "trades," as we called them, at least once a year: I would run away from home, and then he would run away from home. The slog of packed lunches, school drop-offs, and bedtime routines could turn us into resentful business partners, each of us tallying our relative contributions, which typically broke even. This was counter to the domestic inequality so often found in straight relationships, but I still felt the need to get away. We *both* needed a damn break.

My favorite person, the man with whom I'd decided to build a life, became tethered to the place from which I periodically fled. What I really wanted was to flee domesticity *with* him, but babysitters were expensive, and date planning was often lost in the hierarchy of urgent household chores. I had recently told a friend, "I feel like I want a boyfriend . . . and like I want that boyfriend to be Christopher." Instead, we defaulted to gifting each other a couple precious days of selfhood.

It often took only a night before we started sending a stream of love letters via text: "Love you so much." "Feeling kinda lonely." "Wish you guys were here." "Can I see a pic of our beanie boy?" "Send me vids!!" "How's Mr. Stinks [our nickname for Hank]?" This time I stopped an hour into my drive to fill up on gas and tapped out an urgent message: "Miss you already."

By the time I reached Big Sur, the sun was slipping toward the horizon. Snaking between stretches of turquoise water and bands of redwoods, I noticed a couple dozen cars pulled over on the side of the road and heard a voice through a microphone: "Check, check." A trio of twentysomething women walked along the shoulder with their arms around one another. A baguette and a wine bottle poked out of a tote bag. Two of them had their heads pressed together. I hadn't reached out to any of my friends about the day's news, but seeing these women hit me with a pang of longing. I realized how much I did not want to be alone.

I pulled off and walked to a grassy clearing in an amphitheater of trees. People were gathering on a patchwork of picnic blankets in sun-bleached earth tones. A woman with a black corset and a flowing red skirt stepped onto a wooden stage. Her outfit said: *witchy bar wench.* The stage was decorated with a crystal ball, a singing bowl, and some burning sage. *This is ridiculous,* I thought, smiling. I was grateful for it. The woman shouted something into the mic about *Roe* and patriarchy and women's bodies. Everyone clapped and whooped, and my eyes started to burn.

Against a background of echoing chimes, she started to perform spoken-word poetry. "Surrender . . . to the flow of infinite love in your life," she said. "Love is the heartbeat of the universe."

Is it? I thought, looking around at the picnic-blanket islands in a sea of grass. Where was love in the cruel punishment of women and pregnant people—now, then, always? I thought of the various injustices I had been reading about since finding my sister: sterilization, pregnancy, birth, and adoption—all coerced and forced. Depriving Black mothers of adequate resources and saddling them with stigma, harassment, and surveillance. *That isn't love; that's hatred.*

Recently, I had started telling friends what I was discovering through looking into my mom's past. I'd realized how distant it could seem from our current reality. After *Roe* in 1973, the market for domestic adoption, along with the network of homes for unwed mothers, slowly evaporated. I'd felt dreary and ghoulish, pulling out depressing facts about our mothers' generation, dwelling in the dark abuses of the pre-*Roe* era. Now we were all returning to that era, and plenty of people were already there, thanks to decades of systematic attacks on abortion access.

"Humble yourself at the magnitude of love's dazzling mystery," said the woman onstage, stretching out her arms. "Ask it, beg it, to pour into you, to pour through you."

Since finding my sister, I'd felt more open than ever to dazzling mystery. "It almost makes me believe in the moral arc of the universe," I'd told Christopher early on, because Kathy and I had found each other after all this time. I thought of my mom, an agnostic who loved Wordsworth's lines about "a sense sublime / Of something far more deeply interfused, / Whose dwelling is the light of setting suns, / And the round ocean and the living air, / And the blue sky, and the mind of man." She would often say "It's a mystery" in a singsong way, with a twinkle in her eye and a hint of self-ridicule. It was a reference to a character from the film *Shakespeare in Love* who explains the "natural condition" of the theater business, but perhaps also life itself, as one of "insurmountable obstacles on the road to imminent disaster." And yet, he adds, "strangely enough, it all turns out well."

"How?" he is asked on multiple occasions. "I don't know," he says. "It's a mystery." My mom perpetually guarded against disaster, but she also had a sense of faith that, although things were undeniably fucked in so very many ways, it would work out.

The next day, I climbed over and in between car-size boulders to the edge of a river rushing with icy mountain water. I hoped to access my mom's sense of faith and let it *pour into me*. Instead, I found myself doomscrolling on my phone at the edge of this sublime landscape. A viral tweet popped up on my feed: a photo from the day before of a counterprotest on the steps of the Supreme Court. It showed a smiling straight couple holding a sign reading: "We Will Adopt Your Baby." The man looked like he was cosplaying a fifties dad; the woman wore a demure ladylike dress with ruffled sleeves. Their sign echoed the *Dobbs* decision itself: In reviewing anti-abortion arguments, Justice Samuel Alito wrote that "a woman who puts her newborn up for adoption today has little reason to fear that the baby will not find a suitable home." In a related footnote, he quoted a report by the Centers for Disease Control on how the "domestic supply of infants . . . has become virtually nonexistent."

Both Alito and this couple were essentially making the same argument that drove pre-*Roe* adoptions: Women are breeders for respectable middle-class married couples. Then as now, babies and the people who birth them are treated as pawns in the political project of marriage and patriarchal control. Later, I would learn that this creepily wholesome-looking pair had ties to anti-abortion, anti-feminist, and anti-LGBTQ groups. These "antis" went together, of course.

All I knew in the moment was that this picture-perfect couple was portraying adoption as a solution to a problem—with no mention of its profound emotional devastations for both birth parents and their babies. Over the last months, I'd read enough accounts from adoptees to understand that Kathy's sense of wholeness in her adoptive family was tremendously lucky. "My mother had to sever some part of herself to let me go," writes Jeanette Winterson in her memoir about being adopted. "I have felt the wound ever since."

. . . .

My mom hadn't shared many details of her experience around the adoption, but countless other women had, and their stories were all so much the same. Within these homes, social workers pushed women toward the "right" decision, telling them things like: "Write a list of what you can offer this baby. Now write a list of what a married couple can offer this baby." They were often told that adoption meant gifting their child "a better life," which was the same unforgettable phrase that my mom had used when she first told me about my sister.

In *Waiting to Forget*, Margaret Moorman's memoir about placing her son for adoption in 1965—the same year that my mom placed Kathy for adoption—she writes, "I always thought I was the problem, the only thing standing between him and a happy life with loving, grown-up parents who had the resources to raise a child." In the mid-sixties, more than 80 percent of women in these homes placed their babies for adoption. As one woman sent away in this era said, "A few girls, revolutionary girls, talked about keeping their babies but we knew they were crazy. We knew: no one was allowed to keep their baby." Parents often made the adoption decision on behalf of their daughters—and women who didn't go along with it were threatened with disownment.

At the time, childbirth itself was turned into a passive experience. In the midcentury, it had "become exceedingly medicalized and obstetrically violent," writes the journalist Gabrielle Glaser in *American Baby*. Women were given narcotics that made them thrash around, so their hands and feet were restrained. "The drugs were so sedating that women were unable to use their internal muscles to birth their babies and placentas," explains Glaser. "Obstetricians would make incisions, called episiotomies, at the base of the vagina and delivery-room nurses were instructed to apply 'fundal pressure,' using their own weight on the top of the abdomen to force the baby out of the birth canal."

Unwed mothers were told that they shouldn't, or couldn't, see or hold their babies, lest they get attached. One woman told Ann Fessler about screaming to no avail, "Let me see my baby! Let me hold him!" Another woman said, "I just let out the most bloodcurdling scream. I thought, 'Wow. That's kind of scary,' but I guess I wanted [my baby] to hear that in his subconscious . . . to know that I didn't want to do it." One woman described a memory of her parents driving her home as the hospital receded from view: "I flipped out—it was total 100 percent, ripped terror, wailing, screaming, crying—and nobody said a word," she said.

When I first read that woman's words, terror swept through my own body. *My baby, my baby*, I thought, flashing to a memory of Quinn as a newborn cradled in my arms. Nothing, including my own death, fills me with a greater sense of horror than losing him.

Recently, during the final minutes of a virtual spin class, my muscles feeling like jelly slathered on bone, my instructor said, "Imagine whatever it will take to motivate you. What will get you up this hill?" I did not have to search for the right image. I immediately saw myself pulling Quinn in the bright yellow bike trailer we had when he was younger. We were being chased by the Big Bad Wolf of childhood cartoons. This snarly villain wanted my baby, but he would not have my baby. Nothing would stop me, I felt. I could tear a ligament, snap my ankle, and keep going. I would protect my baby. I would never let him go. I got up that hill, tears streaming down my face, knowing that my mom hadn't been able to escape the forces that took her baby away.

I think she was looking over her shoulder my entire childhood.

Moorman went on many years later to have a daughter whom

she kept, and yet she lived in constant fear of losing her. Aside from a single grocery trip, she didn't spend a minute away from her daughter for the first six months of her life. The first time Moorman hired a babysitter, she broke out in hives. She guarded her second child "with the vigilance of a nesting bird who has merely heard a twig snap in a nearby woods." Moorman eventually found a support group for birth mothers and discovered that she was not alone. It was common either to be overprotective with subsequent children or to maintain a self-protective distance. I could see how my mom did both: spinning a cocoon of safety and comfort while never allowing herself to fully join me in it.

My mom had shared so many early stories of maternal anxiety—like the way she demanded postbirth that my dad memorize my every feature, down to the tiny folds of my premature ear, lest I be swapped with someone else's baby. For a long time, I'd connected my mom's love to the way she worried over me. Love *was* worry. It was *The Runaway Bunny*, the book of medical maladies, and our game of ETPT. At her memorial, I told the story of how I'd signed all my Mother's Day cards to her with that nonsensical term. "ETPT became shorthand for saying 'I love you and thank you for always making me feel okay in the world,'" I had said during my speech. Now I was beginning to understand something fundamentally different: I did not feel safe or okay in the world without my mom.

As I made my way through these first-person accounts, I noticed the creep of a familiar feeling. I recognized it from after my mom's death: the hollow, howling ache of mourning. It would stop me in my tracks like a sudden full-body muscle cramp. I'd be folding Quinn's pajamas or loading an odd number of plates into the dishwasher—a reminder of our family of three, just like the trio of my childhood. Then I would think of my mom having her baby taken away. I had known about the adoption for more than twenty years, but now this rarely discussed event from my mom's past was no longer a footnote.

She lost her baby. I felt the reality that those measly, insufficient words concealed. A couple times, the thought left me bracing myself against the nearest surface. Once I started to shake from the built-up pressure of tears that I could not cry fast enough.

"You've got every maternal switch turned on in your body," my mom told me in my early twenties. "You are primed for motherhood. It's like every cell in your body is oriented toward it." She saw this in the way I squealed over puppies on the street and tended to all the "plant babies" in my apartment. It was a caretaking impulse that she had noticed early on—like how, in middle school, I fashioned a baby sling to carry my cat around the house while cooing to her, "You have such a great *kitten-ality.*"

"It wasn't like that for me," my mom continued. "I immediately fell in love with you, before you were even born, but I never felt like I was destined for motherhood, like it came effortlessly and naturally." She spoke slowly, choosing her words.

It was tricky, bringing your kid into the nuances of your parenting experience. She was letting me see a glimpse of herself as human, fallible, and inexpert, which can have such value. The portrayal of women as natural nurturers has not only been essential to our oppression, it also traps mothers in shame and inadequacy when their experiences don't match up with the Earth Mother model. But when I reflected on it, my mom's remark didn't feel like radical candor or brave truth-telling. It felt like a lie that she was sold, and I didn't believe it for a second.

Women like her were told that their motherhood was wrong, that it was unnatural and pathological, that it didn't count, that they weren't real mothers. *What lies did she believe about herself? What parts of herself did she kill just to survive? What parts of my mom were taken from me before she was even mine?*

I wondered whether my own "primed" motherhood was an answer to her stolen motherhood. *What of her sorrow is in my delight?*

....

On my last day in Big Sur, I took a nibble of a mushroom chocolate and sat by a shaded section of slow-flowing river, hoping for transcendence, enlightenment, or just momentary relief from the reality of the world. Was that too much to ask? Instead, I melted into my low-slung camp chair and watched the surrounding forest turn neon green and shimmery like a mirage. I worried that a plant tendril might reach out and grab me. Then the silted river bottom transformed into the sinister cartoon eels from *The Little Mermaid*. They swayed this way and that, summoning me into their murky depths. *Those eels lured Ariel into giving her voice away*, I thought, suddenly nauseated.

This was another childhood fairy tale about desire getting you in trouble, much like in "Rapunzel." Ariel gives up her ability to speak in exchange for a chance at winning a man's love—but really to become human and part of his world, part of *the* world. I leaned over my knees and swallowed the spit pooling in my mouth. *Goddammit.*

In that moment, I saw those cartoon henchmen as a symbol of all the forces that conspire to punish women for their longing—whether it's for sex, love, independence, adventure, or the recognition of their basic humanity. I thought of my mom and all the women whose stories I had been reading over the past weeks—all those forced Faustian bargains. For what felt like hours, I stared at the pebbled ground and begged my body to *please, please, please* not throw up. Eventually, I took small steps back to my hotel, feeling like I had eaten that river silt.

Later that week and back at home, I gathered some friends in our local park. "ur neighborhood aiding-and-abetting-abortion gathering," the subject line of my email invite read. Everything I'd done in the wake of the overturn of *Roe* had been virtual: donating to abortion funds, signing up to volunteer, reposting infographics on Instagram. I wanted to get together in person with my community of parents—all leftists or progressive liberals—even if it was just to vent and share resources for volunteering and donations. "There will be pizza. Kids are welcome," I wrote. "It might be chaos, but we'll figure it out."

Half a dozen people, mostly moms from Quinn's preschool, showed up with tote bags stuffed with snacks and picnic blankets. As our kids took over the play structure across the park, I passed out posters I'd downloaded and printed at Kinko's. "ABORTION IS HEALTHCARE," one read.

Alyson had just gotten off work as a nurse practitioner. She told us about a patient from that afternoon: a mom of two who was unintentionally pregnant. Alyson had to deliver the shocking news to this woman, along with the full slew of options available to her. On her train ride home, Alyson had kept thinking about how those options were drastically shrinking for countless people across the country. "There's wine in here," she said, holding up her insulated tumbler with a beleaguered half smile.

I'd made a point of inviting fathers, but only one showed aside from Christopher, and the two of them had ambled over to supervise the kids on the slide. It was just us women with paper plates of pizza balanced on crossed legs. We told stories of late periods and pregnancy tests, of decisions to get pregnant, stay pregnant, and stop being pregnant. I flashed to a memory of sitting on an exam table in a paper gown. In between my mom's death and Quinn's birth, I got pregnant as soon as we started trying. Then, at my nine-week appointment, the doctor moved the ultrasound probe between my legs like a searchlight, and we listened for a heartbeat that never arrived.

The pea-size embryo had stopped growing several weeks earlier. It was unviable, but my body hadn't gotten the message. A "missed miscarriage," my doctor called it. As I stared at the unmoving ghostly smudge on the ultrasound screen, a nasty voice in my head said: *See?* It asked: *Who do you think you are?*

This was what I'd heard in my early twenties from commentators warning about the perils of hookup culture and delayed marriage. In that moment of medical discovery, in the absence of a heartbeat, I succumbed to those familiar voices. I felt, irrationally, that I was being punished. I wasn't consciously aware of the parallel of my mom being punished for premarital sex with the loss of her baby, but the thought must have been there, hidden under a mossy mental rock on a rarely traveled path. The punishments themselves were incomparable: losing a child, as opposed to the hope for a particular cluster of cells to *develop into* a child.

The doctor explained that I could wait to see if my body would eventually expel the tissue on its own, while not only suffering the nausea, swollen breasts, and hormonal roller coaster of pregnancy but also potentially risking infection. I opted instead for a dilation-and-curettage procedure, the same one used for first-trimester surgical abortions. I had to wait a few days for an appointment, which seemed impossible and darkly laughable. They expected me to *wait* to get this ghost of an embryo out of my body? To go about my day-to-day as an unwilling host?

I spent those days seething over news articles about an unprecedented influx of state laws designed to make it harder, and sometimes practically impossible, to get an abortion: waiting periods, parental notification, forced ultrasounds, and unnecessary medical requirements that forced clinics to close. It was 2015, seven years before *Roe* was overturned. Even so, I read about anti-abortion legislation coming down on people seeking treatment for miscarriages, too. It was only thanks to the privilege of my personal geography, health insurance, and the unviability of my pregnancy that I didn't have to worry about any of that. I felt my own body turn into a cage to which politicians, insurers, and medical institutions held the key.

Of course, miscarriage wasn't a punishment for sex, but forced pregnancy truly was. This was an essential part of the anti-abortion aim: maintaining consequences for women's sexuality. As the journalist Laurie Penny writes, "Criminalizing abortion makes female sexual agency a crime."

"I've never felt quite so passionately pro-choice as I do now," I told a friend at the time, "and that is saying something." Only later, after learning about the framework of reproductive justice, did I realize that "choice" was too narrow a belief. But my miscarriage was a doorway into deeper empathy, a bodily experience that allowed the imagined mental leap toward suffering beyond anything I had known. It was nothing compared to my later experience of carrying a pregnancy to term and giving birth. *Who could go through that and believe that anyone should be forced into it?* Sitting in the park with our pizzas and kids and protest signs, I said as much out loud.

None of us could fathom it.

....

A few days later, I watched the sunset from the hammock chair underneath our deck. Quinn was just down to bed, and the sun was dipping behind Mount Tam, which peeked through a gap between the trees. Our yard was awash in gold. In front of me was a swaying patch of tall grasses dried by the California sun. It was a scene of beauty and calm, and I wanted to scream.

This imagined scream wasn't an exasperated "ahhhh," the kind made while miming the wringing of someone's neck. It was a reverberating full-body scream that would make my face go red and the veins in my neck pop out. Not some high-pitched top-of-head thing but a sound that would reverberate through every muscle fiber. I had screamed like that only twice before.

The first time, I was twelve. My family stopped in Petaluma for dinner on our way to Bodega Bay for vacation. My mom and I stepped into a crosswalk with my dad a few steps behind us, and then everything went black. A red sports car, driven by a sixteen-year-old boy, had come racing around the corner. My mom saw it coming and braced for impact. She bent her knees, planted her feet, and threw an arm around my waist. My mom pressed her hip into mine and tried to use herself as leverage. "I knew I had to get you on top of the car," she told me afterward. "I tried to pull you up and over. I just kept thinking, *Up, up, up*." She pictured a pair of dolphins leaping into the air. "I just kept thinking about your little skull," she said. "I just kept thinking: She *cannot* go under the car."

I did not see it coming. I didn't even see the world fly by as the car hit us. I just saw a dark blob floating in starless space. The blob was shadowy and indistinct, except for its silhouette edged in white. It moved like a bag of marbles hurled into the air, a loose collection of jostling matter. Then my mind replayed the screeching of tires. I remembered that I had been crossing the street. I realized that we were the blob, the jostling marbles. I opened my eyes and saw the world as a whizzing blur.

As soon as I hit the ground, I sat up, grabbed my head, and screamed. I wasn't injured. It was a scream of trespass—not fear but rage. No words came out, but my scream said it all the same: *How dare you.* The first thing I saw was my mom, standing between me and the car. The soles of her shoes were ripped off from the impact. My mom's chest was full and the vein in her forehead bulged. Her arms were out like she was ready to fight, like she might lift the car right off the ground. I believed that she could. "You looked like the Hulk," I told her later. "Hulk Mom."

The second time, I was thirty-three years old and pregnant. When I went into labor, I spent hours in silent agony, swallowing the pain of what turned out to be "back labor," which happens when a baby's head presses on the lower spine and tailbone. What was there to do with the unendurable other than to muffle it, choke it out, pretend it wasn't there? I'd had a vision of a "natural" birth, but then a thought started to loop: *This isn't the Dark Ages.* I turned to Christopher and my doula and broke my silence. "This is *absurd,*" I said with total composure. "I want an epidural." As soon as I'd spoken the absurdity of it all out loud, it was no longer swallowable. So I screamed—while naked, on all fours, and gripping the headboard of the hospital bed. I screamed like I was going into battle. I screamed like sound was poison to my pain. I screamed until my epidural was ready.

I'd never thought much about the sources of actual sound, let alone this sound that I merely wanted to make, but sitting in the hammock, I realized that this scream came from a different place than the screams that had come before. *It's a* uterine *scream*, I thought. I could feel the sound in there, wrapped around this muscle that I had become so much more aware of five years ago. It wasn't just the experience of having a doctor poke, prod, and place a measuring tape across it to determine my baby's growth. Toward the end of my pregnancy, every orgasm would make my uterus tense up. As waves of pleasure rolled through my body, it hardened up, a sudden crystalizing of my unseen insides. We don't usually detect the boundaries of our kidneys or lungs—they float around in there amorphously—but I never lost that precise sense of the pear-shaped organ that housed my baby.

Since finding Kathy, I had started thinking about my mom's uterus. What did it mean for my sister to live there for nine months? What of our mother had she absorbed while inside—her voice, her smell, her laughter, her movements? What did Kathy leave behind for me to pick up decades later—a cluster of cells or maybe something beyond the reach of science, some sort of sisterly transmission, the equivalent of a passed note? It was easy to get a bit woo: No one else had lived in there but us. For all the mysteries of existence, there was the basic fact of our shared origin. It was where we both came from.

So when I say that there was a scream in my uterus, I don't mean it in the way that people wear T-shirts emblazoned with an outline of a uterus giving the middle finger, an ovary serving as a hand. I don't mean to use my uterus as a symbol. I mean that—sitting there in the hammock, totally out of step with the calm of the surrounding scene—I felt a scream originating from this darkest depth of my body.

It was a scream over lost children and forced pregnancies and all the many violations of sexual and reproductive control. A scream for all the women whose stories I had read recently. A scream for Kathy. A scream for my mom. A scream for our relationship. It was the scream that my mom had choked down for most of her life.

The swallowed scream that made her come undone.

10

UNUSUAL WOMEN

"It looks like a mental institution," I said with a laugh.

I was hanging out with my parents in their living room, watching a garden-makeover show on TV. It's hard to place the memory: I might have been a teenager or in my early twenties. I was sprawled on their bloodred Persian carpet, which had been there my whole life, but I could still discover new shapes in its repeating patterns of blue and gold. My parents were side by side on the couch behind me with their feet up on the coffee table.

The makeover show had just done the big reveal: a yard with cement pathways, a closely shorn lawn, and rounded topiary bushes. It was sterile, regimented, and unnatural. A garden as a ceaseless exercise in containment. It made me think of a mental institution, so I had said it out loud. *Mental institution.* Did my mom scoff, or was she silent? Did I read something in her response or non-response? I have no idea. All I know is that I blurted out these words next: "Have you ever been to a mental institution?"

My delivery was matter-of-fact. I had no conscious awareness of having the question, but there it was, hanging in the air, as if someone else had asked it. Behind me, I felt the emotional equivalent of shuffling papers. A heavy breath, a cleared throat, a start, and then a stop.

"Well—" my mom said. "Honey."

I turned around to face her.

"Actually," she continued, muting the TV.

My dad disappeared his lips into a flat, tight smile. My skin tingled in anticipation; we were about to cross another secret threshold.

"After I got pregnant and placed the baby for adoption, I struggled, a lot," she said.

The baby. Her baby. *My sister.*

My mom hadn't spoken her aloud since she'd first broken the news.

She explained that she'd started seeing a therapist to cope with her devastation over the adoption. "I wasn't suicidal," she said. "But my therapist . . . he thought I might kill myself because of how distraught I was." For the second time in her life, she was sent away by a man. This time there were guards and locked doors. My mom didn't say where she was sent or how long she stayed, just that she started plotting her escape as soon as she landed there.

"I figured out what I needed to say to get myself out," she said.

"Wow," I said, because what else was there to say.

"And I got out, as fast as I could," she said.

In retrospect, there had been clues. Long before my mom told me about her institutionalization, she had wryly remarked on the brilliance of Louise Fletcher's portrayal of the tyrannical Nurse Ratched in *One Flew Over the Cuckoo's Nest.* "Disturbingly realistic," she had said of Fletcher's role as a heartless, controlling, and vindictive nurse. "All too believable." I don't remember consciously wondering how my mom was in a position to judge the film's realism, but her comment must have seeded a question in me.

Another clue: In high school, when my best friend, Meredith, decided to move away to boarding school, her mom suggested that the two of us go to a single counseling session to talk through my feelings of abandonment and betrayal. Ahead of time, the therapist asked me to sign a contract consenting to treatment; as my mom flipped through it, she vigorously shook her head. "I don't think we can sign this," she said. "If they decide you're a danger to yourself—even if you aren't, even if it's a misunderstanding, even if you're just struggling with the separation from Meredith—they could send you away, even hospitalize you." I thought she was overreacting; I had no idea that it had happened to her.

One last clue: When I was in high school, my mom bought me Joanne Greenberg's *I Never Promised You a Rose Garden*, a groundbreaking 1964 novel about a sixteen-year-old girl who is institutionalized and diagnosed with schizophrenia—although some later analysis of the book, alongside more rigorous diagnostic criteria, suggests that the protagonist actually has symptoms of a depressive disorder. "I don't know if you will relate to it, but I know I did when I read it," my mom told me. "Just the possibilities of where the mind can go." The protagonist even had my mom's name: Deborah.

At the time, I was a teenager who slept a lot, isolated in my room, and wrote bleakly in my journal. "It feels like there is a layer of glass between me and the world," I wrote. It seemed my mom was always looking at me with pleading eyes and asking with an infuriating level of concern, "How are you *doing*, honey?" This book recommendation scared me: Did she think I was going crazy? But I was also annoyed at her presuming to know anything about what I was experiencing as a teenager. My suffering was mine; it wasn't hers. Aside from reading the first few pages, I left the book on my shelf with the spine uncracked—a message to her.

All these decades later, my memory of *I Never Promised You a Rose Garden* seemed like a gift: a gateway into what my mom had felt during her institutionalization. After all, growing up meant realizing that, in a sense, her suffering *was* mine. She understood the pains of finding oneself as a young woman in this world; and, I had only recently realized, parts of my pain directly arose from her past.

After remembering the book, I drove to my dad's house, ten minutes away from my own. I found the novel still sitting on the bookshelf in my childhood bedroom. I opened it so forcefully that I sent a rippled white tear along its black spine. The book—based on Greenberg's own experience of being committed—tells the story of a traumatized young woman for whom reality has started to feel like being contained in a sarcophagus. "[A]s to the dead, the world was the size of her own coffin," writes Greenberg. The fictional Deborah escapes that suffocating reality by creating an imaginary mental world called Kingdom of Yr, full of gods who control her thoughts, words, and actions. Yr even has its own language, which can express Deborah's emotional torment when the English language fails.

Any time Deborah is scared or threatened, this mental kingdom closes "over her head like water," leaving "no mark of where she had entered." But what starts as a place of refuge from the ravages of reality transforms into a place of "fear and pain," a "sweetness" turned into "total tyranny."

. . . .

I wanted to figure out exactly where my mom had been locked up, so I did some digging. I started dialing Midwest area codes, talking to women who called me "honey" and "my dear" as I told each of them a small piece of my mom's story. "She got pregnant when she was eighteen." "She was sent to a home for unwed mothers." "She gave the baby up for adoption." "She was committed to a mental institution." Again and again, I spoke aloud my mom's greatest shame and pain. Then I spoke aloud my greatest grief: "She's dead." I said it call after call, in different, unbearable ways. "My mom, she died." "My mom, who is now dead." "Oh, well, see, the thing is . . . she's dead."

Sometimes these women—librarians, archivists, and record-keepers—wanted proof before releasing any information. One lady asked very politely for evidence that my mom had "expired." I emailed photos of my birth certificate and her death certificate, rendering the cycle of creation and destruction as email attachments.

I Venmoed forty-five dollars to a stranger off Craigslist to text me photos of some pages of interest from a rare library book in central Indiana: a 1967 directory of all the state's mental and psychiatric hospitals. I reached out to local historical societies. The dossier in my file folder swelled with documents on the long-gone mental institutions where she might have been locked up. I felt like a wild-eyed TV detective pinning documents to a bulletin board, connecting events with red string, trying to solve a murder. I emailed back and forth with Keenan at the Indiana state records office so often that he started showing up in household conversation. Christopher asked me at the end of one day, "So. How's Keenan doing?"

The state records office had no information on my mom, which suggested that she was likely sent to a private institution. I spent hours virtually meandering down rural streets in Evansville, Indiana, looking for the remnants of one such institution. At the address in question, there was no building, just an empty lot with a stand of trees. *Did she look out at these trees? Did they give her an escape? How much have they grown since?*

Beyond a name and an address, I wanted a diagnosis, even though I understood that whatever made it onto her chart would have to be reinterpreted through contemporary diagnostic standards; so many people were misdiagnosed back then. I'd researched enough to know that my mom did not have schizophrenia, but her symptoms could suggest a psychotic break or a severe case of depression. Phone call after phone call, I was told about records that had been "destroyed" or were "long gone." The only thing I knew for certain: My mom dropped all her classes in March 1967, a year and a half after she placed Kathy for adoption.

I called my dad in hopes that he would know more about why she was committed. "I remember her saying that around this time she would mentally sit in too many rooms at the same time, looking at things from different perspectives," he told me. "She was playing some kind of game in her mind." I imagined two rooms opposite each other in a hotel hallway. Instead of numbers, the doors had labels. One door read, "Mother." The other door read, "Not a Mother." She couldn't just sit in the Mother room. Not only had her motherhood been deemed illegitimate to start, but she had legally signed it away. The system itself had demanded a dual consciousness; the whole idea was to pretend it had never happened.

My mom and her older brother, J. R., dressed for church.

My mom, Deb Clark, at around five years old, dressed up as Annie Oakley and standing in front of the apartment in Gary, Indiana.

My grandparents Quen and John in an undated photo—probably not too long after they were married.

My mom as a teenager with (from left to right) her father, John; her brother, J. R.; and her mother, Quen.

My mom and John in 1966, the year after Kathy was born.

My twentysomething mom when she was a graduate student at Indiana University in the early seventies.

Marguerite, Kathy's adoptive mom, in an undated photo—the one that Kathy has framed in her bedroom.

My mom in her early thirties, after she moved to the Bay Area.

Kathy with her mom and siblings. From left to right: JoAnn, Billy, Kathy, Marguerite, and Garrett.

Kathy as a teenager in a school photo from the early eighties.

Kathy at the age of twenty-one, shortly after having her son Sean.

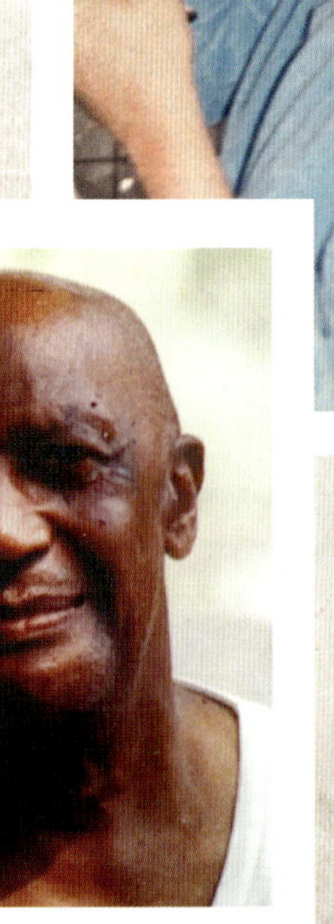

Willie, Kathy's adoptive father, with her son Devin in the late nineties.

Kathy with her sons (from left to right), Justin, Devin, and Sean.

One of the first photos that Kathy sent me of herself.

My parents on their wedding day in 1978.

My mom with me shortly after I was born, in Berkeley, California, in 1984.

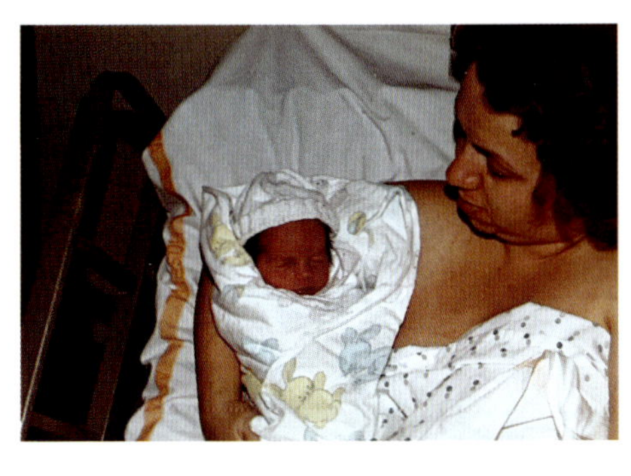

My dad and me happily cuddling one morning—this was my mom's favorite family photo.

My mom and eight-year-old me in our yard.

My mom and me on the front steps of our house.

JoAnn and Kathy at our family brunch in Atlanta.

Me, Kathy, and Uncle Jide at Maggiano's in Illinois in 2022.

The former Florence Crittenton Anchorage in Chicago, Illinois.

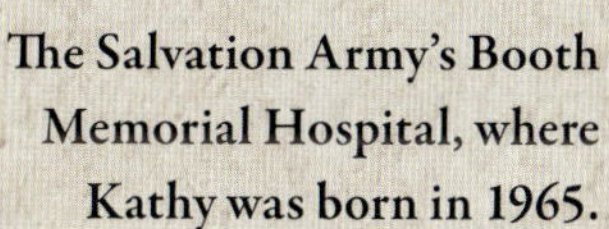

The Salvation Army's Booth Memorial Hospital, where Kathy was born in 1965.

Me and Kathy in 2022, during my first trip to Atlanta.

From top to bottom: Christopher, our dog Hank, me, and Quinn in 2022.

Me and Devin, Kathy's youngest son, during that first visit.

My mom in her late fifties, in her beloved garden.

She couldn't just sit in the Not a Mother room, either. She had grown a baby in her body for nine months and birthed her into the world. As my mom told me herself: She thought about her daughter every single day. I'm sure her body remembered, too. I pictured doubles of my mom, *Sims*-like clones, occupying both rooms at once, going about their days, these realities existing at the same time. Both true, both false.

What other rooms must she have frequented? The one where she kept her baby, the one where her baby was held by an unknown adoptive mother, the one where her baby languished in foster care? I imagined the hotel hallway filling up with labels: a room and its paired opposite for every self-interrogated circumstance surrounding the adoption. Right/Wrong, Choice/Force, Selfish/Selfless.

"She had a mind that could look at things in so many different ways, hold an idea and its opposite as both being true at the same time," my dad continued. "I think she was experiencing being a troubled, very bright, very poetic person."

"She wasn't just committed because she was smart, though," I said. "She got lost in that mental palace, right? Maybe in these con tradictory realities around having a baby and not having a baby, being a mother and not being a mother."

My dad mentioned that she had turned to cutting ahead of her institutionalization. "She showed me spots on her arms where she had sliced herself back then," he said. "It gave her a sense of power. She compared it to taking a drug or a sexual release. It eased her pain." I searched for a mental picture of my mom's arms. Before any images, a tingling wave of sense memory: touching the pale skin on the inside of her forearm, my little-kid fingertips tracing the blue-green line of a vein. This stretch of skin was the softest thing I'd ever felt, until Quinn. Sometimes, running the back of my finger across his baby cheeks, I was transported back to her softness. The first softness.

Then it came to me: a slim knot of white scar tissue. A teardrop shape on the inside of her elbow. "What's that?" I heard little me ask. A scar. She had cut herself a long time ago. "How?" Something about doing stained glass, she had said, a hobby from her twenties. I had been so intimately connected to the landscape of my mother's body. I was *of* it. I had lived in it and on it. My own body had grown a child with her soft skin. Still these mysteries.

"I always sensed that Mom had gone through a crucible and been melted down and come out the other side before I met her," my dad said. "It makes me think of the hero's journey. The test, if you get through it, you're transformed. It's kind of mystical . . ." He sighed in self-mocking, and we both laughed.

I thought of my mom's beloved VHS box set of a six-part PBS series exploring the literary professor Joseph Campbell's take on myth and the hero's adventure. The first episode opens with a montage of heroics—from Martin Luther King Jr. delivering his "I Have a Dream" speech to Neil Armstrong taking "one small step for man." Most of the images are of men. When Campbell was asked about how his scholarship applied to women, he was alleged to have shrugged off the possibility of a *heroine's* journey, saying, "All she has to do is to realize that she's the place that people are trying to get to." Interpretations of that quote range from woman as trophy to woman as spiritual ideal. Regardless, in my mom's journey, the mental institution was what Campbell called "the belly of the whale," the "worldwide womb image" associated with self-annihilation and rebirth.

"She was kind of like the warrior," my dad said. "After surviving what she survived, she was not the girl that she was before. She went through something that could have destroyed her and came out somewhat stronger, sort of tempered, how you heat steel and then dip it in water. It's harder, it's transformed."

. . . .

I kept coming back to something my mom had said in her long-ago email describing her family's puritanism opposite the total acceptance of her brother's stack of *Playboy* magazines. "It was all rather schizophrenic," she wrote. When I'd returned to her email a few weeks back, that line had felt inappropriate in its use of a mental health diagnosis to describe broader cultural schisms and hypocrisies around sex. Then again, for a long time, novelists and feminist critics have drawn parallels, and sometimes a causal line, between the realities of womanhood and schizophrenia.

In Sylvia Plath's *The Bell Jar*—published in 1963 but set a decade earlier—Esther Greenwood, the novel's nineteen-year-old protagonist, knows that she's "supposed to be having the time of [her] life." She has a glamorous internship at a women's magazine and a supposed catch of a boyfriend. "Only I wasn't steering anything, not even myself," she says. "I guess I should have been excited the way most of the other girls were, but I couldn't get myself to react." She constructs a false self to meet outside expectations, especially those of her loathsome boyfriend, Buddy, who belittles her artistic aspirations. He envisions a future of conventional domesticity, but Esther has privately sworn off marriage.

"The last thing I wanted was infinite security and to be the place an arrow shoots off from," she says. "I wanted change and excitement and to shoot off in all directions myself, like the colored arrows from a Fourth of July rocket."

Esther conceals this critical inner voice, along with all the ways that she is out of step with gendered expectations. The disjuncture between outside expectation and internal reality leads to crisis: After a suicide attempt, she's committed to a mental institution. "To label Esther as 'schizophrenic' and leave it at that does not take us very far," writes the critic Marjorie Perloff. "For Sylvia Plath's focus in *The Bell Jar* is not on mental illness per se, but on the relationship of Esther's private psychosis to her larger social situation. Indeed, her dilemma seems to have a great deal to do with being a woman in a society whose guidelines for women she can neither accept nor reject." The feminist critic Elaine Showalter describes the book as a narrative of "schizophrenia as a protest against the feminine mystique of the 1950s."

The Bell Jar was fiction—granted, fiction based off Plath's own experience with mental illness—but I saw so much of my mom's story here. Like Esther, my mom hadn't been able to accept or reject society's guidelines for women. She stepped outside those parameters by having premarital sex and getting pregnant, only to be forcefully pushed back inside when she was sent away. Those homes, of course, were designed to rehabilitate unwed mothers as future wives—essentially, to prepare them for the feminine mystique that had caused Esther to split herself off from reality.

The system *demanded* a split with reality; it was the whole point of homes for unwed mothers. Pretend that your motherhood—*your baby*—does not exist. There were references to division and disassociation scattered throughout the first-person accounts of unwed mothers. "I was like a lobotomized beast," one woman said. "I barely existed . . . I remember pushing the pain down, pushing it down into a place like a steel pipe inside of me, and welding on a steel cap so the pain could never overtake me again."

. . . .

The year before *The Bell Jar*, Doris Lessing published *The Golden Notebook*, which tells the story of a woman whose internal disjunctures led to disintegration. The protagonist, Anna Wulf—a divorcée, mother, lover, writer, and communist—keeps separate notebooks to express and organize the various aspects of herself. This fragmentation leads to a mental breakdown and, as she starts writing in a single golden notebook, Anna moves toward integration of all her roles.

Lessing was influenced by the thinking of the psychiatrist R. D. Laing, who posits in his 1960 book, *The Divided Self*, that the "schizoid" individual develops a split between the carefully guarded "inner self" and the publicly revealed "false self," which "may consist in an amalgam of various part-selves, none of which is so fully developed as to have a comprehensive 'personality' of its own." The false self becomes associated with the body, while the inner self is disembodied. Then the inner self is further divided, erasing its sense of identity and reality, which leads to psychosis, he argued.

Laing, already a controversial figure, went on to have a scandalous and complicated legacy. Still, his analysis struck a nerve with women writers across the decades, although Laing himself didn't actually make a connection to women's gendered experiences. In her 1997 cult-classic novel, *I Love Dick*, Chris Kraus writes:

> R.D. Laing never figured out that "the divided self" is female subjectivity. Writing about the ambitious educated 26-year-old "schizophrenic girl" in the suburban 1950s: ". . . the patient repeatedly contrasts her real self with her false compliant self." Oh really.

All people wear various masks—the sociologist Erving Goffman argues that the "self" is really a series of unending performances—but the cultural realities of womanhood create specific fractures, from the wife/whore dichotomy to the doubling effect of the "male gaze," which leads to a mind-body break. The art historian John Berger famously writes of "a woman's self being split into two" as the result of having to "continually watch herself." She becomes "the *surveyor* and the *surveyed*."

This uncannily echoes Laing's discussion of schizophrenia: "The individual's being is cleft in two," he writes, "producing a disembodied self and a body that is a thing that the self looks at." It is not just women who are cleft in two: The feminist poet Audre Lorde writes of the way that oppressed people as a whole—including Black, working-class, and older people—become "watchers" as a means of survival, familiarizing themselves "with the language and manners of the oppressor, even sometimes adopting them for some illusion of protection."

In the 1985 book *Female Malady*, Showalter studies how feminine cultural ideals in particular have shaped notions of mental illness. She notes the similarities between symptoms of schizophrenia, like depersonalization and fragmentation, and "the social situation of women," and writes, "Some feminist critics have maintained that schizophrenia is the perfect literary metaphor for the female condition." I think my mom's own metaphor is perfect: White patriarchal culture makes women sit in too many different rooms at once. Wife and whore, mind and body, actor and spectator. We are made to walk down long corridors of contradictory reality.

Women writers have used madness and the madhouse as a

metaphor for a very long time. In Mary Wollstonecraft's 1798 *Maria*, a woman is sent to an asylum, which "becomes a symbol of all the man-made institutions, from marriage to the law, that confine women and drive them mad," says Showalter. Nineteenth-century women writers, from Jane Austen to Emily Brontë, used the madwoman as an authorial double, a way to "come to terms with their own uniquely female feelings of fragmentation, their own keen sense of the discrepancies between what they are and what they are supposed to be," write Sandra Gilbert and Susan Gubar in *The Madwoman in the Attic*.

In Charlotte Perkins Gilman's 1892 classic short story "The Yellow Wallpaper," a postpartum mother is put on a "rest cure" for "temporary nervous depression," "a slight hysterical tendency." She suppresses her skepticism about the treatment, her own internal sense of right and wrong, and unravels in her confinement. Gilman wrote the story after her own experience with this isolating prescription, which led her to come "so near the borderline of utter mental ruin that I could see over."

For many of these writers, some of whom wrote from personal experience, madness is more than a dramatic metaphor; it's depicted, at least in part, as the direct result of the constraints on women's lives. Of course, patriarchal culture also defines madness, slinging it over the centuries at women who defy feminine expectation, especially around their expected roles as wives and mothers. The label of insanity has often been applied to women who are seen as inappropriately sexual.

Nineteenth-century doctors assigned the diagnosis of "puerperal insanity" to new moms who "flaunted their sexuality," Showalter explains. Nymphomania symptoms included everything from women's masturbation to "lascivious glances" to obscene language. Most famously, the diagnosis of hysteria—originating from the Greek word for "womb"—was connected to masturbation, sexual frustration, bisexuality, homosexuality, and incestuous fantasies. The various hysteria "treatments" prescribed over the centuries included marriage, marital sex, and pregnancy. "[U]ncontrolled sexuality seemed the major, almost defining symptom of insanity in women," writes Showalter.

There is a direct line to the way unwed mothers in the postwar era were seen as mentally unwell, thanks to their "psychological inability to form a sanctioned relationship to a man," as Rickie Solinger writes. Much like the hysteric, unwed mothers were essentially prescribed marriage—or at least preparation for a marriageable future. I'm reminded again of "The Yellow Wallpaper," whose postpartum protagonist is locked away, alienated from her own wants and beliefs, and deprived of all that makes life worth living.

The cure was the illness.

....

My mom got out of that mental institution, but she never escaped pathologizing beliefs around women's sexuality. When I'd talked to my dad on the phone, he'd made it clear that she had internalized a belief in her own abnormality. "She kind of thought she was a nymphomaniac," he said. "She experienced the intensity of her sex drive as being weird. Mom really believed that she was wired wrong. I mean, who was she to say she wasn't wrong when all of society said she was not what a woman was supposed to be."

Even over the phone, I could tell he was shaking his head.

Back when they first met, though, he was also inclined to pathologize her. They were in their late twenties, living as roommates in a shared house in Berkeley. She was a buttoned-up literary intellectual, and he was a long-haired skateboarding programmer. They saw each other strictly as friends but nevertheless ended up sleeping together, and by my devoutly atheistic father's account, it felt "like they were made in heaven for each other." But he didn't know how to make sense of her "passion," as he put it.

"I had never met a woman who experienced sex as something she couldn't do without," he said. "I thought, you know, 'This is how *men* are supposed to be.' "

Knowing that she had placed a baby for adoption as a teenager, he took a stab at some armchair psychoanalysis. "I built this story in my head that, okay, she's just trying to replace the love that she lost for this baby, and what I'm experiencing is that redirected need to love this lost baby," he told me. "I thought it was sublimation, I guess." When they first started sleeping together, my dad shared his theory with my mom, and her reaction was "Oh, that's crazy." Then she gave him a two-page handwritten letter that read like a treatise on the potentials of sex outside of romantic love.

"From the beginning we both knew that ours would not be a love relationship," she wrote. She believed that sex without love could nevertheless include "caring, openness, and friendship," that it could serve as "a gift of luxurious lust," "a place to be free without judgment, a place to be nurtured, a haven." Much as she saw herself as sexually abnormal, my mom was not going to stick around for my dad's armchair psychoanalysis. "If you cannot conceive of more realms existing than just the opposites of fornication and making love then I don't want to deal with you on that level," she wrote.

They were engaged within six months.

"Eventually," my dad told me, "I concluded that men and women are actually more the same than anybody realizes, and it's society messing things up."

My mom never used the term "nymphomania" with me, but she expressed feelings of being sexually abnormal. There had been that one conversation at the kitchen table in my twenties when she told me that she felt "*unusual* for a woman." *Ah*, I had thought at the time, *that's where I get it from*. My mom had meant what she said to be destigmatizing, but I took it as confirmation that it was my inheritance; I was my mother's daughter. We were unusual women.

Looking back, though, I knew that human desire was varied, complex, and idiosyncratic, and that the concept of sexual normalcy was a powerful form of social control that could both alienate women from their desire and make them feel unusual for having too much or too little of it. I also saw that some of the pleasure I took from having sex, and writing about it, arose from the experience of surviving the shame that came along with it. *That* maternal inheritance existed formidably alongside any theoretical genetic predisposition.

My desire wasn't just about sex, anyway. It wasn't even *mostly* about sex. Across my life, my crushes on boys and men were often tangled with my wish to *be* them, to access some of their freedom and entitlement. The critic Lauren Berlant writes, "When we talk about an object of desire, we are really talking about a cluster of promises we want someone or something to make to us and make possible for us."

Within patriarchy, men have long been pathways to power for women—in the projective capacities of romantic fantasy and, for white women, the economic exchange of marriage. Men have also been part of a trap. It's like that line from *The Bell Jar*: "I wanted change and excitement and to shoot off in all directions myself, like the colored arrows from a Fourth of July rocket." Instead, women's desire is channeled into men and marriage, which impacts so much more than their relationship to sex.

It's an assault on a broader experience of autonomy, exploration, and self-discovery. It severs women from the feeling of being passionately of the world and in the world. In her famous 1978 essay "The Uses of the Erotic," Audre Lorde writes of "the erotic" as a "source of power and information within our lives." Similarly, bell hooks argues in *The Will to Change* that patriarchy had tried to repress the erotic "precisely because of its power to draw us into greater and greater communion with ourselves, with those we know most intimately, and with the stranger."

For all the shame it can bring, a sense of being a "weirdo" can also mean feeling in touch with a potent life force that the world is ceaselessly attempting to reroute and shut down. When the norm is suffocating, abnormality can feel like freedom, but you're still stuck in terms that are not your own.

That day in the kitchen with my mom, while we sat at right angles to each other, in the same configuration as our years-earlier conversation about my sister, she told me that she felt unusual, and I felt a surge of connection. I was proud of our shared unusualness. Specialness is the upside of pathology. I was *a woman like that*.

A woman like my mom.

· · · · · · · · · · · · · ·

After the first time my mom told me about the mental hospital, we never discussed it again. Fine by me—I didn't *want* to talk about it. On a subterranean level, I feared that my mom's institutionalization implied my own capacity for madness. I willed myself to forget about it so successfully that I didn't bring it up even during therapy or routine doctors' screenings around mental health and family medical history.

There was just one time that this buried history came back to life.

A few weeks after her lung cancer diagnosis, my mom was rushed to the hospital with a life-threatening blood clot. By the time I got to her bedside, she was in the clear, but the doctors had put her on a drug that seemed to have triggered paranoia or a flashback. "The *powers that be* transferred me here," she whispered from the hospital bed, her arm a tangle of tubes. "There are guards. This is a locked ward. It's a psychiatric hospital."

She side-eyed the nurse stationed in a chair at her door. "Tracy, I'm putting you on notice. I have a grave concern about what is happening here," my mom said, her mouth barely moving, like she was performing a ventriloquist's act. She looked at me with wild eyes that begged me to understand—and I did. My mom believed that she was being hospitalized against her will. She was flashing back to the Nurse Ratched from her past and reliving the horrors of institutional control. "I understand," I told my mom, taking her hand. "I'm here. I'll take care of you. It's going to be okay."

Soon she emerged from her medicated state and was released from the hospital. My mom started chemo and radiation, which would buy her three more years of life, but I didn't know that at the time. I believed the six-month prognosis given by her doctors. *Half a year.*

My anguish hurled me into a certain kind of madness—exploding the boundaries of self, entering the belly of the whale.

More specifically: I went to dive bars, downed shots of whiskey, and went home with men who I knew, *just knew*, would make visible the pain I felt inside. They roughed me up and tossed me around, while I encouraged them along with smiles and moans. I was left sore and bruised, with rug burns on my knees. It was an act of translation: My all-consuming grief became smaller somehow as a tangible wound.

One man placed his hand on my throat. "Harder," I told him. He left a hand-shaped bruise across the front of my neck. The next morning, in the harsh, flickering light of my bathroom vanity, I noted how this new bruise completed the half circle of my birthmark, which starts with a red thumbprint-like smudge above my right clavicle and wraps around the back of my neck. Seen from the side, it almost looks like a handprint, too.

When I was little, I wondered if my birthmark had been left behind by the doctor who pulled me from the incision in my mom's belly—as though it were permanent evidence of our separation, that moment of being torn asunder. When I was growing up, teachers and camp counselors worried alternately that it was a hickey or a bruise. As a middle schooler, I cared less that people would think I was being physically abused than that they would assume I had made out with some boy. It seemed worse for my birthmark to be seen as a sign of sex than of violence. I told my parents that I wanted to have it removed one day. "It's beautiful," my mom told me, "because it is part of you."

When that man left—or I left, *by way of him*—the hand-shaped bruise on the front of my neck, it completed a startling visual circuit with my birthmark, making it look as though I had been strangled with two hands. As though I, myself, had come close to death. In those days of preemptive grief, I *wanted* the feeling of annihilation from sex. I wasn't interested in an ecstatic, life-affirming experience of oneness and spiritual transcendence. *No.* I wanted repugnant bug-under-the-boot nothingness. When I look back, the bruise seems to have made a metaphorical connection between two points of separation between me and my mom, these marks of my birth and her impending death. Maybe it's a coincidence, or maybe it's the symbolic language of sex, which, like a dream, expresses what we're not yet able to put into words.

In Nathaniel Hawthorne's short story "The Birthmark," a man has a wife with a tiny hand-shaped birthmark on her cheek, "a crimson stain upon the snow." It is "a singular mark, deeply interwoven." The husband comes to see it "as the symbol of his wife's liability to sin, sorrow, decay, and death." The birthmark in the story has been read as a symbol of mortality and natural human imperfection—or, in more feminist terms, the "existential threats" associated with women's "menstruating, childbearing, and lactating" bodies and "men's sexual attraction to them." Feminist thinkers have long argued that men's attempts at controlling women's sexuality and reproduction arise from an anxious wish to be in command of nature and mortality. At the end of Hawthorne's story, the husband gives his wife a potion that successfully removes her birthmark, but it also kills her.

Now my birthmark reminds me of the danger of believing that these deeply interwoven parts of ourselves are stains.

11

HEY SIS!!

It had been four months since I'd found my sister.

Four months, two phone calls, and seventeen emails, but who was counting? *I was counting.* Over and over. Not just the weeks and emails but the number of times I had initiated versus Kathy, which was three to one, which had felt in my moments of doubt and insecurity like a reflection of our respective investment in the relationship. *I am three times more into this sister thing than she is.* Rationally, I understood that this was nonsense, but emotionally, I resisted the urge to initiate again. I waited Kathy out, hoping that thc ratio would shift.

Instead, something shifted in me. I saw how my measured caution with Kathy was part of my mom's emotional legacy. By my mom's own account, she had done what it had taken to get out of that mental institution as fast as she could. That didn't mean she'd healed; it meant she had found a coping strategy. She learned to box up her emotions, as Margie had suggested, lest they overpower her again. My mom had contained her feelings for Kathy to protect herself. Wasn't I doing the same thing? This was easier to see after I'd spent the past weeks reckoning with the emotional wreckage of all my mom's thwarted feelings, the false security of boxing things up, the self-betrayal of catering to outside impressions.

I also started to suspect that I had absorbed some of my mom's insecurities about her first daughter. "I don't want to interrupt her life," my mom had told me when I asked if she had tried to find her daughter. "I don't think that it's my right . . . It is not my right." She saw herself as a burden. Whenever I reviewed my email thread with Kathy, analyzing our messages and the gaps between them, there was a part of me that felt like a gnat buzzing around my sister's head; I felt that she was just too nice to swat at me.

That was part of the destructive story my mom had been fed—the same one that told her she wasn't a real mother. So, when I found myself thinking about Kathy one afternoon, I dashed off an email without scrutinizing it:

Hey Kathy,
I've been thinking of you and hoping that work is not too crazy. Crossing my fingers that some of the chaos has settled. It was really special getting to talk with you a few weeks back. I loved so much hearing about you, your life, your world, and your thoughts.

Anyway, just a quick note to say that I'm thinking of you. I'd be happy to chat again if you're up for it.
Best and love,
Tracy

I was edging toward the end of my workday when my phone rang. I saw it was Kathy and answered with a "*Heyyy!*" This was how I would answer with a close friend. The first time Kathy had called, I'd answered stiffly: "Hi, this is Tracy," like it was a business call. The second time we talked, I'd called and awkwardly stumbled: "Hi, this is Tracy . . . your sister." This "*Heyyy!*" was something else; it was warmth and ease. It assumed and conveyed pages of meaning. It was a declaration and an invitation. The way you answer a phone can change the entire call. I find myself thinking: *Can it change an entire life?* It feels that way now.

"Hey there!" Kathy said right back, returning my brightness. "Is now a good time to talk? I know you're probably still working."

"You know what? I'd love to play hooky right now," I said. "You can be my excuse."

We talked for two hours in a friendly cadence, with some mutual moaning about work, her catching me up on her grandkids, and my giving her the latest on Quinn. I was sitting on my deck awash in afternoon sun, my feet up on a coffee table, and it was like I poured all of that laid-back feeling into the phone. I wasn't *managing my relationship with my sister.* I was showing up—open, curious, and full of love.

"Any luck getting ahold of your dad?" I asked.

"So, I messaged him on LinkedIn a few weeks back but didn't hear anything," she said. "It looks like he hasn't posted on there in years, though, so I don't even know if he's seen the message."

"Hmm, yeah, I feel like I neglect LinkedIn messages for years at a time."

"Right, exactly," Kathy said. "It could be months or years until he sees it. I hate to say it, but I don't even know if he's still alive."

"Oof, yeah."

"I'm so glad we found each other, though," she said. "I'd love to come out to California sometime. I'm a nervous flier. It's something I'm trying to get over. Maybe when work cools down a bit, I could fly out there and work remotely for a while, just to really get the most of it."

"I'm also happy to fly out there, any time," I said. "Even just for a weekend, if you can't get the time off work."

"I would love if you wanted to visit, literally any time," she said.

"I'd be there in a heartbeat if you mean it," I said.

"Oh, I definitely mean it," she said.

"Are you sure?" I asked.

"Are you kidding? I'd be beside myself," she said. "You could meet the whole family."

As soon as we got off the phone, I mentioned the idea to Christopher. Between the flight, a hotel room, and a rental car, it would take a decent chunk out of our vacation savings; and Christopher would have to stay home and solo-parent Quinn, who was starting kindergarten in a matter of days. "Do it, babe," he said without hesitation. "Any time, any day. Don't worry about it, just go for it." I booked a flight a little over a month away and sent Kathy a confirmation. "Wow did I just get so emotional right at this moment," Kathy wrote back. "Honestly Tracy, it means so much to me that you really truly want to come."

My love for my sister wasn't a liability or a vulnerability; it wasn't a burden, either. It was a gift for us both.

. . . .

My flight to Atlanta was a couple weeks away, and I wanted some family photos to bring to Kathy, so I went searching through the sunroom at my dad's house, a light-filled L-shaped space with windows wrapping around the whole way. In a corner, tucked behind a stack of my mom's gardening books, I found a folded-up poster-board triptych from her memorial, with dozens of photographs stuck to it. I carefully pulled each image off, removing the rounds of Scotch tape from their backs, and filed them away in a tattered photo envelope.

I made a mental note to tell my therapist about this memorial poster board, untouched for nearly a decade. A few years earlier, I had mentioned the hospital bed still in my dad's living room—centrally located, right across from the television—and we'd spent the rest of the session talking about it. My dad disagreed with my characterization. "It's not a *hospital* bed," he had once told me. "This is a deluxe reclining bed." Fair enough, but it was the bed they bought and placed in the living room once my mom's cancer progressed. I had asked my dad, gently, whether there was a part of him that didn't want to let go of this great big symbol of grief, this elephant of loss in the living room. "To me," he had said, "it's just a comfortable bed."

Now Quinn went over to my childhood home every Sunday to eat popsicles and watch cartoons with his grandpa while lying in the same bed where his grandma died. The same bed she had been sitting in when she broke down in tears a few weeks before her death and told me, "I want nothing more than to see you as a mother, but I also feel that I know *exactly* the mother you will be. It is crystal clear to me. I see it perfectly."

I found a wicker basket full of family photos—the same basket I had gone searching through as a kid in hopes of finding proof that my mom was really my mom. There were those images of her in the hospital holding me to her bare chest. Whenever we came across these photos together, she had emphasized the importance of skin-to-skin contact for babies bonding with their mothers. She had said it with great emphasis—*skin-to-skin*—and I felt like she wanted me to remember this for my own future motherhood. Now I could only think of it as the act that she hadn't been able to do with Kathy, whom I suspect she was never even able to hold.

Sitting down on the tiled floor of the sunroom, I pulled out a box of photographic slides and held one up to the window. The sunlight brought the image to life, electrifying its bordered shapes like a stained-glass window. I saw my parents on their wedding day at the Berkeley Rose Garden, both of them wearing white with matching flower crowns made of pink carnations and baby's breath. They stood under a wooden pergola blanketed with roses the color of orange sherbet. My mom's dress was cotton and lace with long sleeves and a turtleneck, a little bohemian and a little Victorian.

I saw a woman who had grown up watching her mother's "deal with the devil," who had been marked by a system of punishment designed to create future wives, who had assumed she would live forever as a mistress, and who had eventually, to her surprise, gotten married. In so many ways, she had tried to challenge the institution from the inside—from their separate bedrooms to my hyphenated last name. She sometimes cooked, my dad rarely did, mostly we ate out—something my mom joked about as evidence of her "laziness" and "hedonism." Now I saw that this had allowed her to avoid the kitchen, that classic setting for domestic inequity, as well as the associated emotional drains of litigating such imbalances. Ironically, this dodging was a privilege afforded in part by her inheritance from her traditional patriarch of a dad.

On the handful of occasions when she got money from him

before his death, which she explained to me as his attempt at lessening his own tax burden, my mom had made it clear that there would be no strings attached—he couldn't buy her love, loyalty, or submission. "I never wanted him to have any power over me," she told me.

Never *again*, I assumed she meant. I wondered what strings were implicitly attached back in 1965, long before any inheritance was offered, when choosing to keep her baby might have meant being disowned by her family. Her father had been willing to part with his money for tax purposes. What about the purposes of supporting his daughter in raising her child—his first grandchild?

My mom's inherited wealth, which she maintained as her own, meant that she had financial independence in her marriage. She paid off her half of their house early on, retired at the age of fifty, and lived off investments, while my dad continued working into his early seventies.

She retired just a few months after we were hit by that car while crossing the street when I was twelve. She up and sold her successful graphic design company to her business partner. At the time, my mom told me that this near-death experience had put things in perspective and made her think about the shortness of life. "And I've always hated being across the bridge from you," she said of her office in San Francisco. "I've always worried about the big earthquake hitting and the bridge collapsing and not being able to get home to you."

I thought it was a midlife crisis—she even joked self-deprecatingly about it being one. Now I saw something else: She was worried about being separated from me. It was like she was talking in the over-the-top language of a nightmare—a body of water, a collapsed bridge, a daughter at an impassable distance. Her retirement could have been a reaction to her own mortality as much as the triggering of her trauma.

She was in the thick of perimenopause, often waving her hand in her face during hot flashes, and I was on the cusp of young adulthood, with all the zits to prove it. My mom exited the working world *just* as I entered womanhood. "You're going to be a teenager soon, you'll be going into high school, and this way I can be home and available to you," she told me at the time. I can only imagine how anticipating my puberty must have raised the possibility of history repeating itself.

She sometimes spoke of her retirement with that familiar language of laziness and hedonism, but it seems to me a gilded cage in retrospect. Without a nine-to-five, she retreated more frequently behind her locked bedroom door to smoke and drink. This was less indulgence than numbing; not so much thriving as surviving. The thing being numbed and survived was indelibly tied to my mom's father, the same man who enabled the numbing and surviving. I wondered if this was her deal with the devil, unrecognizable to her because it looked so different from the backdrop of her childhood.

I wondered what I couldn't recognize in my own life. The last months of researching my mom's past had forced me to look at myself as a mother and a wife. I had started talking with Christopher about my growing realizations around how my mom's story fit within a larger history of controlling women's sexuality and reproduction through marriage and the white nuclear-family norm. We always talked about that last bit with a shared sense of irony—a glint in the eye, a subtle smirk. We *were* a white nuclear family. We *were* that mythologized norm.

Much like my mom, I had tried to challenge the institution from the inside. Christopher and I had mutually and enthusiastically agreed to give Quinn my hyphenated last name as a middle finger to patriarchal norms, and Christopher came up with the idea to use his grandmother's maiden name as Quinn's middle name. "Just doing our part to try to make matriarchy a thing," he told his parents with a laugh. Sometimes we made air quotes when calling each other "husband" and "wife" because we didn't experience ourselves or each other as fitting within those boxes. We loved each other as people, as partners.

Despite our shared irreverence toward the institution, we were standing within it. We had generally settled into a lifestyle that looked remarkably conventional. With all my recent digging through the past, I felt that the playful irony of having walked down the aisle to the *Mission: Impossible* theme song was starting to fall a little flat. Now the "impossibility" of marriage felt more like the cognitive dissonance that it required. I had found my greatest comfort, happiness, and sense of intimacy within a foundational system of women's oppression—the same system that trapped my grandmother, fractured my family, and traumatized my mom.

The coercions of that system are very much alive. In *Everyday Utopia*, Kristen R. Ghodsee writes that "our domestic lives—what we do inside our homes, with our families, and in our interactions with friends, neighbors, and members of our wider communities—are still very much shaped by decidedly inegalitarian and sexist traditions."

I sometimes felt trapped by the norms of marriage and parenthood and the overwhelming heteronormativity of our suburban-adjacent existence. "The moms hang with the moms and the dads hang with the dads," I vented to Christopher one day. "It drives me crazy. *Absolutely crazy*. It would be considered extremely weird for me to ask one of the dads out to coffee in the way I routinely ask other moms out to coffee."

"You can go to coffee with Eric if you want, baby," he said playfully, picking a neighborhood dad at random. "Don't let me stop you."

"No, *I don't want to go to coffee with Eric*," I said, laughing, because I really didn't want to go to coffee with Eric. "It's the principle. You know what I mean?"

"I do," he said, nodding.

"We all just follow these unspoken norms, which basically suggest that men and women have nothing in common, but also that we're all in perpetual danger of . . . fucking each other and blowing up our lives," I continued. "Socially, it's like we're all nuns living in convents. And why, for what—to protect the sanctity of traditional gender roles, to protect the fragile foundation of monogamous heteronormative marriage? It probably only further erodes that fragile foundation by draining our lives of richness and connection and yes, too, maybe some friction and complexity and risk."

I paused to think, intending to continue my rant, but instead I just gripped the air above my head and sighed.

Many of us enter these domestic lives with a sense of choice, but our decisions are influenced by everything from the architecture of single-family homes to the lack of a social safety net for which the nuclear family is supposed to compensate. "All of us are seduced, or at least disciplined," writes the feminist critic Sophie Lewis in *Abolish the Family*. "We can't escape it, even when we individually reject it."

I had sprawled out on the floor of the sunroom, still holding the wedding slide in my hand. I looked up from the stained-glass-like image to an actual piece of stained glass hung in the window. My mom had made it in her late twenties or early thirties. It was unlike so many of her other pieces, which depicted scenes of nature in rich greens, purples, and blues: egrets, irises, trees, and mountains. This piece featured just clear and brown glass and two figures: a man and a woman. They appeared to be naked but were shown only from the shoulders up. I had always assumed them to be post-coital, sitting on a bed.

The brown-haired man was in the background, turned away but looking over his shoulder at the woman with a furrowed brow, as if trying to make sense of her. He didn't seem like he was trying that hard, though. I detected a resentful bewilderment in his face. The woman was in the foreground, facing the viewer full-on, her long brown hair flowing powerfully like the forking streams of a river. She was heavy-lidded and enigmatic, her features painted on with nuance.

All the times I had encountered her across my life, I had never quite figured her out. Sometimes I had seen a woman who was strong and independent. She had looked unbreakable, this woman made of glass. Other times, especially as I got older and stopped looking to sex as a source of power, she had seemed tired, detached, resigned, and remote. Now I saw this third invisible entity between them: the presence of everything outside of their private bedroom scene—all those shaping forces, all those traps, all those deals with the devil.

....

A couple weeks later, Kathy sent me an email. It began, "Hey sis!!" *Hey sis.* I don't know how to describe what happened to my heart. It cracked, it exploded, it surged, it skipped a beat. I became my heart and my heart became me. Molten pink heart lava flowed out of my every pore. The world melted into love and oneness. It was a psychedelic trip in a single sentence, an altered state brought on by two words and a double exclamation.

"It actually feels so natural to say that," she continued. "I hope it doesn't weird you out."

It didn't weird me out. For days, I'd been nurturing a fantasy: When I got to Atlanta, my sister and I would get a sister tattoo. A tiny little heart on the outside of the elbow or the inside of the wrist—or maybe a miniature infinity sign. These shapes didn't come to mind from a rational thought exercise, they just arrived, and it was a while before I questioned what they meant. The heart seemed obvious enough, but what about the infinity sign? *Hmm.* Unbreakable connection? The DNA spiral? Time flowing forward and folding backward on itself?

For the past four months, I'd been feeling like a wannabe time traveler, searching for the details of decades-old events, hoping to step back into a historic period in my mom's life. I'd stare so intently at yellowing photographs from the sixties that it was like I believed I could transport myself into the scene, given enough concentration. I'd spent hours on the phone and the internet, searching for records and addresses. Most of the people who had been there were gone. Records had been lost, destroyed, or locked away.

There was so much inaccessible about the past, but I also felt that I had, actually and meaningfully and successfully, traveled back in time by finding Kathy. Our DNA match hadn't changed the events of her life or my life up until that point. It hadn't undone our mom's grief and guilt and fear. It had changed the story, though, forever. Two sisters had found each other and declared the wish to know more, creating a multitude of possibilities and unknowns.

"I feel like we've connected a loop," I told a friend after my first call with my sister. I said this while gesturing vaguely in the air. What did I mean? I wasn't sure. All I could do was say it again. "Some . . . loop was connected." We were flowing backward and forward, connected and unblocked.

I did a Google search about the meaning behind this sideways figure eight, feeling like my subconscious was speaking to me in symbols and I needed a translator. There were different interpretations: life after death, interconnectedness, coming together, the infinite universe, yin and yang—themes of connection and eternity.

Around this time, NASA released historic images from the James Webb Space Telescope, including a snapshot of a cluster of galaxies as they appeared 4.6 billion years ago. Thousands of galaxies glinted like sequins tossed across a vertiginous black expanse. The image covered a piece of sky "approximately the size of a grain of sand held at arm's length by someone on the ground," read a NASA press release, just a "tiny sliver of the vast universe." Who could look at the sky the same way again?

It is one thing to know that you are made of stardust and another to feel it. I felt that atomic connection as I peered billions of years back in time at these collections of stars, gas, and dark matter. I also felt it when seeing photos of my sister, her three sons, and her seven grandchildren. I was awash in wildly different scales of connection. The atomic can make the genetic seem insignificant. I found myself thinking in a stony voice: *What is 27 percent shared DNA next to the atomic interconnectedness of lit-er-al-ly ev-er-y-thing*? And yet that 27 percent match felt more, not less, significant after contemplating thousands of galaxies in every speck of sky. It was the proximity of our genetics amid the infinite possibilities of the atomic.

We were neighboring waves in an endless expanse of ocean, connected nodes in the web of existence. What I mean is, my sister turned me into a New Age parody, I guess.

As I got ready for my trip to Atlanta, I dreamed of matching infinity tattoos, wanting to hold on to these feelings of connection and eternity, grasping for the feeble illusion of permanence with a symbol etched on the skin. I realized I was probably afraid of being rejected—or, in the crude language of the subconscious, I was afraid of being abandoned by the baby my mom had abandoned. This was because of both the guilt I carried on behalf of our mom and the way our family story tested the strength of genetics. If parenthood itself could be relinquished, then what did it mean for our sisterhood?

....

Three days before my flight to Atlanta, I woke up to a text from Kathy. "Hey sis," she wrote, "call me as soon as you're up." A detonation. My entire body demolished in a cloud of dust. I was sure something had happened—Covid, a car accident, a work emergency—and Kathy was canceling the trip. *Fuck*. I knew it had been too good to be true. I called her as I sat down with a cup of coffee in our breakfast nook, the same place where I had answered that first phone call from my sister months earlier.

"Well, sis, do I have a story for you," she said.

"Yeah?" I said uneasily. I watched the swirling steam leaving my coffee, feeling like I was slowly evaporating into the air.

"I got in touch with my dad."

"What," I yelled, lurching forward.

"We've been exchanging emails and texts for hours," she said.

"What!" I said again.

"I've been up all night going back and forth . . . *with my dad*."

I pulled my feet onto my chair and wrapped an arm over my knees as Kathy explained the backstory. Ahead of my visit, she had thought to return to researching her dad. She'd found a news story published just the day before about Babajide critiquing systemic corruption in the oil industry in Nigeria, which had led her to his email address. She'd reached out, just as she had on LinkedIn, but this time she got a response right away.

"He thought it was a scam! He really put me through the paces at first. I told him our mom's name, the timing of my birth, about Purdue, knowing that he was captain of the soccer team, all of that, and he was still skeptical. Then he asked me if I had any unusual markings on my body. He was like, 'All of my children have this particular mark on their bodies.' I wrote back and described in detail the small birthmark I have on my arm, and I kid you not, he wrote back, 'You are my daughter!' "

"Dude," I said. "*Dude*."

" 'You are my daughter,' " Kathy said. "*Exclamation point*."

"I can't believe it," I said. I took a sip of my coffee and looked out our bay window at the collection of pots on our deck exploding with turquoise, baby pink, and lime green succulents—all taken from my mom's garden.

After Kathy had described her birthmark, Babajide had told her that he remembered our mom fondly.

"I have to read you his texts. Hold on," Kathy said. " 'I am grateful to her for giving herself to me fully in a difficult time in the

Midwest. Despite the very little time we had together, we had a very close and intimate relationship.' "

"Wow."

"Here's another one: 'Meeting and getting to know your mother was my most personal experience at Purdue. You are a living legacy of that experience.' "

"A living legacy? Man, how poetic and romantic," I said.

"I guess our mom made an impression," Kathy said. "I was laughing. I hope you don't find this offensive, but I was thinking, *Man, Mom really put it down on him*."

We both cracked up. Our mom would have cracked up, too.

"I haven't even told you the craziest parts," Kathy said.

Babajide informed Kathy that he wanted to give her the Yoruba name Adétòkunbọ̀, meaning "glory from overseas, joyous birth." Our mom's pregnancy and my sister's birth had been treated as a shameful secret by the social systems that swallowed them up, but now Kathy was reunited with a father who saw her existence as a joyous honor.

"Stop," I said, my eyes pooling with tears. "Stop."

It was almost too much. A flash flood of goodness. Now I felt like I was the one being scammed. I mean, *really*. When Kathy had told Babajide about finding me and about our mother's death, he'd asked if my father was still alive—almost as though he were considering taking me under his wing along with my sister.

"He wants to talk with us when you're here this weekend," Kathy explained. "He'll FaceTime us from Lagos."

"Oh my god," I said. "You get to meet your dad."

My voice caught on the last few words. *Kathy will never get to meet our mom*, I thought. *Our mom will never get to meet*

Kathy. I will never get to see our mom again. She was left out of this reunion.

Kathy seemed to read my thoughts. "I figured you could also ask him any questions you want to know about what happened with our mom," she said.

"I'd love that," I said, but I wasn't considering what I wanted to know about the past so much as what my mom hadn't been able to see of the future. "You know, our mom never in a million years would have thought that your dad would respond with such fondness and forgiveness. It reminds me of how you reacted from the beginning—loving, open, full of empathy for our mom. I wish she could have known."

Kathy had told her dad how our mom had been sent away and then locked away. Babajide suggested that the three of us should visit our mom's grave together. "So that she can finally be at peace knowing that we've found each other," he had said. "Unbelievable," I told my sister. "That's so kind. Our mom doesn't have a grave, she was cremated, but maybe we can all visit the spot where we sprinkled her ashes in the ocean."

Twenty-four hours earlier, I had assumed that Babajide would react to the news of his hidden daughter as a betrayal. Much like my mom, I had imagined the anger he would understandably feel toward her. Now I was entertaining the cinematic thought of the three of us visiting her ashes in a gesture of forgiveness and healing.

I had expected the genre of tragedy, but Babajide had shown up and said: *No, that is not our story.*

. . . .

On my flight to Atlanta, in a window seat, everything felt big and profound. I watched as the sun cast shadows off the clouds below onto great dry swaths of apricot-colored earth. A memory slide from childhood clicked into place, an early impression of the sheer scale of the world: standing barefoot in a creek, watching leaves and water skippers floating across the water's surface; then shifting my gaze to their slow-drifting outlines, as well as my own static image projected onto the pebbled bottom.

I had that same sensation now of towering above natural objects and their doubled figures as the sun towered above me. I did not believe in God, but in traveling to meet Kathy, I did have the feeling of forces at play that were beyond me. Maybe it was just the force of my DNA: Released into a vial, it unspooled its story.

I spent the whole plane ride looking out that window, unable to focus on the screen in front of me or the podcast downloaded onto my phone or the book tucked into the seat-back pocket. Instead, I stared at a landscape marbled by deep snaking canyons. *Shaped by water and time*, I thought. It all seemed symbolic, ripe for textual analysis. Apricot earth eventually gave way to geometric patches of farmland in every shade of green, and I kept taking pictures out the window, as though it were my first plane ride. Like, *Holy shit, can you believe this? Are you* seeing *this?* I wondered if my seatmates thought I was on something.

As the pilot announced that we were approaching Atlanta, the clouds turned weird and wild, like nothing I had seen before. I started recording a video, mouth agape, as though documenting a UFO sighting. These were not the fog blankets from back home; these clouds looked like billowing smokestack gases frozen midair, a cityscape of cotton-ball spires, all dramatically lit by the westward sun.

These clouds felt like a cosmic communiqué, an otherworldly message. *Hi, Mom,* I thought, against the objections of my critical-thinking brain. It occurred to me that my mom—even as some sort of disembodied consciousness after death—would paradoxically judge this mushy, magical, and unscientific thinking and yet forgive it, *given the circumstances*. The circumstances being Kathy. *I'm going to get your daughter*, I silently told the clouds, the sun, the sky.

12

LAWS OF PHYSICS

It was dusk by the time I arrived in my rental car in Kathy's northeastern suburb, having blasted the latest Beyoncé album on repeat for an hour down roads walled with lush greenery. A check of my face in the rearview mirror, a deep breath, and a text: "I'm here!" I opened the car door to a humid night abuzz with cicadas, a sound perfectly matched to the itchy feeling of my insides. *Here we go. Here we fucking go, girl.* My mom had often used that word lovingly when talking to me. "My sweet girl." "You silly girl." "You go, girl."

"Hey there," Kathy called from the top of the driveway.

Her silhouetted figure moved toward me across the haze of almost night. *My sister. My mother. My mother's daughter.* I hugged her for myself, and I hugged her for our mother. Just like our mom, she was a few inches shorter than I was, and her forehead grazed my cheek in the same way.

Kathy pulled back to look at me. "You're beautiful," she said, hands clasping my shoulders.

"*So are you,*" I told her.

I felt our mom radiating off her like an aura. Multiple "wows" were exchanged as we looked at each other. It felt less like a meeting than a reunion. We were both wearing jeans, earth-toned T-shirts, and necklaces with a tiny golden charm—hers a simple rounded bead and mine a lowercase *q* for my little Quinn.

We somehow moved our legs sufficiently to walk into her house, a two-story rental that she shared with her best friend, Tru, who was around my age; her son, Devin; his wife, Kellie; their two toddler daughters, Mia and Natalie; and their German shepherds, one of whom pushed her wet nose into my palm as we walked to Kathy's bedroom.

I noted her closet office with a scattering of family photos taped to a bulletin board and a black-and-white framed photograph on the wall of her adoptive mother, Marguerite, in her twenties. "I like to have her there where I can see her each morning," Kathy said. "My mom just always made me feel like I was okay, you know? Even now." We sat on the bed, barefoot and cross-legged, with Kathy on one end and me on the other, and her mom seeming to gaze down at us. Kathy gestured toward a basket of photos sitting on the floor by the bed, explaining that she had pulled out some things from storage for us to sort through.

Looking into her eyes as she spoke, I felt a chill shoot through me. I saw my mother's eyes. I felt her looking at me—really looking at me—for the first time since she died. The moment passed, and Kathy was Kathy again, but I was left with the feeling of having summoned a ghost. It reminded me of childhood sleepovers when we girls gathered around a Ouija board or dared each other to chant "Bloody Mary" into the mirror. This time there was no terror, just awe at the spell of genetics.

Kathy spread out a collection of photos between us on her black faux-fur throw. My eyes scanned back and forth between the images, trying to put together the visual story of my sister's life: Kathy at twenty-one years old in a white wedding gown with long lace sleeves and a matching pouf of a hat; Sean as a baby slumped against her chest during an afternoon nap; Justin at six years old eating a red Donald Duck ice pop; Devin cheesing in a graduation cap with his kindergarten diploma rolled up in his hand. She pointed out photos of her first husband and then her second husband. "I did it kind of backward, you know? My twenties were all about marriage and kids," Kathy said. "Then, after my second divorce, I had my wild era in my forties. Going to bars, staying up until the wee hours of the morning."

Exploration and self-discovery came after motherhood and establishing her career. During one of our earlier phone calls, Kathy had told me that she'd not only "calmed down" since her wild era, she had also given up on sex and dating. "Maybe this is TMI, I figure you're used to it with what you write about, but I've never had an orgasm with a man," she had said. "I'm at that point where I don't have space for a man unless he can really add something to my life. Something I can't give myself."

Now Kathy grabbed a folded pink piece of paper off the bed and handed it to me: the pamphlet from Marguerite's funeral twenty-two years earlier. It told the basics of her life. Born: 1918 in Mississippi. Married: 1951. I was reminded that Marguerite had been born just a year before my grandma Quen and that she was approaching fifty by the time she adopted Kathy. "Together they adopted four children," it read. "Marguerite was a loving wife, mother and friend to all that knew her. She dedicated her life to serving children in need through 46 years of foster parenting."

"She really was an amazing woman," Kathy said.

"It sounds like it," I said. "I guess your mom married kind of late for the time, in her thirties?"

"Yeah, although I only realized after she died that she had married before. I found this nice crystal pitcher in her house etched with the initial *L*, which didn't make any sense. My brother Gary was like 'You didn't know that Mom was married before Dad?' "

"Whoa," I said.

"She had her secrets," Kathy said. "There's so much I wish I could ask her about now."

"Like what?"

"Gary swears he once found a birth certificate in their house for a secret baby."

"A secret baby?" I asked.

Those words brought me right back to the falling feeling when my mom sat me down as a teenager and told me about my sister.

"A baby born from way back, a girl. It's a total mystery around what happened to her—if she was placed for adoption or what."

"I thought she wasn't able to have kids," I said.

"I don't know," Kathy said. "Maybe she had been able to at one point."

The way my mouth dropped, the feeling of life being wilder than fiction. What if my mother's daughter had been raised by another woman who had placed a baby for adoption? *What if.* They hadn't been able to find any evidence of a secret baby, but Kathy said she wondered.

"Man," I said. "I'm just picturing how our mom would have reacted to learning about your mom, getting to see her face, hearing her story."

"I dunno, I feel like my two moms are having tea somewhere, smiling down on us right now," Kathy said.

....

The sound of a car door, a jangle of keys, the dog barking.

Kathy and I were still looking through photos when her twenty-eight-year-old son, Devin, stepped into her bedroom doorway, wearing a T-shirt emblazoned with an image of Bob Marley smoking a joint. Kathy introduced us, and he gave a big smiling "Hey" with all the laid-back ease of his shirt. *My mom's grandson.* How that shirt would have made my pot-smoking mom smile.

A hug, the three of us shaking our heads, the surreality of it all. "Wait a minute," Kathy said, craning her head back as if to get a better look at us. "Seeing you two together right now, wow, that is a trip. I am seeing the resemblance. Let me take a picture so you can see."

We stood side by side, and when Kathy turned the phone around, I saw it: the same smile lines curving from the nose, around the mouth, and down to the chin, which was itself so much the same. Our mouths had the same upturned corners, like the gentle flick of a calligrapher's brush, and our under-eye smile lines were nearly identical.

"You really look like you could be related," she said, and then laughed. "I mean, you *are* related."

....

Early the next morning, after I squeezed in a few hours of sleep at my nearby hotel, I swung by Kathy's house. Mia and Natalie were awake and padding around the kitchen in their pink pajamas. "That's your aunt Tracy," Kathy told them. I flapped my hand dumbly at them. I wanted to cuddle and squish and kiss and coo. Instead, I perched on a kitchen stool, waving and smiling and making random surprise faces while they puttered in their play kitchen. Occasionally, Natalie looked over at me skeptically, and I couldn't blame her. I had none of the ease and confidence that I imagined typically arose around a sibling's kids and grandkids. I felt like a creepy stranger.

We left the girls at home with Kellie and drove to a kids' football game that Devin was coaching. We sat in the bleachers, baking in the Southern heat, as miniature cheerleaders straight from an episode of *Toddlers & Tiaras* rattled their pompoms. When a six-year-old in a clunky helmet and shoulder pads made a surprise touchdown, I watched Devin sprint clear across the bright green field, arms wide open, to bump chests in celebration. It was such a small moment, but I had that same feeling from the first time Kathy called me "sis." Molten pink heart lava.

Afterward, driving to pick up lunch, Kathy and I stopped at a red light across from a Planned Parenthood clinic with half a dozen protesters out front. Back home, a year earlier, I'd been shocked to drive by a group of people randomly standing outside a local shopping center holding signs reading, "I pray to end abortion." It was the first time I'd ever come across anti-abortion protesters in person. Before I even knew what I was doing, I'd rolled down my car window and screamed: "*I pray* you learn to *mind your business* about what other people do with their bodies!" The last word had come out strained and tight, my voice on the verge of collapse. Now, in the car with Kathy, I exercised restraint.

"Yikes," I said.

"Yeah, they're always out there," Kathy told me as I gawked.

"Damn," I said. "We don't see much of that in the Bay Area."

I had no idea where Kathy stood on the issue of abortion, though I'd wondered, given the pre-*Roe* context of her birth. Kathy didn't know that our mom had felt capable of accessing an abortion if she had wanted one but had decided against it; the topic had never come up.

"Back when I was in my wild phase, going out all the time," Kathy started, "I joked to my friend Kendra, 'Protesters be damned, I am *not* having another baby.' "

We both laughed.

"I wasn't sure, you know, where you stood politically," I said, feeling slightly relieved. "I think my politics are pretty obvious."

"I don't know that I'm a Democrat or a Republican," she said. "But I know I was real glad when Trump wasn't reelected. What about our mom?"

"Oh, super lefty," I said. "She watched Fox News just to get mad and yell at the TV."

The light changed and I shifted conversation to the upcoming FaceTime Kathy had scheduled with her dad—another nerve-wracking topic.

"I can totally let you have your moment with him," I said.

"No, no, I really think I'd rather have you there," she said.

"Obviously, you two can mostly talk, I'll just be there on the sidelines for support."

Back at her house, we set up a couple chairs in her closet office and leaned her phone against the laptop screen. Kathy was flitting around the room—tidying things, checking herself in the mirror, folding a piece of gum into her mouth. She rattled the ice at the bottom of the nearly empty fountain drink she'd gotten when we picked up lunch; then she absent-mindedly pulled the straw in and out, making a squeaking sound. I was nervous, too—for my sister and for our mom, who had kept the secret of her daughter from this man for most of her life.

I wanted to represent our mom well; I wanted to explain.

For all the profound weight of the moment, I also felt an irreverent sense of absurdity: *I'm about to FaceTime with one of my mom's college hookups.* I imagined Quinn down the line on a video call with one of the men from my past: the poetry-writing frat boy, the anti-abortion Starbucks barista who didn't use condoms, the airline pilot who liked guns and mixed martial arts. Those men were more representative of my fraught fascination with men's privilege and power at that age than what I had wanted or valued. I had known my mom only in her settled state; meeting this man from her freshman year of college was like getting a glimpse of her early unformed self—the girl before the mom.

We both jumped at the ringing of Kathy's phone. Then Babajide appeared on the screen, wearing a crisp pink-and-blue-striped button-up. He looked much like he did in his yearbook photo, only now he had glasses and a dusting of gray stubble.

"Hello, Katheryn," he said from nearly six thousand miles away. "Hello, Tracy."

"Hello, Baba Mi," Kathy said, using the Yoruba term for "my father," which he had taught her in a text message.

Kathy moved us through some generic pleasantries, powering through the complications of the spotty connection and the pressure of this first meeting. I could see how she led team meetings at work, with a friendliness and curiosity balanced by a sense of destination that kept everything moving along. Eventually, conversation turned to the DNA test.

"Tracy, I wanted to ask: Why did you take the test?" he asked.

"My mom told me about my sister when I was a teenager, and I've wanted to find her ever since. It occurred to me that a DNA test might be a way to do that."

"But how did you find me?"

"My mom told me about you. She said you were captain of the soccer team."

He chuckled at this.

"And that you were Nigerian, too," I continued. "I found a yearbook online, looked up a photo of the soccer team, and there you were, along with your name."

"I remember your mother," he said. "We met in the fall of 1964 at Purdue University. I had no idea about the pregnancy. One day she simply disappeared. I never saw her again."

He waved his hand in the air like the poof of a magician's wand. I nodded and sighed.

"Kathy tells me that she was sent away and that she suffered," he continued. "I was very sorry to hear that. I wish I had known."

"Yes, thank you," I said. "I am sorry, too. I'm so glad that we were able to find you."

Just then Devin got home and popped his head into the room, whispering off camera to ask if he should join. "Oh, Baba Mi, I want to introduce you to your grandson Devin, my youngest," Kathy said, stepping away from her chair so that he could take her place. Devin said hello to his grandfather, making small talk about the game he had coached that morning. The content of the conversation felt less important than the way they beamed at each other through the computer screen. Devin was only a decade younger than I was, but the big, fat grin on his face made him seem like one of those kids from the football field. Later, after our hour-long call, Babajide texted Kathy a message for me:

> *Meeting you, even if just by video, has certainly been one of the greatest pleasures of my life. It is certainly monumental as well. I want to thank you once again for your doggedness in locating Katheryn, and thereby bringing the three of us together, who are united by your mother's memory. May she continue to rest in perfect peace, now that all three of us are united at last.*

He asked me and Kathy to figure out how I would address him going forward. "In my culture, naming has a definite structure which puts the two persons relating in comfort emotionally," he explained. We turned to his wife, whom Kathy had started calling Auntie Yinka, for some guidance on appropriate nicknames and came to a decision.

Now he was my uncle Jide.

....

JoAnn, my sister's sister, flung her arms wide as soon as she saw us. Kathy and I had parked in the historic downtown of Lawrenceville, just outside of Atlanta. JoAnn, a tall and polished woman in her sixties, greeted me with a warm and confident "hello" that was revealing of her work as an executive leadership coach. She had come into town from more than an hour away just to meet me. I had seen photos online of her speaking passionately at podiums and leading breakout sessions in hotel conference rooms. It was clear she would be able to fill any awkward silences and direct the conversation where it needed to go, just like Kathy.

The three of us walked along the sidewalk in a shifting triangular arrangement that inevitably left one of us on the outside. I wasn't sure of my place in this trio. I was Kathy's sister by blood but not bonding. How did the connection of DNA compare to the connection of a shared childhood? I was both jealous of their sisterhood and intent on not threatening it, which meant that I felt a paradoxical mix of relief and danger no matter which of us was walking alongside Kathy at any given moment.

Kathy pointed out the spot where, decades earlier, she had opened a popular restaurant selling Chicago-style hot dogs and ice cream. She had made the newspaper for being the first Black woman business owner on the town square. As we passed the Gwinnett County courthouse, an old brick building with a tall clock tower, JoAnn turned to me. "Now, Tracy, you might find this bit of history interesting, given your subject matter," she said. "That is where Larry Flynt, the owner of *Hustler* magazine, was shot." In 1978, while Flynt was on trial for obscenity, both he and his lawyer were attacked in front of the courthouse. I was touched that JoAnn understood my work enough to make the connection, and her ease in bringing up the topic made me feel like I'd just unbuttoned a tight pair of jeans.

Later, I would read up on Flynt's shooter: He was a white-supremacist serial killer who was incensed by a *Hustler* photo shoot between a Black man and a white woman. "I saw that interracial couple he had, photographed there, having sex," the shooter said. "It just made me sick . . . I threw the magazine down and thought, 'I'm gonna kill that guy.' " I would also read about how, in 1911, right outside this same courthouse, a mob of white men lynched a Black man after he was accused, without trial, of assaulting a white woman.

A couple of blocks away, the three of us sat down at a candlelit restaurant and ordered a bottle of red wine. We picked at a plate of fried artichokes as JoAnn launched into the story of Kathy's adoption. "I remember the phone ringing. They called to tell us about a new baby girl. It couldn't have been that long after that Mom brought you home," she said, nodding toward Kathy. "You couldn't have been older than a few weeks."

"What was that like for you?" I asked.

"I was a girl living with two brothers. The only girl of the family," she said. "I was *so* excited to have a baby sister."

Marguerite had gotten involved through her church with the child welfare agency that facilitated the adoption of her four kids. "Back then white families didn't want to adopt mixed babies," JoAnn said. "They didn't want us, so they sent people around to Black churches looking for Black families willing to adopt mixed babies." *They didn't want us.*

On the drive to dinner, Kathy had mentioned something Devin had said the night before. His wife, Kellie, who was white, had asked Kathy if she wondered what it would have been like if her biological mother had chosen to raise her. Devin had interjected: "No, it couldn't have happened. Her father was probably a racist. She would have had to have run away from home and been all on her own."

I wondered once again about my grandfather. Recently, my dad had told me that my mom never mentioned race as a factor in the adoption; he said he suspected my grandfather never knew that my sister was Black. I thought of my own whiteness and my wish to believe in my dad's suspicion as fact; otherwise, I had to sit with the possibility that my white grandfather had facilitated his grandchild's adoption *because* her father was Black.

JoAnn went to top off our glasses and shifted to talking about her own birth story. "My mother was white, and my father was Black. He was a well-known jazz drummer," JoAnn said. "He played with some of the greats and toured all over the place. He was married to Dinah Washington for a short time. He also had a lot of kids by different women. There's a Facebook group for all of us."

JoAnn went swiping through her phone before landing on a black-and-white photo of her biological father from the early fifties, smiling and handsome in a sharp suit, sitting on top of Washington's piano. Her biological parents met some years after that photo was taken: her mother, an eighteen-year-old secretary, saw him playing at a jazz club in Illinois. "I found this article published in *Jet* magazine after I was conceived," she said. JoAnn turned her phone to show me a screenshot of an article from 1957 written about her parents. The headline: "Musician Faces Ill. White Girl's Bastardy Charge."

"That's how I came into the world," JoAnn said.

....

Dinner gave way to drinks at Kathy's favorite bar, which was tucked away in a strip mall a short drive away. Kathy seemed to know almost everyone, thanks to her wild era. This had been her spot after her second divorce. As we settled onto a row of barstools, JoAnn wanted to know more about my work. "So, Tracy, how did you end up writing about sex?" she asked.

"Well, I used to think it was because I grew up on the internet with porn at my fingertips," I said. "Or because I was raised by a couple of sex-positive hippies in Berkeley, which gave me a sense of permission, you know? That I *could* write about sex without being disowned by my family."

I rotated my pint glass on its coaster. "After finding Kathy and looking into our mom's backstory, though, I realized that our mom's sexuality got her sent away in shame," I said. "She was told to lie, to hide, to pretend, and it destroyed and devastated her, you know? It followed her for her entire life. I think a lot of my writing has been a reaction to that. I've been writing against stigma and shame and secrecy."

"You know, Kathy has told me a bit of your mother's story, and it's awful to learn about her pain after the adoption," JoAnn said. "It's the other side of the joy that I felt when I got my new baby sister."

I took a sip of my beer, wishing that my mom could have known about the joy on the other side of her pain. Just then a smooth-talking man with deep dimples slid up next to Kathy. I listened in as she razzed him about his upcoming nuptials. Was he done with his womanizing ways? Had he really been reformed? Then he looked toward me, and Kathy said, "*Don't even think about it.* That's my baby sister." She was the protective older sister already.

After finishing her beer, JoAnn headed back to her hotel room, and Devin joined us at the bar. I peppered him with questions about his life: work, family, fun. He had served in the navy, specializing in electronics, and now he was working as a technician at a security company, and he coached football on the weekends. I showed him a video I'd captured earlier of him running down the field to chest-bump his player after a touchdown. I felt like a doting aunt already.

That was the mood of my first full day in Atlanta: *already.* It hadn't taken much time to arrive at the feeling of family. Already I was an aunt, a niece, a sister. Already I had a nephew, an uncle, a big sister. It was much more than a biological technicality. This feeling, still shaky and full of doubt, had slowly taken root over the past weeks and then bloomed in the hyper-speed of the past hours. The hugs, the identical smiles, the call to Nigeria, the sister dinner.

I had spent enough time on adoption and reunion message boards to know that this was not how it always went, or perhaps even how it often went. There was no universal meaning to a reunion between siblings. Their shared DNA could feel bizarre or insignificant or profoundly consequential. A first meeting could bring an uncanny sense of sameness or a reckoning with the wide gulf between nature and nurture. It meant what you chose to make it, and half siblings didn't always choose to make it into the same thing.

The three of us sat on those barstools talking for hours. Just before two a.m., I suggested a selfie. Our "already" felt giddy and glowy but tenuous. I wanted proof, like with the sister tattoo that I'd fantasized about. I wanted not to forget the possibility and promise of the moment. And there we were in the photo: sweaty, bleary-eyed, and leaning into one another like it was an undeniable law of physics.

13

A DIFFERENT KIND OF FALLING

The morning after the bar, feeling sleepy and hungover, Kathy and I drove to a popular breakfast spot with a line out the door. Three long tables had already been pushed together for our party of sixteen. Justin and two of his kids were there, along with JoAnn, who waved enthusiastically. The glint in Justin's eyes gave the impression of a discerning sharpness and sense of humor. He stood up to meet me, and every tissue, every cell, every molecule inside me screamed, *My mom's grandson.*

There was a different reality, the one Justin inhabited, where his biological grandmother was a stranger. My whole being reverberated with a feeling of relief and reunion but also caution. I didn't want to invade his sense of reality, hijack his experience, and replace it with my own. *Don't freak out, be normal, play it cool,* I thought. *But don't play it* too *cool.*

There was a "hello," a hug, a "nice to meet you." We went through the motions, which felt rote and profound. I met his eleven-year-old daughter, Isabella, and his six-year-old son, Julius. "They're as cute as they come," I would tell Kathy later, not realizing until I'd said it that it was a phrase my mom had used. Everyone else flooded in: Devin and his family. Then Sean—who was quiet, thoughtful, and a touch mysterious—with his girlfriend and three kids.

I made a show of losing myself in the menu. I mean, really, just studying it like a profound piece of art. I was grateful for this laminated object as a socially acceptable reason to retreat into my mind. I stared right through the pancake and waffle specials while reviewing what I had said and searching for what to say next.

I had ended up in a corner booth between Kathy, who rocked Sean's three-month-old Zya in her arms, and Isabella, who soon commandeered her dad's phone to show me pictures of herself as a baby. It was like she was trying to catch me up on what I had missed of her life so far. This was a kid who had been loved well, a kid who could delight in her own cuteness.

"Look at my cheeks in this one," she said. "So big!"

"Oh my gawd, the squishiest," I agreed.

We got to talking about what was most relevant in her world now: She wanted to be a doctor when she grew up. Next in importance: Her mom had given in and let her get a two-piece bathing suit, *finally*. As our food arrived, I watched JoAnn help the kids cut up their pancakes into little bites and felt inspired to act like an aunt myself. When Julius struggled with the straw for his cup, I launched myself across the table to help.

I knew how to care for little kids and chat with adolescents about what they wanted to be when they grew up. It was harder to find a way in with Justin and Sean, who sat with Devin at the opposite end of our pushed-together tables, which felt symbolic of the emotional distance I hoped to close, and which was far too great for a single brunch, no matter the seating arrangement.

After brunch, most of us went to Julius's basketball game. I sat in the bleachers of the air-conditioned gym, struggling toward small talk, even with Kathy. I was exhausted—from the night before but also the onslaught of up-and-down feelings since I'd arrived. The good felt laced with the bad, just as JoAnn's joy had been the flip of our mom's pain. I was living on both sides of the coin. Watching Justin run up and down the basketball court, much as Devin had done at the football game the day before, there was that molten pink heart lava again, but I couldn't hold on to the feeling; I wasn't sure it belonged to me. I had no entitlement to these boys, who were actually grown men with families of their own.

I could only ooze, like an open wound.

I loved them because I saw my mom in them, because she would have loved them, and because she never got to know them or even know *of* them. I loved them because I loved my mom, and because I carried her in me, not just in my genes but in my memory of her. I loved them because my mom had poured her love for Kathy into me. I felt myself being swept under a wave of mystical thinking. *I've been carrying that excess love my whole life, and maybe it was all meant for this moment. Matter can't be destroyed, only transformed. What about love?*

In the car afterward, Kathy and I talked about how cool it was to see everybody together sitting at one table, and I looked through the photos I had taken on my phone.

"I still have to win over Justin and Sean," I said.

"Oh, you will," she said, fiddling with the air-conditioning. "It's just a matter of time."

"I hope so."

"I can't wait to meet my little nephew and for him to meet his aunt Kathy," she said. "When he's old enough, Quinn could come visit for the summer."

"Ah, that would be amazing."

"That's what my mom did with my boys after we moved from Chicago to Atlanta. Every summer they would go up north to stay with her, and just like she did with me, she really tried to introduce them to different experiences and people and cultures. I would love to do that for Quinn."

"I would love that," I said. "I'm sure he would love that, too."

"I want to share Black culture with him," she said.

I don't remember what I said in response—what words I possibly could have come up with in the moment—but they had to have been insufficient. Kathy was expressing a sense of abundance—in the family who raised her and the culture she grew up in—and she wanted to share it with her white nephew. This was the opposite impulse of the white middle-class nuclear-family values that had gotten so many women and babies sent away. *Those* "family values" were not actually about love and care. They were about maintaining privilege and appearances.

They were about power.

....

That afternoon I passed out for two hours in my hotel room and woke up to the alarm I had set for a home-cooked dinner at Kathy's house. It was my last night in Atlanta. The ache in my jaw told me I had been grinding my teeth for most of my nap. I riffled through my toiletries in the bathroom and caught myself in the mirror. Wild hair, smudged mascara, deep circles under my eyes. I heard my mom's voice. *Oh, honey, you look tired.*

As I shook a couple of Advils into my palm, the sobs came before the tears. I slid down to my knees and plopped onto the cold tile floor. I grabbed a washcloth off the counter and pressed it against my mouth to muffle the whisper of a shaking scream that came out. Then I looked at my distorted reflection in the snaking metal underside of the sink. I told myself: "My mom's grandkids. My mom's grandkids. My mom's *great*-grandkids." I grabbed the washcloth again. "What the fuck," I said into the rough terry cloth. "*What the fuck, what the fuck, what the fuck.*"

I spun the roll of toilet paper and ripped off a long section, blowing my nose so furiously that my ears popped. I had been texting home with updates about meeting Devin, FaceTiming with Uncle Jide, and meeting JoAnn, but with a restrained and matter-of-fact delivery. "It's incredible and amazing," I had said. But I hadn't really let the incredible and amazing in, because letting it in looked like this: snotty toilet paper and screaming into a washcloth.

I thought of a therapist I had seen long ago who would place his hand on his heart with a little scrubbing motion and ask: "What are the feelings?"

Oh, I don't know. The feelings are that I'm mad and sad for my sister, who never got to meet her biological mom. The feelings are that I miss my mom, that I want her here, that it's not enough for me to meet her daughter and grandkids and great-grandkids, that I want her to experience it for herself, that it's so incredibly, unavoidably, inescapably, and irretrievably fucked *that she never did. The* feelings *are that I've found these family members who are of her but don't belong to her, that I've found my mom again in the world but she's not mine, that I've lost her again somehow.*

Just as had sometimes happened with that therapist and his signature question, the list of feelings led to deeper currents that were harder to name. I thought of that phrase JoAnn had said: "They didn't want us." I thought of my own inheritance of that "they," of my whiteness, of my wantedness. *What did my grandfather know? What did Quen know? Did they know that their daughter was pregnant with a mixed-race baby? How did race influence my mom's sense of what was possible or realistic?*

Then I slid into a back-and-forth with myself. *Okay, let's say her parents did know. Would that have been a deciding factor in sending her away?*

I would think so! How would her white patriarch of a dad have felt about that? I mean, really.

But my grandfather probably didn't *know about Kathy's race, according to my dad. And besides, would her parents have helped her to raise a* white *baby out of wedlock? Would it have been any different? Would they have supported her in raising a white baby as a single mother?*

No way. Not a chance. Never in a million years. That's why these homes existed! Most of those babies were white. These white families disowned their white babies because they cared that much about white power and privilege and appearances. Because that *is white culture.*

The adoption would have happened no matter what, right?

Probably. But does that mean race isn't relevant? The outcome might have been the same, but that doesn't mean that race isn't part of this story. You don't want it to be part of this story, but it is.

But what does it mean for it to be part of the story if the outcome is the same regardless of my sister's race?

What about your sister being raised by a Black family? What about a Black family raising your mother's baby? What about a Black woman, born on a Mississippi plantation, raising your mom's baby just a hundred years after chattel slavery was abolished? What about her raising three other white women's babies? What about your mom's race? What about your *race? Your sister was placed for adoption within a system designed to protect white privilege, and you have inherited that privilege as the kept granddaughter of your grandfather.*

There on the cold tile floor, I fell into a pit of sorrow and despair, one that was specific to my family's story and germane to whiteness in this country. Many times over the decades, I had reflected on the privileges I had been afforded because of my class and race. Whenever I pulled on that thread, it seemed the whole tapestry of my life started to unravel. I knew that it should unravel, that it *must* begin to fray, that its tidy coherence was not only an illusion but a kind of spiritual death. I was certain that my mom knew this feeling: In her yellowing copy of James Baldwin's *Notes of a Native Son*, she underlined and circled a passage about how "the white man's world, intellectually, morally, and spiritually, has the meaningless ring of a hollow drum and the odor of slow death."

There are so many ways to avoid the unraveling—from nihilistic overwhelm in the face of systemic racism to the relief of comparing oneself to really, truly "bad" white people. And yet it could be hard to identify avoidance when guilt itself was often a self-flagellating indulgence.

"For the average white person in America, even and perhaps especially the average white liberal person who thinks they are on the right side of racial issues, the privilege is too entrenched," writes Rebecca Carroll in her memoir, *Surviving the White Gaze*, about being a mixed-race child adopted by a white family. "The work and humility required to fully understand systemic racism in this country holds no realistic appeal. Most white people go straight to their own sense of guilt and then don't know how to manage their feelings from there."

I looked at the crumpled length of toilet paper strewn across my lap and resolved not only to keep tugging at that thread of understanding but also to sit with the fraying feeling, inviting that sense of my life as held together by structural privilege to be a more conscious and constant companion.

In *The Fire Next Time*, Baldwin writes that "love takes off the masks that we fear we cannot live without and know we cannot live within." He describes love as "a state of being, or a state of grace—not in the infantile American sense of being made happy but in the tough and universal sense of quest and daring and growth." That was a sentence I had underlined in my copy of the book—a recent printing, unlike my mom's copy of *Notes of a Native Son*, but maybe one that would be yellowing by the time Quinn got his hands on it.

Another thought: When I got back home, I would ask my dad to add Kathy to his will. I wasn't sure what money I stood to ever inherit—my dad had joked that there would be none left by the time he was gone—but there would likely be *something*, and mixed in that something would be my grandfather's money. I thought of the history of marriage—and the control of women's sexuality within it—as a tool for preserving white men's power, privilege, and lines of inheritance. This wouldn't be a stopping point. It wouldn't undo the wrongs of the past or absolve me of my white privilege and the ongoing work of reckoning with it on a personal and cultural level, but it felt meaningful, materially and symbolically. It was a simple and concrete way to reject the values of the racist and sexist system that had fractured my family. It was a way to say: *This is my mother's daughter. This is my grandfather's granddaughter. This is my sister.*

For now, I blew my nose. I pressed a cold washcloth to my eyes and put on mascara in hopes of concealing my breakdown. Then I went to the store to buy a bouquet of sunflowers and a pint of ice cream, and I showed up for dinner with my sister.

....

Kathy was just finishing cooking when I walked in the door. She poked a fork into the sautéed cabbage on the stove and took a test bite. "Damn, that's good," she said. "If I do say so myself." From the smell alone, I knew she wasn't exaggerating. Our mom had been a great cook herself, but she'd never taught me how to do it. I hated to cook, sometimes even felt a visceral rage about it, and had married a man who made almost all the dinners in our household.

On both fronts, I wondered how my mom's backstory might have played a role. After all, homes for unwed mothers had sometimes taught women how to cook because it was supposed to be a tool for their redemption. I wasn't sure whether my mom had been subjected to those lessons, but regardless, cooking was an emblem of proper femininity, and I had pushed that emblem away like poison.

The girls came padding into the kitchen in their pajamas, as they had the first morning I'd met them. They still didn't know quite what to make of me, this lady who kept showing up to gaze longingly at them. I'd spent the weekend watching and loving them at a remove. We were biologically related, but what did that mean to a couple of toddlers who had never met me before? I was waiting for the right opening. Then Natalie stumbled and dropped her pink plastic ball, and it rolled toward me.

"Oop!" I exclaimed, stopping it with my hand. "Wanna catch?"

I gently bounced it toward her, and she caught it with the slightest smile.

"Wanna throw it back?"

She thought about it, watching me quietly, then pushed it forward through the air.

"Good throw!"

Mia wanted in on the action. She wasn't so sure about me but gave the subtlest smirk as the three of us took turns rolling the ball across the kitchen floor.

Soon Kathy and I sat on the couch in the living room with plates of mahi-mahi, cabbage, and rice. Natalie waddled over to me, put her arms up, and started whining. She wanted up, and she wanted me to lift her. I scooped her onto the couch right next to me. She leaned toward my plate and blinked her big brown eyes. I asked Kathy if it was okay to feed her before placing a few bits of rice into her pleading baby-bird mouth. Then some cabbage and fish—and she kept "mmm, mmm-ing" for more. I would have let her eat my entire plate clean. Then Kellie came to take her for a diaper change.

"So." My sister turned to me. "I feel like you've heard a lot about how I'm feeling about all of this, but how are you feeling?"

Could she tell that I'd been late to dinner because I'd been trying to depuff my eyes after sobbing in my hotel room?

"You know, it's a lot," I said. "It's a lot. I keep wishing our mom was here to see this . . ."

My vision blurred. I laughed at myself and took a deep, shaky breath. Kathy tilted her head and put her hand on my shoulder. I could tell she was on the verge, too. Devin quietly floated nearby, picking up toys and getting bottles ready for the girls. Kathy offered that we could go to her room if I'd feel more comfortable, but I had a strong conviction that I shouldn't hide, so she grabbed me a box of tissues instead.

"Our mom would have fallen ridiculously head over heels in love with everyone, and I'm so sad for her missing that," I said, wiping my eyes. "There are all these mixed emotions of joy and grief and sadness."

I knew Devin heard me say this, and I was glad. He should know how much his biological grandmother would have loved him and his kids.

"I know, I know," Kathy said. "I keep thinking of both of our moms—of my mom and our mom—just picturing them seeing all of this. I want to believe that they are."

We had said versions of this all weekend: *Can you imagine our moms watching this? Can you* just imagine *how delighted they would be?*

"I can't believe that this is my last night," I said.

"I know it. It's gonna be hard saying goodbye tomorrow," she said.

We both pulled at the damp, crumpled tissues in our laps.

Ahead of the trip, I had found myself checking my feelings toward Kathy against reality—or at least a technical, sober version of it. "It's weird, I'm flying across the country to visit a virtual stranger," I had told Christopher. "But it feels totally normal and familiar." Meeting Kathy had felt like that, too. Across the weekend, we had laughed over our random similarities, like our style of sitting with a leg pulled up so that it bisected a thigh and the way we danced in our seat after a good bite of food. Privately, I had also observed all the admirable ways that Kathy was quite different from me: She was outgoing, lively, confident, strong, optimistic, and effortlessly warm. She seemed to appreciate my distinct qualities, too: While she showed me a text message from her dad, I had spied the way she described me to him: sweet, gentle, kind, and loving. Our mutual appreciation had bloomed.

Kathy took a deep breath. "After this weekend, I can honestly say that . . . *I love you*," she said, gesturing with her arms out for a hug. As soon as those three words left her mouth, they came rushing out of mine: "*I love you, too.*" I had the same stomach-flipping sensation as with so many past declarations of love, but this was not romantic. It was a different kind of falling in love.

. . . .

Just one weekend away, and my sense of family had expanded exponentially.

When I got home, I sent Devin's daughters a few board books with a note signed from Aunt Tracy. I could own the title now: Kathy had told me that on the last night of my visit, Devin had teared up because, in his own words, he was going to "miss Aunt Tracy." I texted JoAnn with "love and hugs from California," and she wrote back to say, "With Kathy you got a 'twofer' now you have 2 big sisters." Uncle Jide texted that he had found himself having "fatherly feelings" after watching my interactions with Kathy and Devin on FaceTime, and that he wanted to nurture a "familial relationship."

A few days later, a couple packages showed up from Kathy addressed to Quinn. He ripped open the cardboard boxes and discovered three garbage-truck toys. I'd sent Kathy a video of Quinn barefoot in his pajamas running out to the street to watch a garbage truck go by, as he did every Tuesday morning. He was on a waving basis with the truck driver, whom he reacted to like a superhero. "Now he has a FLEET of garbage trucks," Kathy texted. I told her that her gift reminded me of our mom, who had overdone it with presents, often remarking, "I just couldn't help myself." Kathy wrote back: "I can never replace Mom . . . but I sure hope I can fill some of the void."

I was stunned. Our mom had placed Kathy for adoption, and now Kathy wanted to make up for our mom's absence in *my* life and in Quinn's life. Kathy didn't have to do this. She didn't owe it to anyone—but neither did JoAnn with her offer of a sister twofer or Uncle Jide with his fatherly feelings. Neither did I with my auntie care package and California hugs. Somehow we were all bringing our best selves to the moment. *What if we all keep bringing our best selves to the moment?*

I had this sense of mutual creation, harmony, and faith—in this network of human beings tied together by a DNA test and by a refusal of my mom's shame. This went against my mom's cynicism and worst-case-scenario thinking. I was prone to those defenses, too, and had clung to the myth of their protective powers for most of my life, but so much of what my mom had rehearsed and guarded against proved not to be true. Her daughter hadn't lived a terrible life, and she didn't hate her birth mother, and Uncle Jide was not burdened or angry.

In my rib cage, I felt a relaxing, a melting, an opening to possibility. I felt like I could maybe just trust what was happening here. In fact, it seemed kind of rude and dumb to try to think my way out of this beauty.

As I stepped into my life back home, everything felt grand and unified, like the tail end of a psychedelic trip. I even checked my pupils in the mirror. It reminded me of one of my dad's stories from the sixties about LSD. "I really felt I understood the meaning of reality and the truth of the universe," he had told me of one particularly intense trip. "But every time I'd start to put it into words, the understanding melted away like sand through my fingers. The act of making words was incompatible with the knowledge I was having."

I felt that way trying to report back to Christopher, who had been solo-parenting for four days. Now, a few days after my return, I was pitching him on my glimpse of enlightenment. We were on a lunch break from work, sitting in our front yard on a summer afternoon, both of us wearing floppy sun hats with our laptops open nearby. I told him about the melting feeling, the sense of mutual creation, the stirring of something like a human-based faith. Then, while making big, sweeping gestures with my hands, I tried explaining this bigger picture.

All these decades later, my family was coming together in ways that defied the shame and rigid divides of the institutional response to unwed pregnancy. Our embrace of each other underscored the spiritual side of sex and reproduction, too. For so long, I'd focused on sex in the cultural and political arena, thinking about it in terms of individual power and freedom, but this visit had been a testament to its potential for love and connection. It was like Uncle Jide had said to me in a text message: "We are united by a loving memory!"

I got all of this out in a halting, messy, and breathless fashion—and then I paused.

"I have a new sense of openness and interconnectedness," I said. "It's like the boundaries of my heart have exploded."

"Wow, baby," Christopher said. "I'm really happy for you."

"Are you? You sound kind of . . . annoyed."

"Look, man, I'm tired," he said.

While I had been FaceTiming with newfound family in Lagos,

gaining a second big sister, closing down the bar with my nephew, and saying "I love you" for the first time to Kathy, he had been living in the slog of laundry and lunches and picking up LEGOs off the floor. I was grateful to be married to a man who was used to doing his equal share around the house; when I left town, things did not fall apart, and I never worried about how or whether he would manage. By many measures—especially home-cooked meals and the state of the dishes—he managed much better than I did. But solo-parenting was a lot, and I had brought my soaring, wild-eyed feeling of transcendence into the aftermath of his domestic subservience.

"Well, I invite you to catch the vibe," I said, half smiling.

"I want to catch the vibe, I do, but you kinda sound like a cult leader," he told me.

"A *cult leader*," I repeated.

"Look, babe, I'm sorry," he said. "It's just, you went and had this transformative experience, but I wasn't there for any of it."

I wondered whether Christopher's annoyance had anything to do with the fact that I had abandoned him for a weekend and fallen in love with someone else. It was *familial* love, but still, there was a certain romance to the way I'd longed for Kathy for so much of my life, and our DNA match had an undercurrent of "what if" that made it feel miraculous. "It's wild to think about how easily I could have gone with a different testing company," Kathy had said. "Or what if my siblings hadn't pushed to do a test?"

It reminded me of the way Christopher and I talked about the start of our romance. "If I hadn't been offered that job and moved across the country, we never would have met," he had said countless times. Our love had a needle-in-a-haystack quality. With millions of different potential timelines, Christopher and I were living this one, together. It was an utterly exquisite case of luck and chance.

"I'm sorry," he said again. "I'm not sure where I fit into all of this. I feel on the outside."

I imagined the tables being turned: him falling in love with a newly discovered brother and connecting with a dozen other family members. I pictured him announcing "a new sense of openness and interconnectedness," and I felt a twinge of jealousy.

The married monogamous heart is meant to have boundaries, and they are not supposed to be exploded—their structural integrity is sold to us as security. The nuclear family creates a comforting *us*, a dyadic collaboration, a promise of mutual care in a capitalist system that turns even love into a scarce commodity. I could easily see how this exponential expansion of family might feel destabilizing to the balance of our household.

Within a few days, though, Kathy and Christopher started texting back and forth. She sent him a birthday message referring to him as her brother-in-law, along with a Bitmoji of herself popping out of a gift box. "Man, Kathy is great," he told me. "I know I haven't met her yet, but I feel like I can picture her perfectly." He found where he fit and was no longer on the outside; it wasn't just my transformational experience anymore. The contours of our nuclear family and our frequently air-quoted "marriage" were being subtly smudged and redrawn.

....

I wanted the shimmery high forever.

I wanted tiny hearts and infinity signs. I wanted to keep sounding like a cult leader. I wanted the vibe to never, ever end. But a week after I got back from Atlanta, I marked the nine-year anniversary of my mom's death—or it marked me. Labor Day weekend arrived and a dark gauzy curtain descended, veiling everything in black. The pink heart lava turned to ash. It was an emotional flu, a death fever. I simply had to be horizontal; I couldn't keep my eyes open. I found myself lying for hours on our brown leather couch—just being swallowed by it.

This happened every year, but it still surprised me. The symptoms were always what made me realize: *Right, it's the anniversary, of course.* Her death day.

She had been sick for three years, far surpassing her initial prognosis of six months, but there was no preparing for seeing my mother's body, *empty*. She lay in the hospital bed in the living room, and her open mouth gave me the sense of an evacuation, as if she had fled somewhere else. Like she had forgotten to close the door on the way out. *Where did my mother go?* In the first weeks after her death, I curled up on our couch in the apartment I shared with Christopher at the time. I was overcome by waves of sobbing cries that knotted up my insides as items were placed on our doorstep: cards, bouquets, and a potted orchid with a fragile stem attached to a stake with tiny green butterfly clips.

Eventually, the tears dried up and I found myself lying on the couch while staring at the stake and butterfly clips, which propped up the poorly watered orchid. I wanted to be similarly pinned upright, assisted with the unreasonable expectation of verticality. Years later, after Christopher and I had moved into our house, my water broke on that same couch, leaving it slightly discolored. It was my life-and-death couch, my living-room portal. Now, once again, I lingered on that couch, but the death fever was worse than it had been in years.

I felt the excoriation of the past months as a physical fact. I was a pink, raw, wrinkly little rodent spawn with squinty eyes and no defenses. Was I really supposed to move through day-to-day life like I didn't have exposed insides? Four weeks later, it was Kathy's birthday. *The day our mom gave birth. The day they lost each other.* It was a one-two punch of losses—death and adoption. This was the first year that I knew to mark the date: October 3.

While putting Quinn to bed that night, I snapped at him when he pushed to read another book. His response pierced my heart: "Mama, I wish you would stop being grumpy." Later, sitting with Christopher on the couch, my legs draped over his, I told him, "People don't do this. They don't go searching around in their family's past. They don't go digging up all the trauma and pain and shame. There is a *reason* people don't do this. It's fucking hard. I'm not a robot, you can't go through something like that and not *feel* something." I wondered if October 3 had also shifted the mood in my childhood home, if it had ever made me say, "Mama, I wish you would stop being grumpy."

I was more than grumpy. Recently, while sitting on my meditation cushion—something I was trying to do more often—a phrase had popped into my head: "a new season of grief." I recognized its truth immediately. I wanted my mom to be a part of this coming together. The fact that she wasn't made me miss her more than ever. She had missed the full arc of the story, and now I was living it without her.

As we edged toward December, I emerged from our basement with large Tupperware boxes full of Dickensian buildings made of porcelain: a bakery, a curiosity shop, a post office. My mom's Christmas village. There were figurines, too: a woman selling flowers from a cart, children ice-skating on a frozen lake, a puppeteer putting on a sidewalk show. Every year after Thanksgiving, she had spread these scenes across the top of our mantel, placing a lightbulb in each building and sprinkling it all with flakes of pretend snow. When I was a kid, it was the most magical thing I had ever seen. I'd peer in the glowing windows, imagining the miniature family scenes unfolding inside. Now I was telling Quinn about that sense of magic as he helped me unroll long plastic renderings of cobblestone streets.

"Grandma Deb loved baking cookies and putting up these houses and then getting everybody together for Christmas Eve," I said. "It was her favorite holiday. She always made it a very cozy time of year for everybody."

"I wish Grandma Deb was alive," he said.

"Me too, honey."

"Do you ever miss her?" he asked.

"I do."

"Do you miss her right now?"

"Oh, sweetie, I do," I said.

He looked like he might cry as he crawled into my lap and gave me a hug.

"She would have loved the *heck* out of you," I said into his neck. "You know that?"

After all the houses were up, Kathy texted with news. Her dad was visiting three of his other grown children in Chicago for the holidays, and she was going to fly to meet him there. A two-hour plane ride made more sense than the eleven-hour one from Atlanta to Lagos, especially given Kathy's fear of flying. "I so wish you were going to be with me," she wrote. "That would have made the trip so perfect and fun! You will be in Boston, right?"

We were already booked to visit Christopher's family on the East Coast for Christmas, but when I read him Kathy's text, his response was immediate. "Do it," Christopher said. "You cannot miss this." I told Kathy that I could change my return ticket and meet up with her in Chicago after Christmas—but only if she was sure I wouldn't be interrupting time with her dad. "I am 100% sure," Kathy wrote.

"Our first trip," she said, adding a smiley emoji surrounded with hearts. "TKat takes on ChiTown."

14

OPPOSITE OF SHAME

Once again I was on a plane, headed toward my sister.

That morning I'd left Christopher and Quinn cuddling in bed in a Boston suburb. We had spent the holidays with Christopher's family and stayed with his brother, who had two young kids around Quinn's age. The last week had been a flurry of wrapping paper, matching Christmas pajamas, and Disney movie marathons. Now I was getting a needed moment of solitude, and I already missed my little guy.

Above Lake Michigan, the gray expanse of waves looked frozen midcrest, but it was just an illusion, a trick of perspective. From this height, the ceaseless building and crashing of waves appeared like one constant unchanging moment. The snowy blocked-out grid of Chicago came into view. From above, it looked like an easily navigable map.

I imagined placing bright red dots on the landscape below: my sister's childhood home on the South Side of Chicago, the home for unwed mothers on the West Side, and my mom's childhood homes in northwest Indiana. My mom and sister were never far from each other in the months after the adoption—they were ripped apart into a vast mystery while being in *such* close proximity. My mom must have wondered about the possibility of running into her daughter on the street. *Did she ever go looking for her? Did she ever come across a baby Kathy's age and wonder?* I imagined how she might have craned her neck to look into passing strollers. When I was in fourth grade, we flew to visit my mom's cousin Dave and aunt Jewel in suburban Illinois and took a detour into downtown Chicago to visit the Art Institute. *Was my mom keeping an eye out even then?*

In my rideshare from O'Hare to the far-flung hotel where Kathy was staying, I thought of Uncle Jide suggesting months back that the three of us should visit my mom's grave together. "So that she can finally be at peace knowing that we've found each other," he had said. Instead, we were about to get together a few miles away from where it all began, which seemed like its own important ritual.

I didn't have any conscious belief in my mom as a restless soul awaiting peace, but I did have a thrumming wish for our gathering in this place to cause a tectonic shift. A thought: *I'm the restless soul awaiting peace.*

....

As soon as I stepped through the hotel's sliding glass doors, Kathy leaped up from a couch in the lobby. Uncle Jide broke into a big grin, throwing his arms wide over his head before letting them fall at his sides. *The man from the yearbook.* Even across the room, I could see his shoulders gently shake as he chuckled. I could imagine how my mom would have chuckled, too—not just at the three of us coming together across decades and states and thousands of miles of ocean, but also at the surprising simplicity of it. Here we were, after all this time. After everything.

"What a trip," as my mom liked to say.

Nine months earlier, I had breathed my way through the realization that this man didn't even know his daughter existed, and now he was standing right next to her. When I reached them across the lobby, Kathy wrapped me in a hug, and Uncle Jide greeted me with a double-cheek kiss. He was looking sharp in a woolen flat cap, heavy peacoat, cashmere sweater, and loafers. Later, he would tell us that he'd gotten his clothes at a boutique in Italy two decades ago. "Very well made, high quality," he would say. "They don't make them like that anymore."

We sat for a moment on the couch, talking about a storm that had left thousands of flights canceled across the country. Things were especially bad in Chicago's two main airports, where unclaimed luggage spilled out of baggage claim areas.

"But we all made it," Uncle Jide said, eyes shining.

Kathy and I left Uncle Jide in the lobby and went up to our shared room to drop off my luggage. She gave me the quick rundown of her visit so far. The night before, she had driven straight from the airport to meet her dad at his son Remi's house in a wealthy suburb of Chicago. When they opened the front door, eight family members were lined up to greet her with actual open arms: her dad, his wife, two of his adult children, and their families. The dining table was filled with platters of food from a local Brazilian restaurant.

Kathy had worried about being accepted by Remi, who had been the oldest of the family—at least he'd thought he was until she showed up. But everyone was warm and welcoming, and there was no awkwardness or resistance. Remi's twin girls had given her big hugs goodbye and called her Aunt Kathy. "It went better than I could have ever imagined," she said in an almost whisper.

Auntie Yinka had showered her with gifts. Kathy held up a red leather purse embroidered with Yoruba fabric. Laid across the hotel bed were a traditional skirt, blouse, and shawl in gold fabric. The night before, Auntie Yinka had taught Kathy how to style a matching gele, a women's head wrap. She pulled up a photo of her first solo attempt that morning—she had folded the fabric so that it fanned across the top of her head like a halo. Auntie Yinka had given her first try a thumbs-up via text message.

"And now with you here to support me, too," Kathy said, "I just feel so supported and loved."

Kathy was unfazed by having taken a paternity test that morning. Her dad had mentioned the idea to her many months back, along with something of an apology for even asking her to do it. "It's not for me," he had said. "*We* already know." Kathy and her dad met in her hotel room, where they read through the detailed instructions together before swabbing their cheeks. When I'd walked through the lobby doors, they had just gotten back from dropping off the tests at the post office. In a couple weeks, the results would, as her dad had put it, tell them what they already knew: He was her father. But in this moment, I worried. *What if I passed along bad information?* I thought. *What if I caused my sister to bond with a man who is not her father?*

This was absurd. Kathy had already gotten an Ancestry DNA match with one of Uncle Jide's cousins. Her DNA profile had shown her Nigerian ancestry. Uncle Jide remembered being with my mom during the exact period when Kathy was conceived. Still, I felt the pull of what-ifs and the weight of what my actions had helped set in motion. I was playing my mom's role—searching for the shoe left to drop, the loss still to come, the worst possible turn of events.

As we rode the elevator down to rejoin Uncle Jide, I tuned in to the air softly expanding in my chest and exiting through my nostrils—the soft, easy, tender truth of what was. *Me and my sister. Me and my mom's daughter.*

We piled into Kathy's rental car and decided on Japanese food. I directed us to a restaurant with four stars and rave reviews on Yelp. When we pulled up out front, it was just a small storefront with counter service and a scattering of tables.

"No, no, this won't do," said Uncle Jide. "Auntie would kill me if I took you here."

It was on to the next Japanese restaurant, but when we pulled up, Uncle Jide started laughing. It was a little bigger than the last place, and there was table service, but he wasn't having it. He had a vision of what this special occasion demanded.

"Let's go to Maggiano's," he said definitively.

....

Maggiano's was an Italian restaurant chain with a cozy old-school vibe—red checkered tablecloths, plush leather booths, and waiters in ties. My sister and I chose our own dishes, but we left the drinks to Uncle Jide. He seemed like a man who knew his way around a wine list.

We sipped our cabernet sauvignon while he told us about his four other children. They had been born in Nigeria but had gone to boarding schools in the United Kingdom. Now they had an impressive array of job titles: pediatrician, mechanical engineer, chemist, and IT specialist. He detailed a couple of family secrets—not with any sense of embarrassment or scandal but with the matter-of-factness of a man who tells the truth to anyone who deserves to hear it. Eventually, the conversation turned to our mom.

"We had only three or four months together," he said, slowly turning his fork between his fingers.

This was the first time he'd put any kind of timetable on things. I had suspected they weren't in a committed relationship because she would have referred to him as a boyfriend, but I had no clue whether they had gotten to know each other over the course of a semester or a single night.

"Your mother was very quiet," he said. "And I liked that."

I smiled. I knew my mom to be strong, opinionated, and razor-sharp—the kind of woman who wouldn't take well to a man liking her quiet—but that was much later in her life and in the comfort of her own home. Back then she had barely begun to explore adulthood and independence, only just started to figure herself out in relation to men who were not her terror of a father. I felt a pang of regret that Uncle Jide hadn't gotten to know that searingly smart woman—the woman she had become perhaps because of everything that came after their oh-so-brief coupling.

"I'm grateful to her for bringing me joy during a very lonely time," he said.

"What was it like for you back then—at Purdue in 1965, in Indiana?" I asked.

"It was okay," he said. "I would not say that I experienced any obvious racism. We Nigerians don't worry much about what people will think of us. We think, *Judge us on our performance, judge us on how we do in the classroom.* So it was okay."

He was pretty sure they had met at a gathering for international students.

"And then she just disappeared," he said. "She never came back to school. I never saw her again. I didn't know how to find her."

Kathy and I nodded and sighed.

"I knew she lived in Indiana, but it was not a good idea at that time for an African man to go searching around for a white woman," he said. "If she had told me, I would have raised Katheryn myself—or my mother would have. Well, she was gone by then, but my father or my aunts would have."

An alternate timeline seemed to flicker to life on the tablecloth like an old projector film: Kathy being raised by extended family in Nigeria.

"Wow," said Kathy, like she was watching the same scenes play out.

"I just have to ask myself," said Uncle Jide. "Why didn't she *tell* me?"

I took a deep breath.

"From what I've read about this era," I said, "it was very common for girls to be sent away and for the fathers to never be told."

We all twisted our wineglasses.

"I vaguely remember a conversation with her when I was in my twenties," I continued. "I remember her saying something about not wanting to . . . burden you. She didn't want to interrupt your life."

"No, no, it would be no *burden*," he said, shaking his head.

"I know that she went searching for you later on," I said, recalling how she had told me that he worked in the oil industry. "She knew what you did for a living."

"Why didn't she tell me later on?" he asked—not with anger but with vulnerability.

"I don't know."

"Was she angry with me?"

"Not at all. I think she felt a great fondness for you."

He paused, tenderly, with a tilt of his head.

"I am very sorry for everything she went through," he said, casting his eyes toward the table.

I teared up. I took a sip of water. Then I noticed a surprising absence: shame. I went searching for it in the interiors of my mind. I felt myself running down old neural hallways that were now empty and blank, as if the art had been taken off the walls. He had asked that difficult, painful question that I had asked myself so many times before: *Why didn't she tell him?* I had shared some possible answers, but I felt no responsibility for those answers. I had opened myself to compassion for my mom's "choices," their context, and the fact that so many of them were not what I would call choices at all.

Empathy is the opposite of shame, I thought.

We were three people drinking a bottle of wine in a plush leather booth and sharing real, true, honest words—surfacing what had been pushed underground. We were sitting with the uncomfortable and the unknown. We were making space for the path not taken and the path we were on now. It felt awful and beautiful and heartbreaking and triumphant.

After dinner, while Kathy and I were getting ready for bed in our hotel room, my mom's cousin Dave called. He and my mom had fallen out of touch a long while ago, and I hadn't seen him in decades. A few weeks back, I'd searched him out online. That had been a hard message to write. I'd joked with Christopher beforehand about how to deliver the news: "Hi, remember me, haven't seen you in forever, but I'm coming to town and also I found my sister, who I think my mom told you about at some point and, if not, sorry, but now you know—let's hang out!" Now he was calling to firm up our plans for the next day.

"You sound exactly the same," I said with astonishment at his voice.

"Oh, well, I'm sorry about that," he said wryly.

I had forgotten his dry sense of humor. I was brought right back to the last time I'd seen him, some twenty-four years earlier, as an eighth grader. I'd adored him like an uncle. He had been a star football player in college and then worked as a pipe fitter his whole life. Dave was a real guy's guy in contrast with my dad, who was a hippie, a skateboarder, a computer guy, a man who had worn a flower crown on his wedding day. We made plans for me and my sister to visit Dave and his wife, Carol, the next morning, and then for me to stay with them the following night after Kathy headed back home. "Oh, one last thing," he said. "*You* sound exactly like your mom."

That night I slept on the foldout couch in our hotel room, lying in bed and listening for my sister's breath. For the first time in my life, she was right there, across the room from me.

....

The next morning Kathy drove us to Dave's house in Crete, a southern suburb of Chicago right near the Indiana border. The plots of land in his neighborhood were sprawling and farmlike, with single-family homes plunked in the center and a backdrop of woods. We parked and crunched across pristine snow to the front door.

On the phone the night before, I had wondered whether Dave, who was white, knew that my sister was Black. I had worried about what it would mean if her Blackness came as a surprise—and what it would mean for my sister to be *experienced* as a surprise. But I hadn't known what to say, and so I said nothing, which now, after we'd driven past far more American flags than I was used to, felt reckless and unforgivable.

You failed her, I thought.

Later, I would ask Kathy if *she* had any apprehension about going to meet these long-lost white relatives. "Not at all, because I trusted you," she would say. "I was just thinking, *I've got my little sister in the car with me, and we're on this adventure in my hometown. What a blessing and what a treat.*" Then she would add, with a burst of laughter, "I've never met a white person who didn't like me. I could get along with a *rock*."

In that moment, though, I thought of the older white liberal folks I knew who mentioned someone's race only when they were not white. "A Mexican man." "An Indian woman." They always said these things in the context of a positive story—about a pleasant interaction with a stranger or a new friend who seemingly required a contextualizing adjective. But whiteness was never a contextualizing adjective. It was never defining or even worth mentioning; it was invisible.

Please, please, please, I thought, giving a knock on the door before noticing that it was frozen shut. Then Dave called from the driveway. He rounded the corner, and his mouth and arms burst open at the sight of us. "You must be Kathy," he said, giving her a hug. "It is a real pleasure to meet you." I could have fallen to my knees with gratitude. Dave was much as I remembered him—lofty, blue eyes, a halo of hair—save for the mustache that had been replaced by a gray beard. He showed us in through the mudroom, where Carol was waiting.

"Hello, welcome," Carol said, giving me a hug. "You're still tall."

Their two-story home looked out on a pool, an open field, and a snowcapped forest. We sat in a front room surrounded by cabinets filled with glassware that had belonged to my grandma Quen and great-aunt Jewel, Dave's mom. There were crystal serving bowls, pitchers, and vases. It was a museum of the DeRemer women, as they had been called before marriage—the domestic and hostess side of them, at least.

Dave brought out tins and plates of holiday cookies covered in powdered sugar that dusted my palm when I took a bite. We talked for a while about Kathy's childhood thirty minutes north in Markham. Then Dave disappeared and returned with a small square object in his hand. It was a piece of stained glass that my mom had made long ago and given to him. There was a green flower at the center that glinted gemlike in the light.

"I don't know if you've ever seen this," he said, looking to me, "but your mom made it." He looked to Kathy. "I thought you might like to have it."

Dave explained that he had created a wooden frame for the stained glass out of the remnants of a bookshelf that had belonged to his three kids, who had long ago grown up and moved out of the house. "It's so delicate, you know?" he said, rotating the frame between his hands and casting off a flicker of emerald light. I imagined him precisely measuring and cutting the wood to protect this sheet of soldered glass. He was not a flower-crown-wearing hippie, but he was a softhearted caretaker of a man.

"Anyway," he said, clearing his throat and reaching toward Kathy, "it's my pleasure to be able to give this to you."

Kathy's eyes were wet as she took it from him.

....

Later that day, Kathy drove us from Crete to Markham, stopping along the way at a White Castle, our mom's Midwestern fast-food favorite. She had often kept our freezer stocked with the microwaveable version. It was such a trivial thing, but grabbing a bag of burgers at that drive-through felt like a way of bringing her along for this journey. I was going to see a place she must have wondered about so often: her daughter's childhood home.

"Wow, it looks exactly the same," Kathy said, pulling up out front.

It had been many years since she'd been back. After both of their adoptive parents died, Kathy and JoAnn had decided that Billy should inherit the house and live in it. Markham was a predominantly Black suburb full of one-story brick houses on small lots, in contrast to Crete's multistory sprawl. The house next door was abandoned, with boarded-up windows and leaves gathering in the gutters.

I didn't know it at the time, but a recent study had tied the high rates of violent crime and vacant or abandoned homes in Chicago's southern suburbs to the federal government's racist history of redlining, where mortgage lending was discouraged in minority neighborhoods, which forced Black homebuyers into predatory loans and prevented the accumulation of generational wealth. Markham had the second-highest violent-crime rate of all the surveyed neighborhoods.

I thought of one of our early phone conversations when Kathy had put her different modes of being into geographic terms: "There's Sweet Georgia Peach Kathy, and then there's South Side of Chicago Kathy."

As we got out of the car, toting our greasy takeout bag, Billy emerged on the front porch, grinning at his sister. His smile was loving and ironic. It seemed to say: A smile isn't any one thing. He had a small silver hoop earring in each ear, alongside a big sparkling stud, and red rounded glasses that gave him the flair of a favorite art teacher. He showed us into the living room, where he was watching a *Judge Judy*–style daytime court-TV show.

"These floors are looking good," Kathy said of the black marbled tile. "Are these the original floors?"

They were. The bones of the house were the same as when Kathy was growing up, save for the kitchen, which had been partially redone with new cabinets and a fancy chef's stove because Billy loved to cook. "Bit by bit, I'm fixing this place up," he said.

Kathy walked me through the L-shaped hallway leading to the three bedrooms. The first: her parents' old bedroom, a small rectangle with just enough space for a bed, which Billy used for storage. The next bedroom had been shared by Kathy and JoAnn. It was painted white, but the closet was still the same bubblegum pink it had been when they lived there. Kathy walked along its perimeter, showing me how her bed had sat against one wall and JoAnn's against the other, with the ends meeting in the corner. Now the room had just one twin bed where Billy slept.

I thought of my own bedroom growing up. It was about the same size, but I'd had it all to myself. I thought of my parents, each with their own bedroom in our family home. I had grown up in one of the whitest, highest-income, and lowest-crime neighborhoods in Berkeley—and in a house three times the size of Kathy's childhood home, with half as many people in it.

My mom hadn't gotten the relief of knowing about the loving home that her daughter had grown up in, but she also hadn't had to directly face the disparities between Kathy's life and her own. By placing Kathy for adoption, my mom was brought back into the fold of white middle-class respectability; she was allowed to regain the privilege of her race and class. Meanwhile, her mixed-race daughter was adopted by Black parents without those privileges. The disparities between their lives were a testament not only to race and class divides in this country but also to the way that inequities are institutionally and structurally maintained. Those maternity homes had been part of the maintenance, even when it was white babies being placed for adoption with white families.

Kathy pulled a wooden plaque from under a pile of papers on Billy's desk. "Look at this," she said. It featured an etching of smiling children of different ages and races. "In recognition and with deep Appreciation," read an inscription, which featured her parents' names. "For their dedication in providing Loving care for children in need." It seemed those two words—"appreciation" and "loving"—had been capitalized for emphasis, but it also made them seem less like abstract concepts and more like embodied entities, like the difference between writing "god" and "God." For a moment, I felt like I was being unlaced, like everything inside might suddenly pour out. Then I mentally stitched myself back up.

Billy pulled out a large plastic bin of family memorabilia from the last bedroom, which had belonged to the two boys, and brought it to the living room. We sat down on a pair of chairs next to Billy's black leather sixties-style swivel chair, which had a leopard-print throw tossed across the back. I nibbled on fries as Kathy sifted through the bin. She opened a long dusty canister and pulled out her mom's beautician certificates, and then a wedding certificate, but not the one she had seen so many times before.

"Here it is," she said in disbelief.

It was the certificate for Marguerite's first marriage, the one Kathy found out about only after her mother's death. Kathy hadn't been sure of the first husband's name—she just knew that she had found that crystal pitcher etched with the letter *L*, the first initial of his last name. Well, here it was: Edward. They were married in 1938 in New Orleans, when Marguerite was in her early twenties.

Next Kathy held up a photograph of her mom, possibly taken

around her first marriage, likely in Louisiana. She looked regal, in a jaunty hat with an ornamental fold on one side. Then Kathy unrolled a thick piece of paper that turned out to be a photo of Edward. He had smooth skin, a strong jaw, and chiseled cheeks. Later in the car, Kathy would say of her adoptive father, "My dad was good-looking, but that was a *very* handsome man." The marriage certificate and these photographs had started to fill in some contours of her mother's past.

It was a perfect entry point for Kathy to ask Billy about the sibling gossip around an alleged secret baby—a sister—birthed long before they were born.

"Nah," he said with total confidence. "No way."

"Gary is sure he saw something," she said.

Billy shook his head like the idea itself was a nuisance. "Sounds like a conspiracy theory," he said.

"You've never seen any papers like that?" she asked.

"Never."

"What about the attic?"

Billy told us how their mom used to hide money in the rafters, but he wasn't sure why.

"Well, now I *really* want to go up there," Kathy said, looking at the square ceiling hatch. "Do you have a ladder?"

"I used to, but I loaned it to somebody and never got it back," he said.

Kathy pulled a chair over. "No one ever went up there," she told me, wagging her finger at the ceiling. "If my mom was going to hide anything, it'd be in the attic."

I remembered how, in Atlanta, Kathy had told me of her adoptive mom: "She had her secrets. There's so much I wish I could ask her about now." This was how I felt about our mom, too, and I'd done my best over the last months to answer some of those questions. Kathy was doing her own version of that with her adoptive mom. It struck me just how often daughters are left wondering about their mother's lives—especially those parts having to do with love and sex, those parts that are supposed to not really exist. Kathy stood on the chair and peered just over the edge of the attic floor.

"I can't see anything," she said. "I'd have to really get up there with a ladder to be able to see."

Whatever piece of paper Gary might have seen could have been practically in the room with us—right above our heads and just out of reach.

....

I thought of the feelings wheel used at my job to identify our emotional states and imagined it transformed into a roulette wheel. This day had sent me bouncing across its spread of emotions—from taking Kathy to meet our long-lost relatives to Dave's stained-glass kindness to considering my sister's childhood home opposite my own privileged upbringing to the capital-L Loving of her adoptive parents. I had slowed across so many different feelings but never stayed with any one long enough to fully feel it. They had all started to bleed together into one mass sensation. *Worriedthankfulguiltyawed.*

Now I just felt drained.

I imagined the sound my old cell phone used to make when it was running out of battery during a call—a sad, melting digital sound. *Bing-bing-bing.* I needed to power down. Instead, we had plans for a dinner in downtown Chicago with Uncle Jide's family. It would be Kathy's first time meeting her half sister Damilola.

Kathy had bad night vision, just like our mom, so it was my turn to drive. She rode shotgun with Uncle Jide and Auntie Yinka in the back. *Precious cargo*, I thought. Just to add some pressure: It was rush hour, I wasn't used to driving in snow, and we were late for our dinner reservation. I could have fallen asleep right then and there, but I gripped the steering wheel and narrowed my tired eyes.

When we finally arrived, we parked and walked the few blocks to the restaurant, looking up at historic skyscrapers and getting hit with blasts of icy wind. This was the big city of my mom's childhood; she had probably walked down these same blocks. The proximity of our footsteps, in space if not time, made me feel like I could access her somehow.

Look at this. See this. Don't miss this.

An elevator deposited us on the top floor of a building with sweeping city views. There were modernist chandeliers and white tablecloths. We were shown to a private room in the back with one long table set for twelve people. Three of Uncle Jide's grown kids were there, along with their two spouses and three children. The dinner was a blur of decadent food, overlapping chatter, and cocktails with purple orchids frozen inside ice cubes. Kathy's siblings were interesting and profoundly well traveled, and conversation ranged from research on childhood blood diseases to a recent family vacation in France.

I'd ended up sitting between Kathy and Damilola, a doctor in a pediatric residency, and I kept leaning back to try to let them talk. Not too long ago, I had been wracked with insecurity around what our sisterhood meant to Kathy, but those fears had faded. Now I got to be a source of support and a witness in Kathy meeting her other sister. When it was time for a group photo, I jumped up to take it.

The next morning Kathy and I drove to the airport, talking

about the opulence of the dinner and wondering who, exactly, had paid. Her dad, we assumed. It seemed the check had never shown up. By the end, we had been too full for dessert, but Uncle Jide insisted that we take something to go—maybe the butter cake with raspberry sauce? "Eat it for breakfast," he had said, and we had. We dropped off Kathy's rental car and stood in the lobby alongside a row of counters with company logos in harsh primary colors.

"Well, this trip has been amazing," Kathy said.

"It really has," I told her. "It's going to take a few days for it to sink in."

We hugged and said "I love you," and I walked up to one of the rental-car counters. I was about to take a final look at our mom's past—and not through books or college transcripts or Google Street View. I wanted to get as close as I physically could to it.

15

A CROSSROADS

I drove in my rented Toyota Corolla past a red, white, and blue sign: "Welcome to Indiana, Crossroads of America." I laughed as though it were a cosmic joke. I was not a superstitious person, but on this trip, I was looking for signs, figurative and literal. It wasn't as if I thought my mom was throwing down posthumous messages like lightning bolts, but life was starting to feel like a strange, beautiful poem with endless layers for interpretation and analysis.

My car moved across a bridge alongside a rusted semi as I glimpsed a frozen lake dotted with cell towers and dry, pale skeletons of plant life. I was heading toward my mom's first childhood home in Gary, Indiana, a town I had mentioned a few times to people who knew it, only for them to cringe or say something like "Oof." From what I had gathered, it was a once-booming industrial mecca now struggling with poverty and abandonment—the causes being a mixture of white flight, racist housing practices, disinvestment, and deindustrialization.

I was spit off the freeway into the city's downtown area, past the historic City Hall, a Superior Court building, an empty weed-filled lot, and there it was: the three-story apartment building where my mom had spent her earliest years in life. Its brick exterior was the backdrop for one of my favorite photos of her: She is five years old, dressed in an Annie Oakley costume, holding a toy rifle, and giving the camera a fierce look that says, *Try me*, an attitude that probably proved essential to survival in her family.

The building looked unoccupied—the windows were mostly uncovered, and I didn't see any furniture inside. I let my car crawl slowly down the empty street and noted the bits of trash on the lawn: a crushed can of energy soda, the cardboard packaging for a bottle of Patrón, and two empty water bottles. I scrutinized this random detritus as though it had been left behind by my mom. When I reached the end of the block, I circled around again—looking for what, I wasn't sure.

Next I drove twenty minutes away to Griffith, a residential neighborhood with modest, tightly packed one-story houses in muted colors with cinder-block foundations. This move was proof of my grandfather's success—it took them from an apartment building to a single-family home. The white middle-class American dream.

I parked across the street from the house and surveyed all the nearby windows, feeling like someone might be watching. It was that kind of neighborhood: quiet and watchful. Dry leaves tumbled down the street, and an American flag gently rippled on a neighbor's house.

I pictured my mom returning here from college, newly and secretly pregnant. She might have hidden in this house for months on end before being sent away. Even going for a walk around the block with her growing belly would have threatened to ruin her family's reputation.

It would have threatened the coherence of the whole neighborhood, too. Her body would have seemed a dangerous advertisement for improper womanhood; it announced alternative paths, other ways of being. So she was imprisoned within the family home—a symbol of the very thing she seemed to imperil. My eyes started to burn, but I pushed the tears away; crying seemed a disruption to the order of the block.

The family home has long been a tool of concealment, serving not only to oppress women through unpaid domestic labor but also to hide that exploitation behind its private walls. In the fifties and sixties, it isolated unhappy housewives from one another—literally and more abstractly through its normative mythology of feminine fulfillment. It was part of the answer to the question Betty Friedan famously asked in *The Feminine Mystique*: "Why have so many American wives suffered this nameless aching dissatisfaction for so many years, each thinking she was alone?"

As I side-eyed the house, I felt a mix of secretive and suspicious, part undercover cop and part burglar. I put my phone to my ear, pretending to be on a call. "Hi, yeah, totally, I know," I mouthed nonsensically. I was creating a false alibi, maybe because there *was* something sneakily adversarial about this mission. It was a stakeout of my mom's family home—both as a place with a troubling personal history and as a symbol of the coercive institution of the nuclear family.

I noticed a wooden sign on the front door. In cutesy cursive, it read: "Home is where your favorite memories are." At that, I started up the car, laughing and shaking my head, feeling like the absurdity of the sign was as much as I was going to get from this house.

I headed to lunch at a crunchy café called the Green Witch, which sold crystals and ceremonial candles alongside dishes of quinoa and kale. I ordered a salad with turmeric dressing and sat there looking at all the crystals, thinking about a book I'd read recently on the legacy of the witch hunts and the cultural ascendency of the witch as a symbol of women's rebellion. The author, Mona Chollet, writes, "What could have once gotten a woman killed [during the witch hunts] is now available for purchase at Urban Outfitters." What could have once gotten a woman killed was so often her independence—whether she was a widow or a midwife or a single mother.

I'd ended up at this witchy café because I just wanted to eat some vegetables, but it felt like another cosmic joke. It wasn't hard to find connections to my mom's story. Chollet relates the torture and murder of women during the witch hunts to contemporary forms of punishment, including domestic violence, for "women who wish to be free."

Another obvious example of punishment was the recent overturn of *Roe*, which would cause not only untold suffering but also death; it would leave women bleeding out in hospital parking lots. I didn't know it yet, but we were also careening disastrously toward a second Donald Trump presidency, which would prove even in its earliest days to be a regime of punishment, and not just for women and people who can get pregnant but also immigrants, trans people, activists, nonbillionaires, and so many others.

With fingers stained yellow from the turmeric, I headed toward the last home on my itinerary: the final of the family's life upgrades. It was a ranch-style home with a tan brick facade in Munster, Indiana, fifteen minutes away from the old house. Here, the lawns were longer, the spaces between the houses were bigger, and nobody parked on the street. The blinds were drawn on the home's tall windows, but I felt I'd already glimpsed inside from the family stories my mom had told me.

This was the home where Quen had called everybody into the room to give her epic deathbed speech. It was where my mom had stood with me in her arms as her own mother revealed the unhappiness of her life—the unhappiness concealed by a succession of bigger and better homes. *You were the love of my life, and I should have left you the day I married you.* It was where Quen had told everyone about John's false promise that he would die first and give her a second chance at a happy life. This house was where Quen had died instead.

I felt like a balloon blown up to the verge of popping, an experiment in what could be held inside. I ached for Quen, who never got a second chance. I ached for John, who must have been drowning in self-hatred to reassure his wife with the prospect of *his own death.* I ached for my mom, who had rebelled against that domestic misery only to be pulled into an institution designed to reinforce it. I ached for Kathy, who had never gotten to know our mom.

Sitting in my rental car, tears suddenly streamed down my face. I had spent the last nine months trying to make sense of our mom's past—I had mentally wrangled my family history into a comprehendible series of historical causes and consequences—but research could take me only so far. Why else was I here other than to allow this accumulation of sadness, this dam burst of emotion? No amount of understanding could undo my sense of loss. There was nothing left but to feel it.

....

That afternoon I stepped into a florist shop, along a busy thoroughfare lined with squat brick buildings, and found a room stuck in time. Old linoleum flooring led to teal-green carpet with a multicolored scribble pattern reminiscent of nineties clip art. A woman with a half-up hairdo and a waterfall of carefully composed curls asked how she could help me. I'd been hoping for a wall of premade bouquets that I could grab with minimal human interaction, but there were no flowers on display.

"Do you have any bouquets?" I forced myself to say.

"What kind?" she asked.

"Um, just, like, a small one?"

"What's the occasion?"

"Oh, well . . ." I said, feeling my throat threatening to close. "I'm visiting the cemetery. It's to put on a couple graves."

"Oh! You need layout bouquets," she said.

"Ah, I didn't realize there was a term for it."

"Yeah, it just means it's flat, so you can lay it on the ground or a headstone instead of in a vase," she explained.

She wanted to know who it was for—a woman or a man?

"One woman and one man," I said.

She suggested red and white for him and pink and purple for her. Gender norms ruled, even in death.

I took my layout bouquets, festooned with big looping bows, and drove a few blocks down the street to the cemetery, a plot of land that ran two city blocks in either direction. I pulled in, past a white marble Jesus on a wooden cross, and wound my way through the grounds to look for—a directory? An office of some sort? I had never done this before.

There were hundreds upon hundreds of headstones, and there was no way I was going to just spot my grandparents' names in the crowd. I pulled over and googled, "How do you find a grave?" I found the cemetery website. There was no online directory, and the number on the website went to voicemail. Then I saw a couple guys with a yellow excavator digging a grave in the light rain, hunched and squinting.

I pulled up and rolled down my window. "Hi, excuse me," I called as the rain dotted the inside of my car door. "Is there any way to find a particular grave?"

The man sitting on the tractor had a square head with a buzz cut. He wheeled around, placing his arm on the back of his seat. "There *is* a way to find a particular grave," he said, matter-of-fact. "You got a pen?" He rattled off a number and an extension. "They'll help you."

The woman who answered the phone found a record of the plots I was looking for, but directing me to them was another story. She talked me through a series of directions and queries that involved landmarks I couldn't see. "The north side toward the White Castle," she said. I had no sense of direction, and I couldn't see any White Castle through the wooded grounds. She asked about "the house toward Calumet Avenue." Without reliably establishing whether I was facing in the right direction, she started giving instructions. "Right at the flagpole," she said. "Section A is on the left. At the last block in that section, turn the corner and you're at block twenty-two. Lot seventeen. Third row from the very end. Grave number five. Nineteen graves in, the very middle of the third row from the end."

I took copious notes.

I had no idea what the notes meant. At the end of our thirteen-minute conversation, I had some coordinates: section A, block 22, lot 17, grave number 5. I drove around for a few minutes, trying to follow the directions. Then I oriented myself facing the other way and tried again. I pulled up by the men digging the grave.

"Hi, sorry, I have some coordinates now," I said. "I'm wondering if you can help me?"

I read the coordinates out, and the same man from before whispered them to himself on repeat as he trekked off not too far from where I was.

"Clark," he called out, pointing to a joint headstone made of pink granite. "Right here."

My god, I thought. *A joint headstone and neighboring plots with the man she should have left the day they married.* Quen had followed the vows of "till death do us part," and even in death, they were symbolically bound together by stone. CLARK, it read up top in caps, with green lichen growing in patches around the lettering. On the bottom of the headstone: John P. and Querentia A.

I thought of a letter I'd found recently at my dad's house. Quen had written it when her cancer was first discovered, a year before her death. She had assigned certain belongings and responsibilities to members of the family. Quen had also given a clear instruction in her tidy cursive: "Cremate my remains." She was not cremated. I didn't know if she changed her mind or if John ignored her wishes. It would not have been the first time.

Out of the corner of my eye, I saw the gravediggers taking a break from excavating the wet earth. The rain gently knocked on the hood of my coat as I put each of my bouquets on the ground. I thought of my grandparents' caskets—their bones—just under my feet. I crouched down as low as I could. *I found your other granddaughter,* I thought, pressing my fingertips into the crisp pale grass. *We're together now.*

What did it mean to crouch in front of their headstone in the wake of finding Kathy? Even if there was an afterlife—which I did not believe—I hardly needed to physically visit this polished chunk of granite to deliver the news of finding their other granddaughter. Certainly, any kind of post-death consciousness would transcend the exact geography of this cemetery. Why bring this awareness to the site of their bones? Then again, I thought of the essential process that had brought me here: a DNA test of my saliva. Some of that same DNA was in those bones, buried beneath this earth. I was bone and flesh, carrying that DNA and standing on top of this earth.

I wondered how long the bouquets would last, how many months before they dried and decomposed, leaving behind just the frilly bows. Soon enough, there would be no evidence of my visit. There was no guest book to sign. It was quite possible that their graves would never get another visitor.

I had found in my Ancestry searches that a life was often told in the most basic terms: birth date, yearbook photos, marital date, birth-of-child dates, census addresses, obituary, and death date. How was the story of life after death told? I thought of a cosmic *ding*, like a bell at a retail counter, every time someone showed up at the gravesite. Quen's funeral. *Ding.* John's funeral. *Ding.* Then—fast-forwarding through decades of scattered and decreasing visits—their second granddaughter, come to crouch at their headstone because of the first. *Ding.*

I imagined the bell sending a shock wave to the ends of the universe. My grandparents might not know of my visit, but I felt it mattered. I was there, and I had carried my sister with me.

....

That night I went to dinner with Dave and Carol at an Italian restaurant near their house—not a chain like Maggiano's but a local favorite with an elaborate mural of verdant coastlines and turquoise waters. After we ordered an assortment of fried appetizers, I told them about touring my mom's childhood homes and visiting my grandparents' graves. Then, after a pause in conversation, Dave leaned in and placed his elbows on the checkered tablecloth.

"Did you think that I knew your sister was Black?" he asked.

"I wasn't sure," I said.

"Well, I did not know," he said. "And I just found it deliciously ironic."

"How so?"

"Because of what your grandpa John would have thought," he said.

"What would he have thought?"

"He would not have liked it," he said, seeming to take some pleasure in the idea of John being unhappy.

"Would he not have liked it because of . . . *the times*?" I asked with underlined irreverence. "Or because of who he was?"

"A combination of both," Dave said without hesitation.

"He was a nasty man," Carol said with fire in her voice. "A *nasty* man."

Dave wasn't sure whether John had ever known that he had a Black granddaughter, but this much was clear to the surviving people who knew him best: My grandfather was a racist, and he was *nasty.* I thought of the red and white bouquet sitting on his grave. For a moment I imagined taking the flowers back, but I hadn't placed them on his grave because of any fondness for this man who had terrorized my mom and trapped my grandmother. I had wanted to bring the gift of his granddaughter to his grave; I had wanted to announce her as such.

Much later, I would relay to Kathy this conversation about our grandfather and ask how she felt hearing about his racism. "It's not remotely surprising," she would say. "I'm just a realist. I don't feel some type of way about it. I think it's unfortunate." Then she would add with remarkable empathy: "He was probably a product of his environment. My first question with stuff like that is 'I wonder how they got that way.' "

After dinner, driving under an inky, cloudless sky, I followed Dave and Carol back to their house, where I would be crashing for the night. Dave led me to the dining table, where he had placed several boxes of papers and photographs. "I don't know what all is in here," he said, "but I found these in the basement and thought they might be of interest."

Inside the first box, I discovered my parents' wedding announcement, with an Emily Dickinson quote on the front: "That Love is all there is, / is all we know of Love." There was a hospital receipt from Dave's birth in 1955 for $170, as well as Jewel's subsequent unemployment paperwork, which had a checked box that read, "Left work voluntarily to marry, or to perform the customary duties of a housekeeper."

Dave was sifting through another box and handed me a folded yellowing letter. "This is from your mom," he said. "Written to *my* mom." I unfolded it and found that familiar looping script: "Tracy is growing & changing at a quick pace," my mom wrote. "She's starting to say a few more words and once in a while a phrase such as 'Not Bed Time!' She's the sweetest little devil you can imagine." I laughed at my mom's dry humor: "In the photos she's eating ice," she wrote. "I didn't want you to think she was still drooling."

Dave handed me a small bubbled envelope. My mom's writing warned on the outside: "*DO NOT BEND.*" A card inside read, "Here's a batch of our latest Tracy photos. What can I say, I may be biased but I think she's adorable." This was exactly my mom's way: to brag about me in a self-effacing way. She had included a dozen photographs of me around the age of three. In one, I squeezed my bright blue Grover stuffy, his flat red hyphen of a mouth contrasting with my explosive capital D of a grin.

"Oh, look, *more* photos of Tracy," Dave said. He placed a stack in front of me. I flipped through images of myself as a toddler joyfully padding barefoot and naked through the yard, pulling folded clothes out of my drawers to make a heaping mess on my bedroom floor, and sticking my tongue out at the camera—at my mom.

"*More* photos of Tracy," Dave said, unveiling another stack. There I was, cradled in my dad's arms by the ocean, sinking into my mom's lap at a picnic, walking along a garden path holding Margie's hand.

Dave put another stack on the table. "And *more*," he said, smiling.

These boxes cataloged my mom's doting delight. They also documented the way she tempered her doting: I was cute, but she was biased; I was the sweetest and a little devil. I saw her default sense of humor but also the way she specifically guarded against the vulnerability of motherhood—of mother love. I saw her fighting to keep her feet from fully leaving the ground. As a mom, I knew that terror—the risky weightlessness of surrendering to my love for Quinn—but I had never lost a baby.

In these old letters and photographs, I felt the full and undeniable force of my mom's love, as well as her loss. It was right there, all of it. I stared at an image of my grade-school self running through sprinklers on the lawn, right around when I had started to detect a secret sadness in my mom. I saw myself as I now saw Quinn, and as my mom must have seen me. *God, she adored you*, I thought to myself. *You were never not enough.*

"Now," Dave said, clearing his throat, "you might find these especially interesting." He pushed forward a new box with raised eyebrows. "These belonged to your mom's uncle, John David," he said. I reached into the box and pulled out a photograph of a woman wearing a black bra, matching panties, and white high heels. She lounged on a dressing table in front of a big mirror that reflected the camera's flash. Her hair was teased into a Bardot-style bouffant. In another photograph, the woman wore the same underwear set and stood on a stage in front of a red curtain.

"Wow," I said.

"So, that was his friend Glenna," Dave said dryly.

In the mid-seventies, Glenna worked at a club on an infamous two-block stretch of Calumet City known as Sin Strip. It seemed John David was a regular. Dave handed me a greeting card with four openmouthed lipstick kisses inside. Next: a handwritten note from Glenna that read, "You are a very sweet fellow. I really appreciate all your thoughtfulness. Don't ever change." In one of her final notes to John David, she wrote, "I don't know if I'll ever return to dancing."

I wondered where Glenna's story led—all I knew was that her brief overlap with my family's story was more broadly revealing. Within a decade of my mom being secretly pulled into a system designed to produce good women and wives, her own unmarried uncle had frequented Sin Strip, collecting sexy photographs and lipstick prints from a certifiable bad girl. This was not a matter of changing times; it was a matter of sexual double standards, whore stigma, and the sorting of women into categories.

I thought of a quote from the sex-worker activist Gail Pheterson: "The legal difference between marriage and prostitution is a difference between private and public appropriation of women."

She explained that good girls are tied to individual men, while bad girls are "assumed to be 'loose' or for hire." A good woman was owned, while a bad one was free.

Just then Dave stood up and opened the cabinet behind him to reveal Quen's tea set—a collection of white porcelain with gold details. There were coordinating trays, vessels, and silverware, too.

"Quen was basically like, 'Okay, if I have to entertain your businesspeople in my home, then I want to get the *best* china set. I'm not going to just get the fifteen-piece, I'm gonna get the *twenty-one-piece*,' " he said. "That was her deal."

"She exercised power where she could, I guess," I said.

Dave walked me through the house, flicking on lights and pointing out everything that had belonged to Quen—a crystal vase, a porcelain sculpture of an angelic child, a framed etching of a rabbit.

"You should put your name on anything you like," Dave said. "No one cares about it. No one wants it."

Here was the last remaining evidence of Quen's deal with the devil. The furs John had cloaked her in were long gone. His promises of a second shot at a happy life had never materialized. All that was left behind were these objects that no one wanted. I wasn't sure if I wanted to rescue the belongings or smash them to pieces. Each item seemed to hold within it the stolen potential of her life.

16

DOTS

The next morning, leaving Dave and Carol's house, I drove into Chicago to swing by the Art Institute—there was a painting that I wanted to see. My mom had taken me and my dad there during our family trip to Chicago in 1994. Of all the art we saw that day, I remembered only Georges Seurat's pointillist *A Sunday on La Grande Jatte*. It used a luminous symphony of colorful dots and dashes to depict dozens of different intriguing figures on a green riverbank.

At the time, I was ten years old and had never seen a painting that seemed to have its own internal source of light. I had marveled at all the different characters, trying to decipher their relationships to one another. This wasn't just a painting; it was a story.

It was the first time a piece of art had made the hair on my arms stand on end. Most of the vacation existed in my mind as an indistinct blur, but I never lost the memory of lingering with my mom in front of that painting. I could still see her solid stance and crossed arms as she turned her head to explain the piece to me. I couldn't recall what she said, just the feeling of underscored text. My mom, an art history major, was trying to explain something beyond the painting. *Mother to daughter.*

Now, almost thirty years later, I headed straight for it.

I snaked through the museum with a map in hand, breezing past Auguste Rodin's *Eternal Springtime*, a bronze sculpture of two young lovers in a passionate embrace. Then I saw the painting across the room, just as radiant as I remembered. My eyes flitted over the standing and lounging people in Seurat's scene—all of them white—before landing on a woman in the foreground with a large bustle and a pet monkey at her feet. She stands next to a man with a monocle and cane, and she is flanked by mothers sitting on the grass with their children.

When I was a kid, that foregrounded woman *was* the painting to me, and I remembered how my mom had pointed toward the pet monkey. *There's something about the monkey*, I remembered. *There's something about the woman. Wasn't she an adulteress, a sex worker, something like that?*

Later, I would confirm that the woman is widely understood to be, in the sober analysis of art historians, a "cocotte," a "loose woman," a "tart," a "prostitute"—or, as one scholar put it, she is "a woman who flaunts her disregard for society's maternal script." The monkey is a symbol of licentiousness. It's said that a pair of women shown fishing by the waterfront are sex workers, too.

I don't recall what my mom said back then about these women or the monkey, but there is no doubt that she understood the meaning, and it's likely that she shared it with me in that moment. I can imagine what it must have felt like for her to stand side by side with her prepubescent daughter in front of this painting of a "loose woman," just a few miles from where she had been sent away in shame, and in such close proximity to the other daughter whom she had lost as punishment for her own "looseness."

Standing there as an adult, this painting told me a story I knew very well. I had been telling it most of my life.

In the background, past the woman with the monkey, a preadolescent girl runs light and free, her red hair flowing and curling behind her like licks of a fire. Several feet in front of her, an older pubescent girl sits properly on the grass with her red hair tidily combed and fastened into a ponytail. This older girl looks down at a small bouquet of flowers in her hands with a solemn and foreboding gaze. It seems as if she is recognizing that her own sense of freedom will wither just like these flowers—and that she is, in fact, already permanently cut off from her younger, freer, running self.

This was what I had felt, stepping into the world as a young woman. There was a "before" and an "after." A period of joyful possibility followed by a collision with the punishing realities of the adult world.

A third girl, who is maybe three years old, stands at the center of the painting in a ghostly white dress. She is the lone figure shown dead-on and seems to look directly at the viewer. It's as if she's asking, "Do you agree with what's happening here?" The painting has often been interpreted as a commentary on class, bourgeois culture, and modern alienation, but it made me think about the disillusionment of girlhood and the divisions of womanhood: good and bad, wife and whore, mother and lover.

Running my hand along my forearm, I felt the gentle prickle of my hair standing on end.

I walked up to the painting, leaning in to admire the discrete dots of color and the white canvas in between. Up close, a lounging woman's skirt turned into a river of flowing color. The spiky grass became a swath of green periods and hyphens. The light beige trousers of a man reclining in the shade had points of unexpected color: mustard, blue, and green. The impression of the sun glinting off a child's bare shins was revealed as a scattering of soft pink dots. It was like seeing into the secret atomized essence of the world.

A block of text on the gallery wall explained that neo-impressionist color theory prized the placement of opposite colors next to each other to create a "vibrating optical effect." These contrasting pigments became more than the sum of their parts.

I thought about the coexistence of opposites in my mom's life. There was the baby she lost and the baby she raised. "I'm just so grateful to have had my two loves," she told me toward the end of her life, referring to me and my dad. This gratitude for her two loves existed alongside the loss of her first love, perhaps creating a greater vibrating intensity.

I knew my mom was able to find a sense of spiritual comfort in the harmony of life's extremes. "It's the yin and yang," she sometimes said. "Shadow and light." But she also fought to keep her own darkness at bay, so often retreating to her room to numb away the pain. I saw my current task as feeling both sides: the beauty and the sorrow—which was decidedly not the same thing as anticipating and guarding against disaster at every turn.

When I moved back from the painting, the distinct marks on the canvas came to life again. In the shift of perspective from disconnected to interconnected dots, I saw symbolic overlap with so much of what had happened since I'd found Kathy—from my expanding sense of family to the way I'd come to understand myself in relation to my mom, not to mention how our family fit into a larger cultural and historical picture. I had been zooming in and zooming out, allowing a fuller image of my mom—and of myself, too.

Recently, I'd gone out for drinks with a new mom friend, and she asked the question that I had previously dreaded. What was the title of my book, she wanted to know. "*Want Me*," I said, straightforward and smiling. "It's a sexual coming-of-age story about the difficulties of finding yourself as a woman in this world." There was no blushing or stuttering. I felt totally rooted in the fact that most of us go through our own version of that journey. The woman in front of me had likely navigated this terrain—and I figured that, in some ways, she was still navigating that terrain. Similarly, I had stopped worrying about what it would mean for my kid to grow up with a mother "like me." *What, a mother who allowed her own humanity?*

Shining a light on the sources of my shame had caused so much of it to slowly evaporate. This wasn't true of just my roles as a mother and a sexual being. It felt like I had laid down a barrier against that sudden landslide of self: *They don't like me. They hate me. I am bad.* In those moments, I could see that I was doing to myself a version of what had been done to my mom. That recognition alone helped to prevent any further collapse.

And now, standing in front of Seurat's work, I looked again from the sex workers to the mothers to the little girls on the canvas, those same figures that my mom had talked to me about decades earlier. As with plenty else around my mom's story, I had forgotten what she'd said at the time, or maybe I'd pushed it away because I wasn't ready to hear it, but I had remembered enough to bring me back to this painting, to the memory of standing there with her, and to the deeper meaning embedded in that moment.

In so many ways, she was still right there, waiting for me.

••••••••••••••

That afternoon, before my evening flight back home, I drove to the West Side of Chicago. This part you already know: I stood on that sidewalk, gazing up at the red brick Victorian building that had been the Florence Crittenton Anchorage. I took in the rounded tower on one corner with its witch-hat roof. In the tiny attic window, I felt like I might catch a glimpse of the young woman my mom had been back in 1965.

Walking up to the locked front gate, I grabbed one of its cold iron spikes with my bare hand. I thought of Toni, who had called herself an "inmate" of the Anchorage, and who had changed rooms to escape the constant crying of her roommate. Just above the building's foundation were a series of rounded windows that looked out from the basement where that "lech" of a maintenance man had called Toni for a kiss.

Somewhere in the recesses of this house, the "haughty" nurse had shamed young women for leaving toilet paper in their pubic hair. I remembered the gallows humor of the girls joking in the resident-run newspaper about urine specimen bottles and the "unwed mother mice" skittering through their rooms.

As I stood on the sidewalk, still holding the icy gate, I felt worshipful—not for this building but for the women who had lived inside it. I imagined hopping the fence, kicking down the front door, and running up the stairs, as if I would find them all still there. Then I noticed a sign in a second-story window with the building manager's phone number. I called and left a voicemail asking for an impromptu tour, explaining my connection to the building, and offering to pay for his time.

Across my career, I had run after shame—writing about my sex life on the internet, being called a "slut" by anonymous trolls, reporting on women who were pushed to the taboo margins. Now

I was standing at shame's front gate and asking to be let inside, but not because I wanted to prove how much I could endure or withstand. I wanted to pay tribute to all those girls and women, to stand there with clarity and understanding, as a witness and a friend.

I stepped back from the gate to take pictures of dried leaves blanketing the front walkway and a fallen security camera dangling from its cord. Then my phone rang. It was the manager explaining that he was out of town. "Sorry about that, but there's not much to see, anyway," he told me as I walked the length of the fence. "It's already been emptied out. It'll be turned into condos soon."

There's not much to see. I pictured empty hallways, peeling paint, and buckling wood floors. I imagined running my hand along the walls. I saw myself saying, "I'm here to pay my respects," in an empty, echoing room. I didn't care that they had carted away the books and beds and exam tables. This building had been emptied of the evidence of its past, but coming here felt like a way of saying: *My mom never forgot, and neither will I.*

In several months, the building would be saved from demolition at the last minute when the city recognized it as a historic landmark. Instead of being turned into condos, it would become a community center. For decades, this home had helped to reinforce the atomized nuclear-family ideal, but its future is as a shared gathering place. I didn't know that then, though. As I hung up with the building manager, all I knew was that it felt totally predictable that this piece of history would be lost, along with so much else from this time.

All told, I had spent weeks trying to track down a piece of paper that definitively said my mom had stayed in this home. I believed she had lived here, but I couldn't prove it. In 1973, after *Roe v.*

Wade was decided, and with the end of "maternity care services" at the Anchorage, resident records were handed off to a charitable organization whose archives eventually ended up at the library of the University of Illinois Chicago.

When I had asked a librarian to look for the resident records, though, they were missing—or perhaps uncataloged and hiding in a box, waiting to be found. "My sense is that there just might be an unfortunate gap in the record," the librarian had told me.

Recently, Kathy had obtained her original birth certificate, which showed that she was born at Salvation Army's Booth Memorial Hospital in Chicago. That explained my mom's disdain for the Salvation Army bell ringer so many Christmases ago. But I knew she had also talked about a Florence Crittenton home—and even listed the organization on her adoption registry paperwork—and this one was close to her parents' house and thirty minutes from Booth Memorial.

Ann Fessler's guess still seemed a good one: Maybe my mom had started at one home and switched to another because she was that unhappy. Part of me felt it didn't really matter. I was here for all those women I'd read about, for everything this building represented, as much as for my mom.

I got back in my rental car and drove to my next destination: Booth Memorial, my sister's birthplace. This was not a residential home but a complex of rectangular brick buildings with mirrored windows that reflected the flat gray winter sky. An institution. It had the labyrinthine quality of the building where I had been born in Berkeley—the same hospital where I had given birth to Quinn—under profoundly different circumstances.

I had seen an archival photo online showing Booth Memorial's bright red exterior. Now it was a muted orange, an understated piece of the past. I sat in my car in the complex's large parking lot, blasting the heat but shivering. I felt dispatched here—through the unfolding of colliding influences, like a rippling wave sent across the oceans of time to arrive at this building. My DNA had been the direct path to Kathy, but what had made me go searching for her in the first place?

I could point in so many different directions: my mom's love for her lost daughter and my love for my mother; the muddled mess of my family's history and mythology; and the person I had become as a result of the tangle of nature, nurture, and culture. I felt the spirit of my mom acting through me, but not in a sense of spectral possession. I am her daughter, by biology and care. I came from her and from her pain. I stared at the sky reflected in the windows until my vision blurred the borders of the building, merging the sky with its own reflection.

I thought of *The Runaway Bunny*. "If you run away, I will run after you." It had been my mom's pledge to me, entangled with her previous loss, and now I had a weird sense of symmetry. After finding the baby she'd lost, I had gone running after my mom. Ever since the "crossroads" of Indiana, I had been looking for evidence of her—in those pieces of trash outside the apartment building in Gary, the rustling of leaves in front of the house in Griffith, the emptiness of the residential street in Munster, and the attic window of the Anchorage.

I didn't find her anywhere. The obviousness of this thought made me realize that, on some level, I felt that my mom literally had left behind pieces of herself in 1965. It's like I wanted to retrieve all her broken bits and glue her back together.

I turned the key in the ignition and drove toward the parking lot exit, taking a final look in the rearview mirror at this building full of sky. "It is your mother's redemption," Wini had recently said of my search through my mom's past. She didn't mean the false redemption offered by homes like this one—the Faustian bargain of abandoning essential parts of yourself in order to be seen as good. She meant the redemption of truth and perspective, aided by the arc of history.

Turning onto a street clogged by rush-hour traffic, I realized that I *had* collected bits of my mom over these past months. I had sought out the secrets in her past, the parts of her that had been sent away, the feelings that she had boxed up just to survive. I couldn't put her back together, exactly, but I had come to understand her fractures and missing pieces.

I had picked up shard after shard and insisted with love: *Yes, this, too, every single part, belongs.*

AFTERWORD

"Hey sis." Almost three years ago, when Kathy first wrote those words to me, I turned into molten pink heart lava. Now that phrase marks my every week. It's how we start our regular text-message check-ins. I will wake to those two words first thing in the morning or send them off in the evening before bed. "Hey sis, love you, sleep tight." It's the first thing we say when calling each other, too.

These days, "sis" feels less like a volcanic eruption than a wave of a familiar warmth. Every time, though, it's like a coin is deposited in a shared bank. It feels the same with the rare moments when we're able to physically be together—like last summer when I flew to Atlanta with Quinn and Christopher so they could meet Kathy in person for the first time. I was left with a slideshow of memories that feel as profound as they are prosaic.

Kathy handing Quinn a homemade milkshake with an extra dollop of whipped cream while saying, "Anything for my little nephew." Mia climbing into Christopher's lap and pressing Play-Doh onto his face for a "beauty treatment" while Natalie gently scrapes a pipe cleaner across his face, pretending to give him a shave. Quinn and four of Kathy's grandkids piling on top of one another and tumbling around on the floor while giggling hysterically. Walking the kids to the park in the buzzing summer heat with Mia's tiny hand in mine. Shooting hoops with Julius in the middle of a sudden downpour.

Every memory, every "Hey sis," feels like another line in a story that we're writing together.

May 2025

ACKNOWLEDGMENTS

Thank you, Mom, for all that you were—and for the love that you poured into me. I'll spend the rest of my life trying to share you and your love with the world. Kathy, you are more than I ever could have dreamed. Along with Uncle Jide, you have overhauled my sense of what's possible in this life. I'm grateful to Devin, Justin, and Sean, too, as well as your beautiful kids. Meeting and knowing you is a privilege beyond words. To JoAnn: I'm so lucky to get this "sister twofer."

Christopher, you are an unreal gift of a person and partner. Thank you, my bb, my love, for your humor, passion, ideas, support, tenderness, and annoyingly good edits. From the earliest seed of an idea to the final manuscript, you have consistently understood and had faith in the importance of this story. QB, loving you has opened me to the world in whole new ways. It opened me to my mom's story, too. I don't think I ever could have embarked on the journey told by this book without first becoming your mama. You are a joy and a blessing.

Dad, thank you for all the pieces of Mom's story that you have held and preserved, and for the talks and cries along the way. I am glad for all that you have gotten to see in Mom's stead. Dave,

Carol, and David, it was a delight to reconnect with you after all that time. I'm grateful to the Flory fam, as well as the family I've been lucky enough to inherit through Christopher.

Thank you to my Slothy Aunties, Margie and Wini, for all the conversations, hugs, and memories. The whole Berkeley family taught me early on about love, community, and connection outside the usual boxes. To Snow and Ben for being a chosen brother and cousin, respectively. And to all of my mom's women friends for being "unusual" in their own way. You surrounded me early on with a sense of possibility, as opposed to restriction. I am so lucky to have been shaped by your examples. To Sharon: Your vital memories unlocked details that helped to bring my sister together with her dad.

To my editor, Rebecca Strobel, for believing in this project from the get, embracing its full complexity, and swooping in with essential guidance along the way. Thanks also to the incredible team at Gallery and Simon & Schuster, including Aimée Bell, Jill Siegel, Pamela Cannon, Sarah Westergren, and Taylor Rondestvedt. And thank you, endlessly, to Jamie Carr for being a tireless, real-talking, trustworthy, and die-hard literary agent.

I am so grateful for my writing community. Thank you to Amanda Montei and Sarah Wheeler for coworking conversations, making each other lunch, and that magical DIY retreat where I had a breakthough on a crucial chapter, and where Anna Pulley brought the fruitful end-of-day hot tub chats. To my "sister" Elissa Bassist, one of the first people to hear this book idea, and who immediately "got it" in the deepest way. I know you are always just a voice note away.

Thank you to Alexis Madrigal, Amanda (again!), Koa Beck, and Savala Nolan for vital and transformational feedback on my manuscript, but also for providing inspiration and influence through your own writing. To Courtney Martin and Myisha Battle for chats about this book and creative life more generally. Thanks to my former colleagues at *Jezebel*, *Salon*, and Vocativ for shaping me as a reporter.

To all the friends and family members who listened as this story unfolded, but most especially: Anna Leddy, Carrie Whealy, Emily Hartman, Gabi Carmo, Jill Heinke, Liz Linden, Page Rockwell, Ryan Heryford, Sarah Mattes, Sarah Schulweis, and Serena Donovan. To my original "mom group" friends for being part of my discovery that "mom friends" are just friends, no scare quotes needed, and for that witchy night by the firepit in my backyard: Rebecca Weissman, Sarah Stamatiou, and Stacy Weibley.

To my former therapist, Deborah Krow, you were essential to so much of the transformation that is captured in this memoir. Much appreciation to my newsletter subscribers, who witnessed some of my early grappling with these events and themes. (If you aren't a subscriber, you could be: tracyclarkflory.com.) Thanks to Gardenseal Ranch for providing a beautiful space for a DIY writing retreat with other feminist writers, and Maria Schoettler for letting me turn cat-sitting into a retreat.

Thank you to Ann Fessler, Gabrielle Glaser, Karen Wilson-Buterbaugh, Regina Kunzel, and Rickie Solinger for mapping these important adoption histories. To the memoirists who have told personal stories of adoption, most especially Dani Shapiro, Margaret Moorman, Nicole Chung, and Rebecca Carroll, for their beautiful books.

To Elaine Tyler May and Loretta Ross for their research on the birth control pill and reproductive justice, respectively. To bell hooks, Patricia Hill Collins, and Dorothy Roberts for shaping my thinking on the intersections of race and "good" womanhood. To Gail Pheterson, Margo St. James, and Melissa Gira Grant for illuminating whorephobia and its associated ills. To Angela Saini, Gerda Lerner, and Silvia Federici for research on patriarchy; Stephanie Coontz for following the story of marriage; and Deborah Tolman and Laina Bay-Cheng for vital thinking on feminism, sexuality, and notions of empowerment.

Thanks to the librarians at the Berkeley Public Library for keeping up with all of my holds, and to the Internet Archive for being an invaluable resource. I'm indebted to all the archivists, record keepers, and librarians who I leaned on for research, especially those at the University of Illinois Chicago Library. I appreciate all my local booksellers and bookstores, but especially Womb House Books (for creating a local feminist gathering space), Point Reyes Books (for being an all-time favorite), Green Apple Books (for hosting such great events), and Pegasus Books on Solano Avenue (one of my favorites since childhood). And to Lynn at the Florence Crittenton Home Reunion Registry for the work you do reuniting families.

And, finally, thanks to Hank, the most perfect dog in the world, who napped in my lap while I wrote 75 percent of this book.

NOTES

Chapter 2: The Call

35 *an estimated three million girls and women:* Gabrielle Glaser, *American Baby: A Mother, a Child, and the Shadow History of Adoption* (Atria Books, 2022), 117.

35 *thousands of parents sent their young pregnant daughters away:* Rickie Solinger, *Wake Up Little Susie: Single Pregnancy and Race Before Roe v. Wade* (Routledge, 2000), 110.

35 *burn "witches at the stake":* Solinger, *Wake Up Little Susie*, 129.

35 *"Once exorcised, denied its subversive potential":* Silvia Federici, *Witches, Witch-Hunting, and Women* (PM Press, 2018), 23–31.

36 *compared the homes to prisons, asylums, and leper colonies:* Solinger, *Wake Up Little Susie*, 103.

36 *They were controlled by house rules:* Solinger, *Wake Up Little Susie*, 140.

36 *a "white only" policy:* Solinger, *Wake Up Little Susie*, 4.

36 *When Black unwed mothers tried:* Solinger, *Wake Up Little Susie*, 27.

37 *"sexual power" was turned into "pathetic powerlessness":* Solinger, *Wake Up Little Susie*, 25.

37 *"socially unproductive breeders":* Solinger, *Wake Up Little Susie*, 24.

Chapter 3: Scarlet Letter

40 *"putting feminist ideals of equality into sex":* Tracy Clark-Flory, "In Defense of Casual Sex," *Salon*, August 1, 2008, https://www.salon.com/2008/08/01/chastity_books.

50 *"A mother is a woman whose sexual being":* Jacqueline Rose, *Mothers: An Essay on Love and Cruelty* (Farrar, Straus and Giroux, 2018), 36.

Chapter 4: Feelings Wheel

58 *"the human right to maintain personal bodily autonomy":* SisterSong, "Reproductive Justice," SisterSong Women of Color Reproductive Justice Collective, accessed February 21, 2025, https://www.sistersong.net/reproductive-justice.

58 *It crucially pushes beyond the issue of individual "choice":* Abortion Care Network et al., *Systemic Racism and Reproductive Injustice in the United States: A Report for the UN Committee on the Elimination of Racial Discrimination* (CERD, 2022), https://reproductiverights.org/wp-content/uploads/2022/08/2022-CERD-Report_Systemic-Racism-and-Reproductive-Injustice.pdf.

58 *Then there were fascinating phenomena like "microchimerism":* Viviane Callier, "Baby's Cells Can Manipulate Mom's Body for Decades," *Smithsonian Magazine*, March 2, 2021, https://www.smithsonianmag.com/science-nature/babys-cells-can-manipulate-moms-body-decades-180956493.

59 *These hitchhiking cells could migrate:* Blanca Cómitre-Mariano et al., "Feto-Maternal Microchimerism: Memories from Pregnancy," *iScience* 25, no. 1 (2022): 103664, https://doi.org/10.1016/j.isci.2021.103664.

64 *Black women are three times more likely to die:* U.S. Centers for Disease Control and Prevention, "Working Together to Reduce Black Maternal Mortality," CDC.gov, last reviewed July 13, 2023, https://www.cdc.gov/womens-health/features/maternal-mortality.html.

65 *Amanda Montei writes in her memoir:* Amanda Montei, *Touched Out: Motherhood, Misogyny, Consent, and Control* (Beacon Press, 2023), 83.

65 *"bodies and psyches, to put them to work for free and call it love":* Montei, *Touched Out*, 82.

66 *"a vast body of knowledge":* Silvia Federici, *Witches, Witch-Hunting, and Women* (PM Press, 2018), 34.

Chapter 5: Good and Bad

69 *"they discovered that moving on":* Ann Fessler, *The Girls Who Went Away: The Hidden History of Women Who Surrendered Children for Adoption in the Decades Before Roe v. Wade* (Penguin Press, 2006), 187.

75 *He'd asked to follow them on their vacation:* Bill Castanier, "How an MSU Professor Helped Popularize Spring Break into a National Rite of Passage," *MSU Alumni Magazine*, summer 2011.

75 *the number of spring breakers in Florida more than doubled:* Pagan Kennedy, "Who Made Spring Break?," *New York Times Magazine*, March 24, 2013, https://www.nytimes.com/2013/03/24/magazine/who-made-spring-break.html.

75 *MTV started broadcasting from spring break:* Louise Hart, "MTV's First Spring Break VJ Remembers What Spring Break Was Like Before Camera Phones," *GQ*, March 13, 2023, https://www.gq.com/story/mtv-spring-break-vj-alan-hunter.

76 *Joe Francis, a man who would eventually be accused:* Krystie Lee Yandoli, "Five Takeaways from the 'Girls Gone Wild' Documentary," *Rolling Stone*, February 21, 2023, https://www.rollingstone.com/tv-movies/tv-movie-news/girls-gone-wild-joe-francis-peacock-doc-1235191346/.

81 *Contemporary feminist research suggests:* Deborah L. Tolman, Stephanie M. Anderson, and Kimberly Belmonte, "Mobilizing Metaphor: Considering Complexities, Contradictions, and Contexts in Adolescent Girls' and Young Women's Sexual Agency," *Sex Roles* 73 (2015): 298–310, https://doi.org/10.1007/s11199-015-0510-0.

82 *As the feminist scholars Deborah Tolman and Jennifer Chmielewski:* Jennifer Chmielewski and Deborah Tolman, "From Tightrope to Minefield: How the Sexual Double Standard 'Lives' in Adolescent Girls' and Young Women's Lives," in *The Cambridge Handbook of Sexual Development: Childhood and Adolescence*, ed. Sharon Lamb and Jen Gilbert (Cambridge University Press, 2018): 198–220, https://doi.org/10.1017/9781108116121.011.

82 *"compulsory (sexual) agency":* Rosalind Gill, "Empowerment/Sexism: Figuring Female Sexual Agency in Contemporary Advertising," *Feminism & Psychology* 18, no. 1 (2008): 35–60, https://doi.org/10.1177/0959353507084950.

83 *"the degree of control":* Laina Y. Bay-Cheng, "The Agency Line: A Neoliberal Metric for Appraising Young Women's Sexuality," *Sex Roles* 73 (2015): 279–291, https://doi.org/10.1007/s11199-015-0452-6.

83 *"Some girls are bolstered or shielded by race":* Bay-Cheng, "The Agency Line."

83 *"Whether a woman is an actual virgin":* Patricia Hill Collins, *Black Feminist Thought: Knowledge, Consciousness, and the Politics of Empowerment* (Unwin Hyman, 1990), 134.

83 *We were told to go ahead and marry:* Lori Gottlieb, *Marry Him: The Case for Settling for Mr. Good Enough* (Penguin Press, 2009).

Chapter 6: Our Mom

89 *The birth control pill:* Claudia Goldin and Lawrence F. Katz, "The Power of the Pill: Oral Contraceptives and Women's Career and Marriage Decisions," *Journal of Political Economy* 110, no. 4 (2002): 730–770, https://doi.org/10.1086/340778.

90 *Some college health officers:* Elizabeth Siegel Watkins, *On the Pill: A Social History of Oral Contraceptives, 1950–1970* (Johns Hopkins University Press, 1998), 65; Bernard Asbell, *The Pill: A Biography of the Drug That Changed the World* (Tarcher Perigee, 2014), 195.

90 *most young and sexually active single women:* Elaine Tyler May, *America and the Pill: A History of Promise, Peril, and Liberation* (Basic Books, 2010), 83–84.

90 *"were afraid of . . . aligning themselves":* Pagan Kennedy, "Could Women Be Trusted with Their Own Pregnancy Tests?," *New York Times*, July 31, 2016, https://www.nytimes.com/2016/07/31/opinion/sunday/could-women-be-trusted-with-their-own-pregnancy-tests.html.

91 *In the sixties in New York City:* Rachel Benson Gold, "Lessons from Roe: Will the Past Be Prologue?," *Guttmacher Policy Review* 6, no. 3 (2003), https://www.guttmacher.org/gpr/2003/03/lessons-roe-will-past-be-prologue.

91 *The illegality of abortion made the procedure dangerous:* Maggie Koerth, "What the History of Back-Alley Abortions Can Teach Us About a Future Without Roe," *FiveThirtyEight*, May 3, 2022, https://fivethirtyeight.com/features/what-the-history-of-back-alley-abortions-can-teach-us-about-a-future-without-roe.

93 *"no longer portrayed as sexual":* bell hooks, *Ain't I a Woman: Black Women and Feminism* (South End Press, 1981), 31–33.

93 *"pure White womanhood possible":* Patricia Hill Collins, *Black Feminist Thought: Knowledge, Consciousness, and the Politics of Empowerment* (Unwin Hyman, 1990), 142.

93 *"justify the economic exploitation of house slaves":* Collins, *Black Feminist Thought*, 71.

93 *"American culture reveres no Black madonna":* Dorothy Roberts, *Killing the Black Body: Race, Reproduction, and the Meaning of Liberty* (Pantheon Books, 1997), 15.

93 *"The conception of motherhood confined to the home":* Roberts, *Killing the Black Body*, 14–15.

94 *"lost the privilege of whiteness":* Elaine Tyler May, foreword to *Wake Up Little Susie: Single Pregnancy and Race Before Roe v. Wade*, by Rickie Solinger (Routledge, 2000), x.

95 *The visibility of Black single mothers:* Solinger, *Wake Up Little Susie*, 24.

95 *"essential in reproducing racialized notions of American womanhood":* Collins, *Black Feminist Thought*, 50.

95 *They developed laws, policies, and a culture:* Loretta J. Ross and Rickie Solinger, *Reproductive Justice: An Introduction* (University of California Press, 2017), 18.

95 *"the fertility of the enslaved woman into the essential":* Ross and Solinger, *Reproductive Justice*, 18.

96 *"fundamental to racializing the colonies":* Ross and Solinger, *Reproductive Justice*, 15.

96 *"children of 'immoral' unmarried mothers":* Ross and Solinger, *Reproductive Justice*, 36.

96 *"reproduction to regulate who could live":* Ross and Solinger, *Reproductive Justice*, 37.

96 *"make sure that the* right *white women":* Ross and Solinger, *Reproductive Justice*, 93.

Chapter 7: Rapunzel

105 *She is sent away:* Jacob Grimm and Wilhelm Grimm, "Rapunzel," *Grimms' Fairy Tales*, 7th ed., vol. 1 (Verlag der Dieterichschen Buchhandlung, 1857), accessed February 26, 2025, https://sites.pitt.edu/~dash/grimm012.html.

106 *"a supreme pity for the":* Otto Wilson, *Fifty Years' Work with Girls, 1883–1933: A Story of the Florence Crittenton Homes* (The National Florence Crittenton Mission, 1933), 17.

106 *"rescue bands" would invade "concert halls":* Wilson, *Fifty Years' Work with Girls*, 33.

106 *Soon the Salvation Army:* "Booth Memorial, White Shield, and Door of Hope Hospital and Maternity Homes," Salvation Army Maternity Records West, accessed February 27, 2025, https://maternityrecordswest.salvationarmy.org/maternity_home_records/booth-records-maternity-home-and-hospital-records.

106 *"dark, dingy, forbidding":* Wilson, *Fifty Years' Work with Girls*, 249.

107 *"pure white lily":* Wilson, *Fifty Years' Work with Girls*, 250.

107 *"women do not voluntarily restrict their own liberty":* Regina G. Kunzel, *Fallen Women, Problem Girls: Unmarried Mothers and the Professionalization of Social Work, 1890–1945* (Yale University Press, 1993), 17.

107 *"rogues, scoundrels, and unscrupulous cads":* Kunzel, *Fallen Women, Problem Girls*, 22.

108 *a larger "girl problem" in the culture:* Kunzel, *Fallen Women, Problem Girls*, 18.

108 *"Social workers called on 'sex delinquency'":* Kunzel, *Fallen Women, Problem Girls*, 52.

109 *"postwar white family imperative":* Rickie Solinger, *Wake Up Little Susie: Single Pregnancy and Race Before Roe v. Wade* (Routledge, 2000), 149.

109 *"psychological inability to form a sanctioned relationship":* Solinger, *Wake Up Little Susie*, 16.

109 *"the absence of psyche":* Solinger, *Wake Up Little Susie*, 24.

109 *"The matriarch represented a failed mammy":* Patricia Hill Collins, *Black Feminist Thought: Knowledge, Consciousness, and the Politics of Empowerment* (Routledge, 2000), 83.

110 *"public health duty":* Solinger, *Wake Up Little Susie*, 210.

110 *"Everyone knows what The Pill is":* "The Pill and the Sexual Revolution," *American Experience*, PBS, accessed February 27, 2025, https://www.pbs.org/wgbh/americanexperience/features/pill-and-sexual-revolution.

110 *"a species of mental patient":* Solinger, *Wake Up Little Susie*, 206.

110 *"neuroses of the era":* Solinger, *Wake Up Little Susie*, 220.

113 *Jill Nagle calls this "compulsory virtue":* Jill Nagle, "Introduction," in *Whores and Other Feminists*, ed. Jill Nagle (Routledge, 1997), 1–15.

113 *When a woman fails at "compulsory virtue":* Gail Pheterson, "The Category 'Prostitute' in Scientific Inquiry," *Journal of Sex Research* 27, no. 3 (August 1990): 397–407, https://doi.org/10.1080/00224499009551568.

114 *In the late nineteenth century:* Silvia Federici, *Revolution Point Zero: Housework, Reproduction, and Feminist Struggle* (PM Press, 2012), 13.

114 *"the destiny of the unwed mother":* Silvia Federici, *Patriarchy of the Wage: Notes on Marx, Gender, and Feminism* (PM Press, 2020), 113.

114 *"Like the profession of prostitution":* Nickie Roberts, *Whores in History* (Feminist Press, 1998), 8.

114 *The feminist historian Gerda Lerner:* Gerda Lerner, *The Creation of Patriarchy* (Oxford University Press, 1986), 8.

114 *Lerner also notes that Middle Assyrian law:* Lerner, *The Creation of Patriarchy*, 140.

115 *"illegitimate or illicit femaleness":* Pheterson, *The Prostitution Prism* (Amsterdam University Press, 1996), 70.

Chapter 8: Sorry About Her

123 *"through their pregnancy and delivery":* Mary T. Dresser, "Booth Hospital: Haven for the Unmarried," *Daily Herald*, June 7, 1967, 17.

123 *only 11 percent of women at the hospital:* Dresser, "Booth Hospital: Haven for the Unmarried," 17.

Chapter 9: Uterine Scream

129 *"a woman who puts her newborn up for adoption today":* Samuel Alito, majority opinion, *Dobbs v. Jackson Women's Health Organization*, 597 U. S. ____ (2022), 34, https://www.supremecourt.gov/opinions/21pdf/19-1392_6j37.pdf.

129 *My mother had to sever:* Jeanette Winterson, *Why Be Normal When You Could Be Happy?* (Grove Press, 2013), 220.

130 *"I always thought I was the problem":* Margaret Moorman, *Waiting to Forget* (Kensington Publishing, 2004), 152.

130 *more than 80 percent of women:* Ann Fessler, *The Girls Who Went Away: The Hidden History of Women Who Surrendered Children for Adoption in the Decades Before Roe v. Wade* (Penguin Press, 2006), 53.

130 *"A few girls, revolutionary girls":* Fessler, The Girls Who Went Away, 49.

130 *The drugs were so sedating:* Glaser, *American Baby: A Mother, a Child, and the Shadow History of Adoption* (Atria Books, 2022), 159–160.

131 *"Let me see my baby!":* Fessler, *The Girls Who Went Away*, 176–179.

131 *"I flipped out—it was total 100 percent":* Fessler, *The Girls Who Went Away*, 61.

132 *"with the vigilance of a nesting bird":* Moorman, *Waiting to Forget*, 120.

137 *"Criminalizing abortion makes female sexual agency":* Laurie Penny, "The Criminalization of Women's Bodies Is All About Conservative Male Power," *New Republic*, May 17, 2019, https://newrepublic.com/article/153942/criminalization-womens-bodies-conservative-male-power.

Chapter 10: Unusual Women

145 *later analysis of the book:* Dava Sobel, "Schizophrenia in Popular Books: A Study Finds Too Much Hope," *New York Times*, February 17, 1981, https://www.nytimes.com/1981/02/17/science/schizophrenia-in-popular-books-a-study-finds-too-much-hope.html.

146 *"[A]s to the dead":* Joanne Greenberg, *I Never Promised You a Rose Garden* (Signet, 1964), 48.

150 *"All she has to do":* Maureen Murdock, *The Heroine's Journey* (Shambhala, 1990), 2.

150 *"the belly of the whale":* Joseph Campbell, *The Hero with a Thousand Faces* (Princeton University Press, 2004), 74.

151 *"supposed to be having the time of [her] life":* Sylvia Plath, *The Bell Jar* (Harper & Row, 1971), 2–3.

151 *"The last thing I wanted was infinite security":* Plath, *The Bell Jar*, 83.

152 *"For Sylvia Plath's focus in* The Bell Jar*":* Marjorie G. Perloff, "'A Ritual for Being Born Twice': Sylvia Plath's The Bell Jar," *Contemporary Literature* 13, no. 4 (Autumn 1972): 507–522.

152 *"schizophrenia as a protest":* Elaine Showalter, *The Female Malady: Women, Madness, and English Culture, 1830–1980* (Pantheon Books, 1985), 216.

152 *"I was like a lobotomized beast":* Karen Wilson-Buterbaugh, *The Baby Scoop Era: Unwed Mothers, Infant Adoption, and Forced Surrender* (self-published, 2017), 299.

153 *Lessing was influenced by the thinking of:* R. D. Laing, *The Divided Self: An Existential Study in Sanity and Madness* (Tavistock Publications, 1960), 73.

153 *"R.D. Laing never figured out that":* Chris Kraus, *I Love Dick* (Serpent's Tail, 2016), 225.

154 *"a woman's self being split into two":* John Berger, *Ways of Seeing* (Penguin Books, 1972), 47.

154 *"The individual's being is cleft":* R. D. Laing, *The Divided Self*, 162.

154 *Audre Lorde writes of the way:* Audre Lorde, *Sister Outsider: Essays and Speeches* (Crossing Press, 1984), 114.

154 *"Some feminist critics have maintained":* Showalter, *The Female Malady*, 213.

155 *"becomes a symbol of all the man-made":* Showalter, *The Female Malady*, 1.

155 *"come to terms with their own":* Sandra M. Gilbert and Susan Gubar, *The Madwoman in the Attic: The Woman Writer and the Nineteenth-Century Literary Imagination* (Yale University Press, 1979), 78.

155 *"so near the borderline of utter mental ruin"*: Charlotte Perkins Gilman, *The Yellow Wallpaper* (Wisehouse Classics, 2016), 7.

155 *"puerperal insanity"*: Showalter, *The Female Malady*, 57.

155 *Nymphomania symptoms included everything:* Carol Groneman, *Nymphomania: A History* (Pantheon Books, 2003), 5.

156 *"[U]ncontrolled sexuality seemed"*: Showalter, *The Female Malady*, 74.

156 *"psychological inability to form a sanctioned relationship"*: Rickie Solinger, *Wake Up Little Susie: Single Pregnancy and Race Before Roe v. Wade* (Routledge, 1992), 16.

158 *"When we talk about an object of desire"*: Lauren Berlant, *Cruel Optimism* (Duke University Press, 2011), 23.

159 *"source of power and information within our lives"*: Lorde, *Sister Outsider*, 54.

159 *"precisely because of its power to draw us into"*: bell hooks, *The Will to Change: Men, Masculinity, and Love* (Washington Square Press, 2004), 183.

162 *"as the symbol of his wife's liability"*: Nathaniel Hawthorne, *The Complete Short Stories of Nathaniel Hawthorne* (Doubleday, 1959), 127–128.

162 *"menstruating, childbearing, and lactating"*: J. L. Goldenberg and T. A. Roberts, "The Birthmark: An Existential Account of the Objectification of Women," in *Self-Objectification in Women: Causes, Consequences, and Counteractions*, ed. R. M. Calogero, S. Tantleff-Dunn, and J. K. Thompson (American Psychological Association, 2011), 77–99, https://doi.org/10.1037/12304-004.

Chapter 11: Hey Sis!!

171 *"our domestic lives—what we do inside our homes"*: Kristen R. Ghodsee, *Everyday Utopia: What 2,000 Years of Wild Experiments Can Teach Us About the Good Life* (Simon & Schuster, 2023), xii.

172 *"We can't escape it"*: Sophie Lewis, *Abolish the Family: A Manifesto for Care and Liberation* (Verso, 2023), 10.

175 *"approximately the size of a grain of sand"*: "NASA's Webb Delivers Deepest Infrared Image of Universe Yet," NASA.gov, July 12, 2022, https://www.nasa.gov/image-article/nasas-webb-delivers-deepest-infrared-image-of-universe-yet.

Chapter 12: Laws of Physics

193 *"I saw that interracial couple he had"*: Kyung Lah, "Serial Killer Joseph Paul Franklin Prepares to Die," CNN, November 19, 2013, https://edition.cnn.com/2013/11/18/justice/death-row-interview-joseph-paul-franklin.

193 *I would also read about how*: "Historical Marker Unveiled in Gwinnett County, Georgia," Equal Justice Initiative, February 18, 2020, https://eji.org/news/historical-marker-unveiled-in-gwinnett-county-georgia.

Chapter 13: A Different Kind of Falling

205 *"the white man's world"*: James Baldwin, *Notes of a Native Son* (Beacon Press, 1955), 64.

205 *"The work and humility required"*: Rebecca Carroll, *Surviving the White Gaze* (Simon & Schuster, 2022), 309–310.

206 *"love takes off the masks"*: James Baldwin, *The Fire Next Time* (Vintage Books, 1995), 94.

Chapter 14: Opposite of Shame

230 *a recent study had tied the high rates:* Maria Pappas, "Maps of Inequality: From Redlining to Urban Decay and the Black Exodus" (Scavenger Sale study), Cook County Treasurer, July 2022, https://www.cookcountytreasurer.com/pdfs/scavengersalestudy/2022scavengersalestudy.pdf.

Chapter 15: A Crossroads

239 *"Why have so many American wives":* Betty Friedan, *The Feminine Mystique* (W. W. Norton & Company, 1964), 28.

240 *"women who wish to be free":* Mona Chollet, *In Defense of Witches* (Melville House, 2021), 66.

249 *"The legal difference between":* Gail Pheterson, *The Prostitution Prism* (Amsterdam University Press, 1996), 16.

250 *"assumed to be 'loose' or for hire":* Pheterson, *The Prostitution Prism*, 134.

Chapter 16: Dots

252 *in the sober analysis of art historians:* S. Hollis Clayson, "The Family and the Father: The Grand Jatte and Its Absences," in *Readings in Nineteenth-Century Art*, ed. Janis Tomlinson (Prentice Hall, 1996), 222.

ABOUT THE AUTHOR

Tracy Clark-Flory is a journalist, essayist, and author of the memoir *Want Me: A Sex Writer's Journey into the Heart of Desire*, an NPR Best Book of the Year. She has written for *Cosmopolitan*, *The Cut*, *Elle*, *Esquire*, *Marie Claire*, *Glamour*, *The Guardian*, *The Washington Post*, *Wired*, *Women's Health*, and many others. Previously, she was a senior staff writer at *Jezebel* and a staff writer at *Salon*. She writes a weekly newsletter and cohosts *Dire Straights*, a feminist podcast critiquing hetero love, sex, politics, and culture. You can find more at tracyclarkflory.com.